BlackBerry Planet

BlackBerry Planet

The Story of Research in Motion and the Little Device that Took the World by Storm

Alastair Sweeny

John Wiley & Sons Canada, Ltd.

Library and Archives Canada Cataloguing in Publication

Sweeny, Alastair
    BlackBerry planet : the story of Research in Motion and the little device that took the world by storm / Alastair Sweeny.

Includes index.
ISBN 978-0-470-15940-8

1. Research in Motion (Firm)—History.   2. BlackBerry (Computer).   I. Title.
HD9696.2.C34R46 2009   338.7'610041670971   C2009-902929-4

Production Credits
Cover design: Ian Koo
Interior design: Adrian So
Typesetter: Thomson Digital
Printer: Tri-Graphic Printing

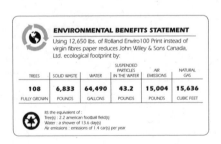

ENVIRONMENTAL BENEFITS STATEMENT

Using 12,650 lbs. of Rolland Enviro100 Print instead of virgin fibres paper reduces John Wiley & Sons Canada, Ltd. ecological footprint by:

TREES	SOLID WASTE	WATER	SUSPENDED PARTICLES IN THE WATER	AIR EMISSIONS	NATURAL GAS
108	**6,833**	**64,490**	**43.2**	**15,004**	**15,636**
FULLY GROWN	POUNDS	GALLONS	POUNDS	POUNDS	CUBIC FEET

It's the equivalent of :
Tree(s) : 2.2 american football field(s)
Water : a shower of 13.6 day(s)
Air emissions : emissions of 1.4 car(s) per year

John Wiley & Sons Canada, Ltd.
6045 Freemont Blvd.
Mississauga, Ontario
L5R 4J3

Printed in Canada

1 2 3 4 5 TRI 13 12 11 10 09

This one's for Gaëtane and Sophie.

Contents

Preface

Welcome to BlackBerry Planet.

When I started to research this book and study Research in Motion (RIM), I simply wanted to explore how a Greek-Canadian wireless geek and his Harvard MBA hockey jock sidekick invented, perfected and took to market the world's most addictive device, the BlackBerry. Another typical high-tech success story, right?

But as I dug deeper into the remarkable history of Research In Motion, I found there's a lot more to this tale than just a company romance, although on its own it is an extraordinary story. The birth of RIM's BlackBerry and other mobile Web devices like Apple's iPhone marks a major turning point in how we live and work. It also points the way toward a much more spectacular device that is now emerging—a tool I call the TeleBrain.

It soon struck me that the world has suddenly changed course and is evolving in ways that seem like 1950s science fiction. As my old teacher Marshall McLuhan famously put it, the human race is starting to plug deeply into electric technology, and we are increasingly wearing our brains outside our skulls.

But how did this change of course happen so fast? It's as if a light bulb switched on in a dark room. Suddenly, there is a huge tribe of 25 million people who simply cannot get along without RIM's electronic organizer. The change started in the enterprise, and virtually all major corporations use BlackBerry servers. In a few short years, the BlackBerry has become the world's foremost mobile business tool, and the planet's elite electronic communicator—the US government alone runs over 500,000 BlackBerrys—and some say that BlackBerrys now run the US government.

But RIM's success story also has a dark side. In the book, we explore the various court cases RIM has faced—including the grueling five-year legal grind that ended in a $650 million payout—the largest technology patent settlement in U.S. history. And we look at abusers of the BlackBerry, people trapped in an always-on world whose personal and family lives are suffering from their dependence on this device.

Big good things often come in small packages, and radical new businesses can rise out of tiny start-up companies.

In 1984, the year Steve Jobs brought out his first Apple Macintosh, Research In Motion (RIM) began life in Waterloo, Ontario, as a two-person tech start-up in a one-room office. The founders were a twenty-three-year-old college dropout named Mike Lazaridis and his boyhood friend Doug Fregin.

From the get-go, RIM was a company with a difference: Mike and Doug were both practical and visionary at the same time, and the pair turned out to be superb engineers. Financed at the start by family funds and a $15,000 government loan, RIM's first big job was a $600,000 contract making networked LCD display screens for the General Motors Canada assembly line. Ten years later, Mike Lazaridis stood onstage at the Academy Awards and accepted an

Preface

Oscar from actor Anne Heche for RIM's Digisync Film Barcode Reader, a device that revolutionized Hollywood.

In the late 1980s, Research In Motion got in bed with AT&T, Rogers and Ericsson and started to build miniature radios and modems to let PCs send data and messages over mobile networks. In 1996, RIM came up with the Inter@ctive Pager 900, the world's first pocket-sized, two-way pager. Two years later, it built its first BlackBerry, the 950, a wireless wonder that synchronized with a user's desktop computer and corporate e-mail.

Since 1992, Mike Lazaridis and co-CEO Jim Balsillie have been the tandem team driving the RIM story. *BlackBerry Planet* details their passion to build and deliver the foremost mobile business tool on the planet. Their BlackBerry has become a compulsory communicator, used by 85 percent of the Fortune 500 companies. The Queen has a BlackBerry and shares her e-mail address with favored subjects. Today's politicians can't operate without it—U.S. President Barack Obama's struggles to keep his device in the White House gained him enormous sympathy. He's the first BlackBerry president!

With input from RIM veterans and competitors, *BlackBerry Planet* tells the story of the BlackBerry from its early days, starting with its use during the 9/11 attacks, which earned RIM a reputation for security and reliability. Now the Swiss Army knife of smartphones, RIM's super-secure e-mail device and Web browser is becoming what the company calls a "lifestyle platform," packed with applications and features that can do everything from online banking to opening your garage door.

I wrote *BlackBerry Planet* as a business biography of Research In Motion, but I soon became drawn to the social side of BlackBerry

xi

use—the cultural adoption of this iconic device as a must-have status symbol, as well as the backlash against the addictive properties of what quickly became known as the CrackBerry. This little device is having a profound effect on daily life, family relations, and manners, beyond the world of business.

Most governments and businesses which use BlackBerrys get major productivity gains with the devices—studies tell us that BlackBerry use can boost employee productivity by more than 30 percent. It's helped change the way we communicate in the enterprise, being "always on, always connected." But at the same time, it is leading to major headaches for managers and employees. Digging deeper into BlackBerry Planet, I found that there is a serious downside to BlackBerry use.

Lazaridis and Balsillie knew they had an addictive device right from the start, but they have always stressed the sunny side of device dependence—Balsillie calls it "calming." It's true that BlackBerry-addicted execs who use their device to excess may be more productive, but they can develop an addiction as strong as that experienced by alcoholics or chemical abusers. E-mail-checking junkies who can't live without their BlackBerrys can't laugh off the truth—they are addicts.

So, what makes BlackBerry users tick? If you're a BlackBerry outsider, from another planet, you've seen these people:

- hunched over their devices on the train or bus or subway, *tip tip tapping* with their thumbs, more productive than thou;
- heads bowed in the meeting room, as if in prayer, fiddling over something under the table;
- thumbing in their cars looking as if they are pushing on the horn. When the light turns green, there is a furious beeping as cars honk to get the BlackBerry bozo's attention.

Or you're out in a social setting. You're talking to someone and have her full attention, and then you hear a gentle buzz and suddenly her eyes glaze over. She pulls a BlackBerry out of her pocket, turns her head, and without saying sorry, she is gone, lost in the reply.

Or you and your wife have just forked over a fortune to get tickets for *Don Giovanni*, and now you are in your seats, entranced by the majesty of the voices. Suddenly your eye is drawn to a little pool of light off to your left, and yes, there is a BlackBerry barbarian, tapping on his infernal little device. The performance is ruined. If you're a citizen of BlackBerry Planet, however, you're Lord of the Ringtones. Entering the elevator, as the door closes, you pull out your precious device and check your urgent e-mail, in sync with all the other passengers.

You arrive early at a meeting, and you note with satisfaction that most people sitting at the table have their heads inclined, their eyes cast downward in contemplation, assuming the BlackBerry Prayer Position. You sit down quietly and join them in worship, in tune with the sound of little clicks.

Later, the meeting becomes boring, and you feel a gentle buzz, which sounds kind of like a cross between a bee and a far-away cow. Without attracting notice, you remove the BlackBerry from your pocket, under the table, and sneak a quick peek at the screen.

On Sunday, you're in church and the sermon is wandering. You find it hard to concentrate, and only with great effort do you resist the urge to answer the buzz in your pocket.

Or you take a winter break with your family, and you're sitting in a lounge chair on the beach. You tell your family you're reading an e-book when in fact you're checking in with the office. You've been told that the project cannot go on without your input.

Such is the life of the citizens of BlackBerry Planet.

The addictive, immersive properties of smartphone use are now challenging the whole world of work, and we're a long way from being able to cope with the new power it gives us.

In offices around the world, workers are drowning in e-mail excess, and BlackBerry use is very much part of the problem. It's now clear that constant BlackBerry checking can actually nullify gains made in productivity. BlackBerry bondage can also make family life suffer, as employees bring their work home and never really leave the office behind. Any gains people make in organizing family messaging and scheduling, can get cruelly offset by upsets in work-life balance. Says Canadian business professor Linda Duxbury: "Moderate users of the BlackBerry are okay, but for a growing number of people, the BlackBerry only contributes to stress and depression, and a decline in healthy personal and family life."

How can managers and employees deal with this growing problem? In *BlackBerry Planet*, I explore the roots of device dependence and show how some people are handling it in creative and practical ways. I also suggest that we must come to terms with the power of mobile computing—and quickly—or risk suffering real social upheaval.

The problem will certainly get worse before it gets better, as many more powerful features are being crammed into new releases of the BlackBerry and rival devices.

In the next twenty years, we're going to have to learn how to cope with whole new generations of advanced superphones. These in turn will evolve even further into what I call the TeleBrain, a portable device more capable than the human brain itself, one that we can carry around in our pockets or even install under our skin, expanding our powers and connecting us directly with the whole intelligence of the planet.

What of the future of Research In Motion? For a few weeks in 2007, RIM became the largest company in Canada in terms of market cap. Today, battered by the global economic downturn but still driven by the need to compete, RIM is fending off Apple and its superb iPhone while rapidly expanding its own reach across the planet, especially into the billion-fold markets of India and China, where it is tackling the giant Finnish phone company Nokia head-on.

In *BlackBerry Planet*, I have tried to probe the personal and corporate DNA that has driven Research in Motion and propelled the company over a 25-year period to become a global technology powerhouse, and one of the top three NASDAQ tech favorites—the other two being Apple and Google.

BlackBerry Planet also explores the challenges of taking a dream to market, and meeting the desire of customers all around the world to manage how they communicate to colleagues, clients, friends and loved ones, in the easiest and most secure way possible.

Above all, *BlackBerry Planet* is about the vision of Mike Lazaridis and his team of engineers, who were at the right place when it mattered and are still turning their vision of the future into reality.

Acknowledgments

Scores of people gave me input and wise counsel with this book. In particular, I'd like to thank John Albright, Sam Archibald, Dale Brubacher-Cressman, Denzil Doyle, Linda Duxbury, Dick Fadden, Robert J. Fraser, Bill Frezza, Iain Grant, Sophie Le Blanc, Gaëtane Lemay, Stephanie MacKendrick, Joe Martin, Don McMurtry, Tim Meyer, Don Morrison, Gary Mousseau, Tony Patterson, Rebecca Reeve, Susan Stranks, Malcolm Sweeny, Kevin Talbot, Matt Walkoff and Elizabeth Woyte, as well as a number of present and former RIM employees who spoke on conditions of anonymity. At Wiley Canada, I would like to thank Karen Milner and her splendid crew: Meghan Brousseau, Michelle Bullard, Deborah Guichelaar, Liz McCurdy, Jennifer Smith, Lucas Wilk and Brian Will, as well as CrackBerry widow Heather Sangster of strongfinish.ca, Carol Long of Wiley Technology Publishing and Joe Wikert, now with O'Reilly Media.

A Web Support Service for Readers

If you are a buyer of this book, you'll enjoy and profit from my *BlackBerry Planet* Web Support site at:

http://blackberryplanetbook.com.

You'll find chapter-related images and video, and a full resource base of BlackBerry related audiovisual files and pictures, documents, patents, financial history, device models, useful Web links, and a bookstore with direct links to order pages at online retailers.

The Web Support site also has clickable Web-linked references that take you right to the original article that I've cited. **These are indicated at the end of appropriate footnotes in the book with the symbol < * >.**

And while I have tried making RIM's technology features as reader friendly as possible, if you need help with technical terms, and want to understand the mobile universe better, I invite you to use the glossary on the site at: http://blackberryplanetbook.com/index.php/BlackBerry_Planet_Glossary.

I will also be posting from time to time on the BlackBerry Planet Weblog at: http://blackberrynationweblog.blogspot.com/.

Thanks for reading *BlackBerry Planet*. I hope you enjoy this book and that it gives you insight, context, and understanding about the amazing saga of the BlackBerry. As the story unfolds, and as RIM tackles global giants such as Nokia and Apple in the emerging superphone marketplace, I invite you to look to the *BlackBerry Planet* Web Support site for future developments.

I welcome your feedback, questions, and comments.

Alastair Sweeny
Ottawa, Canada
blackberrybook@gmail.com
May 9, 2009

The Planet
Goes BlackBerry

"When they go to work, people expect a phone, a desk, a chair, a light. And a BlackBerry has really taken on that status."

—Mike Lazaridis

Mike Lazaridis's little device is the favorite fruit of 25 million people across the planet who just can't get along without their innovative electronic organizer. But a scarce ten years ago, the BlackBerry was known to only a few movers and shakers in Washington, on Wall Street or in big high-tech firms like Intel and IBM.

Back in 1999, Research In Motion (RIM) built the first reliable product to offer two-way mobile e-mail and messaging. At that time, pagers holstered on belts were part of the MD's or Wall Street broker's uniform. But they allowed only one-way communication. Lazaridis had realized that corporate technophiles wouldn't want to be tethered to their computers and would, instead, love to work anywhere, sending and receiving e-mail directly on their pagers.

So, the BlackBerry easily won a favored spot on the belts of hard-charging political staffers and business professionals, from wireless warriors, out in the field and battling for market share, to cubicle cowboys lunching at their desks, hunched over BlackBerrys and juggling work and home.

Today, the BlackBerry monopolizes the world of work—nobody else comes close. An astounding 85 percent of public corporations are supplying staff with the devices, and more than 175,000 BlackBerry Enterprise Servers are installed worldwide. The US Congress was RIM's first big client, and Uncle Sam is still the biggest consumer of BlackBerrys. Today, more than 500,000 devices are installed in every department of the U.S. government and throughout the US Senate and House of Representatives.

Some larger corporations are handling tens of thousands of e-mail accounts securely and efficiently, and the top three or four companies each manage close to 100,000 BlackBerry users. Security is key. BlackBerry messages are secured with NATO–grade encryption, and network managers love the ability to freeze or wipe data from a lost or stolen BlackBerry.

The BlackBerry is also super-efficient. Studies show users can boost their productivity by 30 percent, and BlackBerry messaging is compressed, sometimes twenty times more than competing systems, so companies save a bundle in bandwidth costs.

But RIM has also adapted the BlackBerry to serve the consumer as well, and today more than 60 percent of users are outside the enterprise, buying their services from telecom providers.

RIM's original wireless devices were just glorified two-way pagers, used mainly by police, firefighters, and ambulance drivers. But that was a maturing market. When the company added enterprise servers with e-mail, calendars and contact lists to its first BlackBerrys, RIM started to get some real traction on Wall Street and inside the Washington Beltway. RIM co-CEO Jim

Balsillie was so confident that they had a winner on their hands, he seeded hundreds of those first BlackBerrys to influential users. Soon, a growing number of leading executives, bankers, opinion makers and politicians were adopting the addictive little devices.

Unfortunately for RIM, the BlackBerry was still unknown on Main Street, and growth sputtered. The big telecom providers weren't helping the picture. At the time, they were obsessed with selling their cell phone services, and wireless texting was a distinctly unsexy secondary market.

It took a tragedy to get the BlackBerry to launch velocity, and it happened suddenly, on September 11, 2001.

During the horrific attacks that day in New York and Washington, the only people trapped in the World Trade Center's Twin Towers who were able to contact their loved ones after cell service failed were those with BlackBerrys. Police, firefighters, and ambulance drivers and U.S. Vice President Dick Cheney all used their BlackBerry devices during the crisis.

According to a RIM insider at the time, "During 9/11, RIM staff were PINning [messaging] the hell out of the Mobitex and DataPac networks used by people with BlackBerrys caught in the towers, while the support workers relied on them to communicate even while the regular cell lines were dead. The text network survived while the cell network died because it was barely used and signal strength was possible from remote nodes."*

Throughout the evacuation and collapse of the Twin Towers and during the surge in traffic, Cingular kept its text-only Mobitex network running despite losing many base stations in lower Manhattan. While slow at 12.5 kilobits per second, Mobitex on BlackBerrys kept running while others failed because it did not

---

* Personal correspondence.

have to share precious bandwidth with voice. Also, even if an e-mail got delayed because of network congestion, it was queued and sent just a few seconds later.

After 9/11, more and more police and fire departments as well as U.S. federal authorities signed up for BlackBerry services. BlackBerrys also shone during the great 2003 Northeast Blackout and hurricanes Anita and Katrina. But it was in the U.S. Congress where the BlackBerry first gained a serious foothold, when all the politicians and their staffs were given the device, and all the lobbyists and people doing business in Washington followed. Capitol Hill became the first dedicated metropolis on BlackBerry Planet.

RIM's BlackBerry first came to the notice of congressional leaders during 9/11 when poor communications hampered the evacuation of the Capitol building. Washington was literally under attack for the first time since August 1814. It was only by luck that the third plane did not crash into the Capitol or White House. Michigan Representative Fred Upton, who already owned a BlackBerry, was one of the few able to get messages in and out during the chaos. RIM suddenly had a sterling reputation for security, and the U.S. Congress took notice.

A few short weeks later, the October 2001 anthrax scare focused even more attention on BlackBerrys, since Congress had to start sterilizing mail for biological hazards and screening it for bombs. This event delayed regular mail delivery to lawmakers by up to two weeks.

Faced with these two crises, a rattled U.S. Congress promptly spent $6 million to buy BlackBerry Enterprise Servers and 3,000 devices for all 100 senators, 435 House members, and thousands of staffers. There were really no other contenders, and Capitol Hill was soon hooked. Within a few years, Congress had more than 8,200 installed BlackBerrys, and congressional servers were handling more than 25 million e-mail messages a month.

The BlackBerry quickly became a congressional essential. In 2006, Congress panicked and nearly declared a second American Revolution when Judge Spencer in Virginia, trying the NTP patent case against Research In Motion, threatened to shut down the BlackBerry service completely. Members of Congress rose unanimously against any threat to their constitutional right to bear BlackBerrys.

Today, BlackBerrys have become so pervasive in American politics, the show could probably not run without them. New Jersey Representative Scott Garrett, recently interviewed by *Politico*, had this to say about his BlackBerry use:

Garrett: Yeah, today I was without it for about 45 minutes, and the whole time it was like panic.

Politico: I don't understand how members can outright not use one. It almost seems impossible.

Garrett: Well, obviously we did it before there were BlackBerrys.[1]

THE AGE OF TELEPOLITICS

U.S. politics today is a fast-moving, lobby-driven profession, and the BlackBerry is a perfect prop and timely tool for lawmakers. In Washington, D.C., every congressional committee meeting is like an electronic trading pit, where competing vote traders watch the action intently, thumbing messages to and from their home offices. And behind every successful politician you'll find an army of BlackBerry toting "telepols," all plugged in to their leader.

(Continued)

---

1. Daniel Libit, "The Shuttle: Rep. Scott Garrett," *Politico*, May 16, 2008.

(*Continued*)

Florida Representative Adam Putnam, who was part of the first freshman class to be issued a BlackBerry, says that member-to-member messaging is now pretty routine in the House. He says his party's leadership has started e-mailing key materials directly to members each morning, bypassing press people and staff. He feels the handhelds have broadened members' horizons by boosting their comfort level with the Internet: "So, you have members talking about what's on Drudge or Town Hall or Red State." Black-Berrys have "dragged members out of the Dark Ages and into the information age. You now have members conversant about blogs, online news sites, signed up for breaking news alerts. So they're actually less insulated today ... than they were before BlackBerry."[2]

⊕　　⊕　　⊕

"Karl Rove has more bandwidth, I think, than any presidential advisor has ever had in history."
　　　　　—*Mark McKinnon, Bush media consultant*

The White House installed its first e-mail services under George Bush Senior, but he personally never used them. Now, however, the elder Bush describes himself as a "black belt wireless e-mailer." During Houston Astros' games, he sits behind home plate with his BlackBerry and waves back on TV when he gets e-mails from friends.

Bill Clinton was not a BlackBerry fan and sent only two e-mails during his entire term, preferring to use a secure cell phone and dedicated fax line. Even then, he felt increasingly isolated in the Oval Office, a place he liked to call "the crown jewel of the federal penal system." According to Clinton aide Paul Begala,

---

2. Daniel Libit, "Are Members BlackBerry Addicts?" *Politico*, June 11, 2008.

"Presidents can stay in touch with their pre-presidential friends, but they have to work at it. In the pre-BlackBerry age, presidents gave their friends their special, secret ZIP code, listed their names with the White House operator, with instructions to put the calls through, even gave out the cell phone numbers of close aides."[3]

George W. Bush was expecting to be the first BlackBerry president, but he had to give his up on assuming office due to concerns about e-mail security and the Presidential Records Act (PRA). The PRA puts each president's correspondence in the official record and ultimately up for public review or able to be subpoenaed by Congress or the courts. So, three days before Bush's first inauguration, knowing he was about to be locked into the Oval Office, he sent a mournful message from G94B@aol.com to forty-two friends and relatives that explained his predicament: "Since I do not want my private conversations looked at by those out to embarrass, the only course of action is not to correspond in cyberspace. This saddens me. I have enjoyed conversing with each of you."

But for Bush's entourage, some of whom used their Republican National Committee BlackBerrys and e-mail accounts, it was business as usual. During the 2002 election season, Bush's friend and operative Karl Rove "wore his war room on his belt." Rove's BlackBerry held his Rolodex and e-mail system, which he used to flash marching orders to campaign workers and soothe worried lobbyists. Rove was such a BlackBerry devotee that *Time* magazine reported his device had "every appearance of being surgically attached to his hand."

Rove, a.k.a. "The Boy Genius," amazed people with his BlackBerry use. "It's like haiku," said a friend. Even in the middle of meetings with Bush, Rove would spin the thumbwheel and punch out pithy messages with his big thumbs. "Sometimes

———
3. Paul Belaga, "Obama Should Keep That BlackBerry," CNNPolitics.com, January 9, 2009.

we're in a meeting talking to each other," said a colleague, "and BlackBerrying each other at the same time."[4]

Unfortunately for Rove, his attempt to do an end-run around the PRA by using Republican National Committee e-mail accounts was slammed by a Washington judge, who called it an "apparently flagrant violation of the Presidential Records Act."

George W. Bush's lack of a BlackBerry may have insulated him more than he wanted to be. In *Angler*, Barton Gellman's book about the Cheney vice presidency, Cheney was facing a growing revolt by the Justice Department over warrantless wiretapping, and the acting attorney general finally came to see Bush and told the president he was refusing to go ahead. This crisis had been going on for six weeks, and nobody had been able to tell the president.

Bush was completely shocked when he realized how insulated he had become.

Says journalist Julian Sanchez, "Nobody wants to give the boss unwelcome news, and so the person at the top of the hierarchy often ends up least aware of what's going on. It's all too easy to imagine an online president getting bogged down in an unmanageable flood of correspondence, but there's also clear value in finding some way for folks at a few steps' removed from the inner circle to circumvent the minders and get the attention of the president directly. Maybe it's time for Digg.gov?"[5]

Bush recalled that when he was governor of Texas, "I stayed in touch with all kinds of people around the country, firing off e-mails at all times of the day to stay in touch with my pals." When he returned to private life, says aide Karen Hughes, he immediately signed back on.

Bush's brother, Florida Governor Jeb Bush, was also a BlackBerry addict and called himself "America's first e-governor."

---

4. James Carney and John F. Dickerson, "W. and the 'Boy Genius,'" *Time*, November 9, 2002.
5. Julian Sanchez, "The First BlackBerry President?" *Ars Technica*, November 24, 2008.

He listed his e-mail address publicly, and personally answered hundreds of constituent e-mails a day. He feels his administration helped change how the government and people interrelate and helped make Floridians generally more hopeful and optimistic. In December 2006, Jeb Bush unveiled his official portrait at the governor's mansion in Tallahassee. It showed him standing beside a bookshelf, with his personal BlackBerry next to a picture of his family.

🌐   🌐   🌐

"In just the first few weeks, I've had to engage in some of the toughest diplomacy of my life. And that was just to keep my BlackBerry."

—Barack Obama

During the 2008 U.S. election campaign, Barack Obama campaign director David Axelrod got more and more frustrated when team attention wandered away during strategy meetings and participants went into BlackBerry Prayer Position. Even candidate Obama would sneak a peek at his device. So Axelrod came up with a brutal way of dealing with the problem: during work sessions, at the first sign of people getting into position, he ordered all participants, Obama included, to unholster their BlackBerrys and place them in the center of the table.

Obama was the first true BlackBerry candidate. During the campaign, aides did not send him printed stacks of briefing books but rather e-mailed digests to his BlackBerry for review. He looked at longer documents on his laptop computer, putting his editorial changes in red type. He also relied on his BlackBerry to keep the home fires burning, e-mailing his wife and daughters constantly. And before bed, he played a few games of BrickBreaker to unwind; reports say the president's high score is around 15,000.

Right after Obama's election win, he replied to a friend's congratulatory e-mail from his BlackBerry with the line "How about that?"

Ultimately, Obama had to face the same BlackBerry issues as George W. Bush. Even though he was elected in "the most technologically sophisticated presidential campaign in history," the Secret Service told Obama he would have to give up his BlackBerry for security reasons, once installed as chief executive. Hackers around the world would rise to the challenge of getting into the e-mail of the most important smartphone on Earth—look how easily amateur hackers got into Sarah Palin's personal e-mail account (gov.palin@yahoo.com) during the election campaign. Also, every word a president generated by way of correspondence had to be archived. Finally, the White House was heavily protected by an electronic security field, and wireless didn't work too well inside.

"Imagine you're Barack Obama," said Michael Agger in *Slate*. "Your operatives played social media like a fiddle while coordinating field operations via text message, e-mail blast, and iPhone app. You proved yourself to be a modern info-executive with your 3 a.m. e-mails and your preference for reviewing docs on your BlackBerry .... Now, you're preparing to enter the White House, and your BlackBerry is about to be ripped from your clutches."[6]

Said Obama advisor Linda Douglas, "Given how important it is for him to get unfiltered information from as many sources as possible, I can imagine he will miss that freedom." Campaign manager David Plouffe said that losing his BlackBerry would be more than just an inconvenience for Obama: "It's an important way for him to operate with his colleagues, but also it's very important for him to stay in touch with ... his friends and his family. It's

---

6. Michael Agger, "Luddite in Chief: Why Barack Obama Should Keep His BlackBerry," *Slate*, November 21, 2008.

something he's really struggling with. He does live his life through technology."[7]

Barack Obama had the guts to quit smoking during the election campaign; now the most powerful man on the planet was told he was going to have to go cold turkey on his "BarackBerry" as well. No doubt his wife, Michelle, had mixed feelings. An amateur video clip taken in Chicago showed her slapping her husband's hand when he took his BlackBerry from his holster to check his e-mail during his daughter's soccer game. He quickly put it back. Later in the game, the clip showed him patting his holster absentmindedly but not daring to pull out the device.

Obama was well aware he would have a harder time kicking his BlackBerry addiction, and in a post-election interview with Barbara Walters, he said that he was trying to find a way to keep both his BlackBerry and personal e-mail account:

> One of the things that I'm going to have to work through is how to break through the isolation, the bubble that exists around the president. And I'm in the process of negotiating with the Secret Service, with lawyers, with White House staff ... to figure out how can I get information from outside of the 10 or 12 people who surround my office in the White House. Because one of the worst things I think that can happen to a president is losing touch with the struggles that people are going through every day.

Some commentators felt that breaking his BlackBerry habit would be a good thing for Obama. Would the United States have wanted a BlackBerry president anyway, and a self-confessed CrackBerry addict to boot? Some studies show that BlackBerry-wielding

---

7. Jeff Zeleny, "Lose the BlackBerry? Yes He Can, Maybe," *The New York Times*, November 15, 2008.

multitaskers end up performing each task a bit more poorly since they are afflicted by "continuous partial attention." Better a president who can concentrate on one crisis at a time.

But Obama continued to resist, even after his inauguration, and senior advisor David Axelrod told ABC News: "He's pretty determined."

In a *New York Times* interview, Obama told John Harwood: "I'm still clinging to my BlackBerry. They're going to pry it out of my hands."

> **HARWOOD**: Well, are you, in fact, going to overcome this idea as anachronistic that presidents can't use the most modern ...
>
> **President-elect OBAMA**: Well, here's what I think I can get. I think I'm going to be able to get access to a computer somewhere. It may not be right in the Oval Office. The second thing I'm hoping to do is to see if there's someway that we can arrange for me to continue to have access to a BlackBerry. I know that ...
>
> **HARWOOD**: As of this moment, you still have your BlackBerry.
>
> **President-elect OBAMA**: As of this moment, I still do. This is a concern, I should add, not just of Secret Service, but also lawyers. You know, this town's full of lawyers. I don't know if you've noticed ...
>
> **HARWOOD**: Yeah.
>
> **President-elect OBAMA**: ... and they have a lot of opinions. And so I'm still in a scuffle around that, but it—look, it's the hardest thing about being president ...
>
> **President-elect OBAMA**: I don't know that I'll win, but I'm still—I'm still fighting it. And—but here's the point I was making, I guess, is that it's not just the flow

of information. I mean, I can get somebody to print out clips for me, and I can read newspapers. What it has to do with is having mechanisms where you are interacting with people who are outside of the White House in a meaningful way. And I've got to look for every opportunity to do that—ways that aren't scripted, ways that aren't controlled, ways where, you know, people aren't just complimenting you or standing up when you enter into a room, ways of staying grounded. And if I can manage that over the next four years, I think that will help me serve the American people better because I'm going to be hearing their voices. They're not going to be muffled as a consequence of me being in the White House.[8]

In a third interview with John King on CNN, Obama was a little more belligerent about hanging on to his BlackBerry. "I think we're going to be able to beat this back," he said. "I think we're going to be able to hang on to one of these."

Obama said he would be careful about how he used the device: "Now, my working assumption, and this is not new, is that everything I write on e-mail could end up being on CNN. So I make sure that—to think before I press 'send.'"

Describing his BlackBerry as "just one tool among a number of tools that I'm trying to use, to break out of the bubble," the yet-to-be-inaugurated Democrat said he wanted "to make sure that people can still reach me. But if I'm doing something stupid, somebody in Chicago can send me an e-mail and say, 'What are you doing?' You know? Or 'you're too detached' or 'you're not listening to what is going on here in the neighborhood.' I want to

---

8. John Harwood, "John Harwood Interviews Barack Obama," *The New York Times*, January 7, 2009.

be able to have voices, other than the people who are immediately working for me, be able to reach out and—and send me a message about what's happening in America."[9]

PRICELESS PUBLICITY

All this "will he or won't he" commentary about Barack Obama's BlackBerry was a godsend for RIM.

Doug Shabelman is president of Burns Entertainment, which arranges deals between celebrities and companies. He estimates the worldwide publicity value of the president's struggles to keep his beloved Verizon BlackBerry 8830 World Edition Curve on assuming office at about $50 million. "He's consistently seen using it and consistently in the news arguing—and arguing with issues of national security and global welfare—how he absolutely needs this to function on a daily basis ... Think about how far the company has come if they're able to say, 'The president has to have this to keep in touch.'"

Laura Ries, president of marketing-strategy firm Ries & Ries and co-author of four books on brands and marketing, pegs the publicity value to RIM at more than $100 million a year if Obama were able to make product endorsements. That would top the marketing take of Tiger Woods, she said. "How often does a president get photographed? Every five minutes. The potential of him being in a photo using a BlackBerry in all likelihood is incredibly high. That would be very powerful."

A big chunk of the public sympathized with Obama's problem. In a *San Francisco Chronicle* poll, 50 percent of respondents said "NO" when asked whether Obama should have to give up his BlackBerry, and 24 percent argued he should keep it to create a

(Continued)

---

9. "Obama Plans to Keep His BlackBerry," Hindu News Update Service, January 17, 2009.

record of his presidential doings. A further 18 percent said he'll be too busy with other matters to bother with checking his e-mail.

Lori Sale, head of artist marketing at the Paradigm Talent Agency, says that the fact Barack Obama was not paid to promote his BlackBerry is even better for Research In Motion. "What makes it even more valuable than that is how authentic it is," she said.

Fran Kelly, CEO of ad agency Arnold Worldwide, said that Obama's tacit endorsement worked both ways. While he did a lot for the BlackBerry brand, the smartphone boosted Obama's image in turn. "The BlackBerry anecdotes are a huge part of Mr. Obama's brand reputation," he said. "It positions him as one of us: he's got friends and family and people to communicate with just like all of us. And it positions him as a next-generation politician."*

John McCain suffered in comparison, when he confessed to reporters that he didn't know how to check e-mail and relied on his wife for computing. On the other hand, his running mate, Alaska Governor Sarah Palin, "governs by BlackBerry." She has two devices and confesses she "feels naked without her BlackBerrys."10

"President Barack Hussein Obama has changed everything about America already—not just by being what he is but by being who he is. He is not just the first black president. He is the first BlackBerry president."

—*Tina Brown*

---

* For BlackBerry, Obama's Devotion is Priceless, by Stephanie Clifford. *New York Times*, January 8, 2009; also Clayton Harrison, BlackBerry flattered, but it'd be easier if Obama let gadget go," *Bloomberg News*, Jan. 17, 2009

10. Ross Douthat, "The Palin Record: One More Look", The Atlantic, Oct. 2008.

Even after the inauguration, Obama transition co-chair John Podesta kept up the spin, putting Obama's need to connect on a higher plane. "Obama's politics are interactive, solutions-oriented and open to the citizens," he said. Obama's BlackBerry enhanced his decision-making by helping him reach outside his inner circle. "Let the man have his BlackBerry," Podesta declared. "An off-line Obama isn't just bad for Barack. It's bad for all of us."

Others argued that the 1978 Presidential Records Act was obsolete in light of thirty years of information technology (IT) advancement. Congress needed to hold hearings to update the law rather than puzzle over whether it applied to e-mail and messaging.

Still others suggested that President Obama use other National Security Agency–approved smartphones, such as General Dynamics' Sectéra Edge or the new Guardian from L-3 Communications. But there's a learning curve with switching to a new operating system. Some said that the phone was the major security problem.

The Secret Service and National Security Agency saw that the main danger to the president lay with the cellular radio in the device, which constantly syncs with nearby wireless networks so calls can be routed to the phone. If bad guys ever got access to the cell phone systems that handled Obama's BlackBerry, they might be able to ping his smartphone to a wireless tower and track his movements. Or they could scan cellular frequencies over several days to triangulate his exact position, even down to one of several identical limousines, even though they could not decode the AES-128 encrypted BlackBerry data.

So, maybe RIM could supply the president with a more secure PIN device only?

Obama's BlackBerry battle was priceless PR for RIM in the short run. But Roger Entner, an analyst with market researcher Nielsen Co. in Boston, said the device would be a magnet for spies, and "a significant share of Russia's signal intelligence and China's signal intelligence and cyber intelligence budgets would be targeted to break it." This would put RIM's "sterling" reputation at risk.[11]

Security expert Bruce Schneier said about Obama, "Look, he can decide to paint the White House blue if he wants. The Internet is the greatest generation gap since rock and roll .... The NSA will tell you the risks, but they will never say here's what the benefits are." Obama might be productive and effective with a BlackBerry, but the risk of hacking the presidential BlackBerry is high, and, in any event, it is not possible to have absolute certainty that e-mail actually came from Obama. "No encryption program solves that," he said.[12]

Gartner security analyst John Pescatore said the problem was switching to unclassified mode to use the regular Internet. "Internet e-mail is totally unacceptable for a president to use," Pescatore said. "There is no strong authentication—how can anyone prove an e-mail came from the president? There is no integrity—how can anyone prove the content wasn't changed?" And use of encryption "doesn't stop anyone from forwarding an e-mail from him outside that closed loop."

Obama advisor John Podesta urged him to find a work-around to satisfy the security team: "They'd keep you in a lead container in the basement if you let them."

In the end, presidential security could not trump Barack Obama's CrackBerry addiction, and he didn't have to kick his tech habit, at least not entirely. He won the battle to keep his beloved BlackBerry, albeit a crippled "custom" version without a phone, for personal use only, that connected through a secure base station. His address would change regularly, and friends could not forward his e-mails or send him attachments. The National Security Agency

---

11. Crayton Harrison (Bloomberg News), "BlackBerry to Obama: Thanks, Now Lose It," *Rocky Mountain News*, January 13, 2009.
12. Bruce Schneier, "Why Obama Should Keep His BlackBerry-But Won't," *The Wall Street Journal*, November 21, 2008.

also limited his address list to an elite group of West Wing staffers, family, and friends, who were all given security briefings. He and his wife, Michelle, insisted on family contact. Vice President Joe Biden has access to Obama, as do White House Chief of Staff Rahm Emanuel, advisors David Axelrod and Valerie Jarrett, and press secretary Robert Gibbs. It is not known whether Secretary of State Hillary Clinton, talk show diva Oprah Winfrey, or actor Scarlett Johansson have the president's ear or thumb.[13]

For any phone calls in the wild, President Obama first had to use the clunky but powerful $3,350 Sectéra Edge made under special contract by General Dynamics, which has dedicated channels not on the public cell networks. In June 2009, he took delivery of a custom BlackBerry 8830 running special SecureVoice encryption software developed by Washington DC tech firm The Genesis Key, in concert with RIM. The software scrambles phone calls, emails and text messages to the highest possible level required by the NSA. But it can be used only to hook up with other BlackBerrys running the same encryption software. And the President may have to wait up to 50 minutes for an email reply, since the system actively sniffs out incoming messages for viruses or Trojan horses.

The Presidential Records Act says anything President Obama e-mails, IMs, and PINs will have historic value and must be saved. But historians will have to wait as long as twenty years to read them.

While Washington learned to cope, similar BlackBerry tensions also arose in other democratic assemblies around the world. Canada, home base of the BlackBerry, was not immune. In May 2004, the speaker of the Ontario Legislature in Toronto, Alvin Curling, told

---

13. Peter Baker, "Symbol of Elite Access," *The New York Times*, January 31, 2009.

the members that the use of BlackBerrys had "gotten out of hand, especially since the electronic devices are prohibited." Curling declared a "war on CrackBerrys" when he saw a minister reading a statement off her BlackBerry.[14]

Ottawa, Ontario, Canada, is a political town, chock-full of BlackBerry addicts. Overall, the city shares with Washington, D.C., a kind of frantic machismo about using the device. Prime Minister Stephen Harper does not use a BlackBerry, but his staffers and most other politicians on Parliament Hill are dependent. All Members of Parliament (MPs) and their staffs are given four BlackBerrys by the office of the Speaker of the House.

Former Liberal MP and financial author Garth Turner is a self-confessed connection junkie, who sleeps with his BlackBerry next to his bed. Turner particularly hates long flights when his precious device no longer works. "Traveling is hard enough," he says, "but traveling without your BlackBerry vibrating reassuringly on your hip is absolute digital hell."[15]

Durham MP Mark Holland says he felt "phantom vibrations" when away from his device for three days, and notes that there is a BlackBerry-driven "subconversation" going on all the time in committee and in the House. There is also an "emergent BlackBerry etiquette," where it's okay to use the device, even at a dinner, when everybody else is also tapping away, but it's important to be aware if there are any non-addicts in the room who might be insulted.

But there are islands of sanity on Parliament Hill. All parties ask their MPs to check their BlackBerrys at the door of caucus meetings, and the Liberal Party caucus even went so far as to pass a rule banning them outright. You can also find a few people off the Hill with some decent perspective on RIM's invention and how it ought to be used.

---

14. "Sour Grapes over MPPs' BlackBerries," *Toronto Star*, May 3, 2004.
15. Harris MacLeod, "Call Them CrackBerrys," *Hill Times*, June 2, 2008.

Chapter One

Dick Fadden is former Deputy Minister of Citizenship and Immigration in the government of Canada.* Fadden became a hero to his department and to scores of government employees when in January 2008 he banned BlackBerry use for business from seven o'clock at night and on weekends. Well, not exactly *banned*. Fadden called the new policy *"operating rules,"* designed to help "attack some of the stresses around work":

- BlackBerry blackout between the hours of 7:00 p.m. and 7:00 a.m. and on weekends and holidays;
- Meetings should not be held during the lunch hour;
- BlackBerrys should not be used during meetings;
- Meetings should start and finish on time as a means of managing workloads.**

I visited Fadden a year after the famous memo and asked him whether the policy had any effect. Right away he said, "Look, we consider the BlackBerry has great value in the department. It's a useful tool and boosts productivity. But it has to be managed."

I asked him whether he had done any analysis of the BlackBerry blackout. He said he brought it up regularly with his managers and found "the main result was a major drop in the amount of e-mail delivered in the department. Although it is creeping up again."

How did Fadden manage his own personal use as a senior public servant? He said he never uses e-mail on his BlackBerry, but only PINs or sends messages for security. E-mail stays on his PC. He turns his off at eleven at night, but of course he still has to be available for emergencies by phone 24/7.

---

* In June, 2009, he was appointed head of the Canadian Security Intelligence Service (CSIS)
** See Fadden's memo on the *BlackBerry Planet* Web Support site under Texts and Documents.

Fadden says public reaction to his policy was mixed. Some newspaper letter writers said he should "get a life" or "join the 21st Century." One senior manager sniffed that the BlackBerry blackout was "a stupid decision that pretends to deal with the real issue of workload and stress. So would we have banned telephones on bureaucrats' desks at the turn of the century?"[16]

But overall the policy struck a nerve. People in Fadden's department were clearly suffering under the onslaught of e-mail and the expectation of always being on. They knew they needed to manage their addiction and attack their BlackBerry abuse. One employee told CTV News, "We're feeling the pressure trying to get a lot of stuff done in a short period of time and the fact that they're recognizing our families are suffering the consequences of it, I think it's a great idea."[17]

I asked Fadden why these kinds of operating rules were not more popular and why they weren't government policy across the board. He said other departments were bringing in similar guidelines to a greater or lesser extent, but that it was not something that should be imposed from above. Policies had to be tailored to each department, and managers had to be convinced they were useful in their particular cases.

Fadden acknowledged his measures might seem a "bit artificial" to some. Obviously you had to be flexible and recognize that some meetings had to go on longer or you had to keep your BlackBerry on at critical times. But finding ways to respect the needs of employees to balance their work and life was worth it. And the very fact of having a policy—not a ban—still makes people aware of the dangers and time-wasting if they don't respect others in the amount of e-mail they send.

---

16. "'BlackBerry Blackout' Imposed on PS," *Ottawa Citizen*, February 1, 2008.
17. "Immigration Canada Calls for BlackBerry Blackout," CTV.ca, February 1, 2008.

Chapter One

Linda Duxbury, a professor at Carleton University's Sprott School of Business in Ottawa, hailed Fadden's move as "visionary" since, in her opinion, many people in the public service were too "wired" to do their jobs efficiently and productively. "Good for him, it's the kind of leadership the public service needs, and this is leadership because he's doing something that is not easy. The whole public service revolves around the BlackBerry and being available 24/7 and he's the first to go beyond talking about balance."

⊕   ⊕   ⊕

Queen Elizabeth II is a thoroughly modern, high-tech monarch. She gets a buzz from her Royal BlackBerry, a gift from Vodafone. She is by all accounts only moderately addicted and gives trusted reporters a business card with her e-mail address. Apparently it's not oneself@houseofwindsor.uk.

The Queen got her first mobile phone in 2001 but never uses it in public. She also banned her staff from using them while on duty at Buckingham Palace, Balmoral, Sandringham, and Windsor Castle. Several waiters and butlers were nearly sent off for beheading when they were caught fumbling with their ringing phones during an official banquet for a foreign dignitary.

As befitting her regal status, the Queen normally dictates replies to an aide rather than writing them herself. However, Buck House insiders say she does use her handheld to send short messages to Princes William and Harry, who taught her how to text.

The eighty-three-year-old Queen was turned on to BlackBerrys in 2005 by her son Prince Andrew, the Duke of York, who equipped himself and his staff with the devices. Her Majesty already owned an Apple iPod, which she filled with patriotic tunes such as "Land of Hope and Glory" and other favorites from *The Last Night of the*

Proms. In 2007, she delivered her Christmas Day message for the first time as an MP3 podcast.

The Palace, like any other well run business, is now properly equipped with a secure BES and BlackBerrys to enable members of the Royal Family and their staff to keep in discrete but constant touch with their offices while out and about on official engagements.

The Duke of York himself is a technology fanatic and regularly attends conferences. He is enthusiastic about BlackBerry innovations, and in 2008, he joined Mike Lazaridis to officially open the new U.K. headquarters of Research In Motion in Slough, England.

Apparently "By Appointment to Her Majesty the Queen" still rules the waves, the electromagnetic ones.

⊕　⊕　⊕

Across the Channel in France, it was another story. President Nicholas Sarkozy clearly had a problem with his BlackBerry manners. By 2007, he was becoming known as "the King of Bling" for his serious attachment to clunky watches, Ray-Ban aviators, and obsessive BlackBerry use. The French were shocked when he risked offending Pope Benedict by sneaking a peek at his BlackBerry during an audience with the pontiff. Presumably it was an urgent call from his gorgeous new lady, now his wife, Italian model and singer Carla Bruni.

By early 2008, Sarkozy's popularity ratings had plummeted, and he was forced by his advisors to adjust his lifestyle before a state visit to England to visit Queen Elizabeth. With this excursion, the rebranded and "re-presidentialized" Sarkozy soon redeemed himself in the eyes of the French. He and Madame Bruni appeared in understated yet elegant couture befitting a head of state and consort. The notoriously impatient president's BlackBerry was nowhere to be seen, and his ratings recovered as he re-emerged as a leader of "elegance and discretion."[18]

⊕　　⊕　　⊕

"According to the emerging etiquette of the online era, it's the height of rudeness to take out your handheld device and check your emails while friends or colleagues are talking. But what if they've been talking for seven hours?"
　　　　　　　　　　　　　　—Oliver Burkeman, The Guardian

Downsides to BlackBerry politics are emerging. For one thing, BlackBerrys are now the new techno–crib sheet, allowing handlers to provide real-time feedback to their politicians. In the 2004 U.S. election, Senate Democratic candidate Representative Peter Deutsch was caught checking his device during a live-TV debate in Florida. He said, "He was getting words of encouragement from his staff and only checked it during commercials." WPTV producer Tom Kastanotis said he will consider asking candidates not to wear or hold BlackBerrys during debates in the future.[19]

Another downside to BlackBerry use can be obsession with the device over the job. During the 2008 Democratic leadership campaign, it emerged that Hillary Clinton's staffers were spending more time relating to the media and interfacing with star reporters than promoting the fortunes of their candidate.

New York Democratic National Committee member Robert Zimmerman, a prominent Clinton supporter, publicly grumbled that "Hillary Clinton has a very powerful populist message about issues that impact people's lives, and it's being undermined by all these group therapy discussions the campaign staff is having with the media."

---

18. Henry Samuel, "Nicolas Sarkozy to Shed 'King of Bling' Image," *Telegraph*, March 18, 2008.
19. Margaret Kane, "BlackBerry Season in Florida Politics," CNET, August 6, 2004.

"The most important innovation this campaign could pursue," said Zimmerman, "is confiscating all the BlackBerrys so they do their jobs."[20]

The Washington obsession with BlackBerrys is even spreading onto the august floor of the U.S. Senate, where members now openly flaunt the ban on electronic devices. In 2005, Sergeant at Arms Bill Pickle warned that "These devices are not only disruptive to the legislative business on the Senate floor, but they cause interference with the chamber's audio system." However, only two years later, in December 2007, Missouri Senator Christopher "Kit" Bond was caught glancing repeatedly at his BlackBerry as he delivered his oration, marking the first time anyone in the chamber had seen a fellow member of Congress reading his speech directly from a PDA.

It's not just e-mail any more. It's Google. Senators are using the BlackBerry as an instant information tool. *The Washington Post* described the scene on Valentine's Day 2008:

In the presiding officer's chair, Sen. Robert Menendez (D-N.J.) read a briefing book during a vote but had his BlackBerry next to the binder, dutifully checking the device infamously known by Capitol Hill staff as a "CrackBerry." Menendez took the precaution of lowering his BlackBerry onto his lap so his colleagues couldn't see him typing.

Even senior staff openly use their BlackBerrys these days. Yesterday, the top Republican floor adviser, David Schiappa, used his to conduct quick research in response to a question from Sen. Olympia J. Snowe (R-Maine).[21]

Congressional activities are getting more and more virtual. In April 2008, Senator Sam Brownback (R-Kan.), a self proclaimed "BlackBerry hound," used his BlackBerry to e-mail his chief of

---

20. Ben Smith, "Hillary Banks on a Game-Changing Event," *Politico*, March 4, 2008.
21. Mary Ann Akers and Paul Kane, "BlackBerrys in Hand, Senators Thumb Their Noses at Ban," *The Washington Post*, February 14, 2008.

staff from his seat at the Papal Mass at the Washington Nationals' ballpark to change the language of a resolution welcoming Pope Benedict XVI, since the wording had offended Senator Barbara Boxer (D-Calif.).

Brownback loves how his BlackBerry cuts down meeting time and workload but says, "I do see it as distracting at times. When you're in meetings and you get hit with a BlackBerry message and you get so trained to respond to the jolt at your side, I see it as distracting people, and in a way that is not very mannerly."[22]

The Mother of Parliaments in Westminster was not immune to the BlackBerry dilemma either. In February 2005, Michael Martin, the speaker of the British House of Commons, issued a ruling that MPs would be ejected from the chamber if they used their BlackBerrys or other handheld devices during debate. He also cautioned members against using hidden earpieces.

Speakers and their deputies had long frowned on the use of electronic devices in the Commons chamber, and the chirp of a mobile or pager could result in a strong rebuke or ejection by the sergeant at arms. At the time, messaging in and out of the chamber during debates was restricted to slips of paper passed by lackeys wearing black tail-coated uniforms.

Speaker Martin's raspberry to the BlackBerry came one day after he spied several MPs tapping on their BlackBerrys during debates. When questioned by the press, most MPs agreed with his ruling, although Labour MP Sir Peter Soulsby later admitted, "Many of us use them rather covertly, both in committees and in the chamber."

Yet only two years later, it was clear to the speaker that a boundary line had been crossed. He was finding his 2005 dictate

---

22. Daniel Libit, "Are Members BlackBerry Addicts?" *Politico*, June 11, 2008.

too hard to enforce—more and more members seemed lost in prayer during the most long-winded speeches, and he knew exactly what that meant.

Finally, in 2007, the Commons Modernisation Committee asked the speaker to allow handheld devices in the Commons "so backbenchers could make better use of their time." Most agreed with committee chair Jack Straw, who said that "lengthy speeches and long waits before being called upon to ask a question can mean backbench MPs are left twiddling their thumbs for hours. And that boredom leads to low morale and may even be discouraging some MPs from attending parliamentary debates." His report, entitled *Revitalising the Chamber: The Role of the Back Bencher*, concluded that "The use of handheld devices to keep up to date with emails should be permitted in the chamber provided that it causes no disturbance."

On October 29, 2007, after three hours of debate, the members voted seventy-four votes to thirty-six to allow handheld use in the House of Commons.

Meanwhile, in Norway, where BlackBerrys and other PDAs are allowed, one bored parliamentarian was censured after he was found playing BrickBreaker on his BlackBerry during a debate on Norway's military action in Afghanistan. So, apparently e-mailing in Parliament is okay these days, but entertaining yourself is definitely not.

"Technology is part of our bodies. Electric technology is directly related to our central nervous systems ... Those parts of ourselves that we thrust out in the form of new invention are attempts to counter or neutralize collective pressures and irritations. But this counter irritant usually proves a greater plague than the initial irritant, like a drug habit."
—Marshall McLuhan

In Washington, world capital of workaholism, many young professionals find BlackBerrys a godsend. They're proud of their capacity for suffering, for not having a life off the Hill, and for their 24/7 work culture, and the BlackBerry is a big part of that culture. But in that same Washington milieu that has so enthusiastically adopted BlackBerrys, there are signs of dissent, and they come from more senior politicians and pundits. Some are arguing that the device has put too much power of access in the hands of donors, lobbyists, and friends, with a hotline to the member's BlackBerry, while regular constituents have to e-mail a general inbox.

Former Oklahoma Representative Mickey Edwards, who now lectures on government at Princeton University, thinks all the constant input from linked-in constituents makes partisan politics worse. "It's just going to lock you in tighter and tighter to your preconceived positions. It works toward more polarization."

Steve Frantzich, a professor of political science at the U.S. Naval Academy, says handheld usage "reduces George Washington's 'cooling saucer' by allowing members less time for deliberation and more tendency to respond without much thinking." Having a BlackBerry makes a member of Congress "always 'on,' with little downtime or little ability to say, 'I don't know.'"

"They're not really free agents anymore," adds former House historian Raymond Smock. "They're captives of whoever contacts them next."[23]

Other Capitol Hill BlackBerry users feel that this new technology is enslaving them even as it sets them free. On the one hand, most love to feel untethered and free with mobile smartphones such as the BlackBerry. But many also hate it when e-mail interrupts their lives, shackling them to a new ball and chain when they feel compelled to use them wherever and whenever.

---

23. Ibid.

So they grumble that BlackBerrys have become wireless leashes that bind them to work off hours, whether they like it or not. "I still believe the premise that someone in my position is entitled to some personal time," said one U.S. Defense Department employee. "I've had guys say they'd kill for one, but I don't like the fact that I am electronically tethered twenty-four hours a day, seven days a week."[24]

While Barack Obama treasures his BlackBerry as a way to stay connected with the outside world, others welcome any excuse to ditch the device and go on an enforced digital holiday. In April 2007, when RIM's North American networks went down for ten hours, one major investment bank warned that important deals might fall through. But many other users breathed a sigh of relief, grateful for the break from their BlackBerry shackles.

The smarter BlackBerry users in government learn that the key is knowing when to turn it off, when to avoid being *always on*. Some leaders have taken direct action to give people a break. Ontario Premier Dalton McGuinty banned BlackBerrys from Cabinet meetings, saying that "It's really hard to receive information and be thoughtful at the same time." Others have instituted "BlackBerry blackout."

The wisest of Washington's wireless warriors know there is a time and a place for everything. D.C.'s exclusive Metropolitan Club, "incorporated for literary, mutual improvement and social purposes," lets its members cope with the surrounding Sahara of silicon by offering a green digital oasis and watering hole. The club rules state simply that members and their guests must not take notes at the tables or use their BlackBerrys.

So how did a device such as the BlackBerry become so addictive that managers actually need to control its uses and abuses? The best place to look for clues is in the story of the BlackBerry's birth and early development.

---

24. Alina Tugend, "Blackberry Jam," *Government Executive*, November 1, 2004.

The Birth
of the BlackBerry

"Mike is a modern Leonardo da Vinci."
—Ken Wood, Microsoft Corp. Cambridge, England

The founder of Research in Motion and the lead architect of the BlackBerry was born Mihalis "Mihal" Lazaridis in 1961 in the bustling Greek quarter of Istanbul, Turkey. Mike's father, Nick, worked as a clothing salesman, and his mother, Dorothy, was a seamstress. In 1966, they grew worried about rising Turkish-Greek tensions in the Aegean Sea and Cyprus. Eager to make a fresh start, the family decided to pull up stakes and start a new life in Canada.

Nick and Dorothy sold their business and, packing all their belongings into just three suitcases, flew to London, England, then took an ocean liner to Canada. One of Mike's first boyhood memories was flying his bird-shaped kite over the stern of the ship as it steamed over the Atlantic Ocean. He was captivated by the motion of the boat and how the wind kept the kite in the air.

Reaching Montreal after a six-day voyage, the family caught a train to Toronto, then Windsor, Ontario, across the river from the great motor city of Detroit, Michigan. Nick got a job on the

Chrysler Canada assembly line and Dorothy settled into working from home. Mike was just five years old.

Young Mike grew up in a hard-working, blue-collar neighborhood with good schools and libraries. His parents and teachers soon realized he was a sponge for knowledge, and they encouraged his lifelong love affair with science. At age four, he made a model phonograph out of LEGO and then at age eight, a working pendulum clock. He got turned on to electricity by an electric train. At age twelve, he won a prize at the Windsor Public Library for reading every science book on the shelves.

"I was fascinated by all of it, particularly physics and electronics," Lazaridis said. "One book that really caught my attention was *The Boy Electrician* by Alfred Morgan, which showed me how to make amplifiers and generators and things like that. I got a few electric shocks making them."[1]

"He was always in the basement concocting something," says his younger sister, Cleo. In grade six, Mike and best friends Doug Fregin and Ken Wood (a pastor's son who later became a Cambridge professor) set up a rec room workshop, where they built radios, rockets, and iodine bombs made from chemicals supplied by Ken's mother, a science teacher. One Halloween, the boys constructed a mechanical haunted house in the church basement of Ken's father, with screaming heads, grasping hands, and flying bats.

Mike and his friends were all rabid fans of the *Star Trek* TV show. The original Gene Rodenberry series, starring Montreal actor William Shatner as Captain James T. Kirk, was packed with gadgets, including wireless handheld communicators, scanners, and tricorders, cloaking devices, laser surgery, and desktop computers.

Star Trek's futuristic tools inspired the boys to start some serious tech tinkering. Mike and Ken Wood even decided to see

---

1. Paul Marks, "Beyond the BlackBerry," *New Scientist*, March 12, 2008. < * >

whether it was possible to build force fields using wires, switches, and chemicals. In the end, the young Trekkies gave up. "That's one of the things that, however much tenacity either of us had, we never managed to finish," Wood later said. But in high school, he and Ken did succeed in building their own computer and programming it using primitive toggle switches.

The boys got a lot of guidance from their electronics shop teacher, who ran the local ham radio and amateur television club. Doug Fregin recalled that if Mr. Micsinszki thought you had a good idea, he'd allow you to come in after hours and try out your thinking. "There was something called ATV [amateur television], which allowed ham operators to put their call letters on a television screen, and people around the world could pick that up. Most of this is done in people's basements, but we designed a way to send that information over the air. Automated television."[2]

Mike and Doug soon developed a passion for wireless technology. They spent hours in Micsinszki's labs tinkering with the equipment that a wealthy benefactor had donated to the school and sending ATV signals between Windsor and Detroit. Micsinszki let the boys use the lab during the summer holidays and took them to ham-radio swap meets, where they could buy parts on the cheap.

"I loved problem-solving," Mike says, "and electronics became almost instinctive to me. I felt a tangible connection with how the electrons flowed. To me it wasn't an intellectual exercise. I could almost feel my way through circuit designs. I always wanted to be an electronics engineer, but what really inspired me was the fact that you could use mathematics to predict things—and some pretty amazing things, such as the way Maxwell's equations predicted electromagnetic waves to give us radio."[3]

2. Laura Pratt, "Persistence in Motion," *PROFIT* magazine, May 2001.
3. Paul Marks, "Beyond the BlackBerry," *New Scientist*, March 12, 2008. < * >

In fact, it was another Canadian, Reginald Fessenden, who used Maxwell's discoveries to come up with the heterodyne technique and transmit speech over radio waves for the first time on December 23, 1900.

Mike vividly remembers his teacher's foresight: "Don't get too hooked on computers. Someday the person who puts computers and wireless technology together is really going to come up with something special."[4]

The friends always entered the Windsor science fair, and Mike and Doug won first prize with a solar-powered water heater that tracked the sun. In his final year of high school, Mike sold a buzzer system he had developed for *Reach for the Top*, a high school quiz show. The funds paid the tuition fee for his first year of college.

Mike Lazaridis still calls his old shop teacher, Mr. Micsinszki, every Christmas, to say hello and send his very best wishes.

"Going back and forth between work and university gives you a whole different view on what you're learning, and how it gets applied."

—*Mike Lazaridis*

The city of Waterloo, Ontario, sits on gently rolling hills along the Grand River, bounded on the north by the fertile fields of prosperous Mennonite farmers. You can see them, dressed head to toe in black, driving their buggies to church or pitching hay onto wagons in scenes right out of the Middle Ages.

There are about 100,000 citizens in this bucolic community an hour's drive west of Toronto. Most people work for Research In Motion or other high-tech outfits, or for one of three big insurance

---

4. Laura Pratt, "Persistence in Motion," *PROFIT* magazine, May 2001.

companies, or for one of the three universities and colleges. Waterloo is a student haven, with about 50,000 swelling the regular population.

The University of Waterloo (UW), founded in 1957, was the first accredited university in North America to create a Faculty of Mathematics. It has the largest co-op program in the world, with students gaining credits for work in one of the local companies.* UW's intellectual property policy wisely leaves ownership rights with the inventor rather than the university. This has helped to foster a dazzling galaxy of high-tech spin-offs, more than any other Canadian university. UW's Faculty of Engineering, considered one of Canada's best, holds the world record for the longest distance traveled by a solar car.

In the fall of 1979, at age eighteen, Mike Lazaridis enrolled at the University of Waterloo in electrical engineering with an option in computer science. The university, sometimes called "the MIT of the North," was a breeding ground for computer buffs with big ideas. A burgeoning Microsoft was about to start cherry-picking many of the best tech grads and shipping them off to its Redmond, Washington, campus.

But Mike and his friends were more charged up about wireless technology and determined to start their own companies. Many of their courses combined study with work experience, and this fired them further.

Mike got co-op credits in his first year at the Waterloo branch of supercomputer maker Control Data Corporation (CDC). His job was to research automatic error detection and correction in computer memory. He recalled, "This made me realize that I could get

---

* RIM today hires more than 600 co-op, intern, and summer students every year from local and national universities and colleges. Lazaridis often tells people that he "built his factory right next to the mine," referring to the nearby University of Waterloo, Wilfred Laurier University, and Conestoga College.

paid to improve other research teams' operating systems, or build computer circuits for them."[5]

CDC's Programmed Logic for Automated Teaching Operations (PLATO) computerized learning system, launched in 1978, was pretty amazing for its day, pioneering concepts such as online forums and message boards, online testing, e-mail, chat rooms, picture languages, instant messaging, remote screen sharing, and multiplayer online games fifteen years before they became mainstream.

While working at CDC, Mike learned an important lesson about business that made a huge difference to his later success. CDC was on the downslope as Japanese competitors were entering the supercomputer market. The CDC corporate culture was crumbling, and Mike saw firsthand the damage done when engineers with cutting-edge ideas had to butt heads with the marketing department, who demanded simple products to attract customers. Many of the CDC engineering staff were so frustrated that they were quitting for the greener pastures of Silicon Valley.

His CDC work left a lasting impression on Lazaridis and gave him an insight that he would carry on into his RIM career—that technology companies have to nurture engineers. Simplifying a product does not encourage customers to purchase newer models. "The kiss of death," he says, "is when you allow marketing to dumb down innovations."[6]

Mr. Micsinszki's caution about not getting too captivated by computers still echoed in Mike's brain. So he focused on marrying computers and wireless technology with e-mail and the new local-area networks that were emerging in university. He did some more

5. Paul Marks, "Beyond the BlackBerry," *New Scientist*, March 12, 2008. < * >
6. Amy Gunderson, "26 Most Fascinating Entrepreneurs," Inc.com, Feb. 18, 2009.

tinkering with wireless radio and the automated display system he and Doug Fregin had worked on in high school, and in 1984, he wrote a program that generated a video signal to send data to any computer monitor. He thought about taking it to market as a display system for stores, but wisely realized he had zero business experience. So he decided to talk to Larry Smith, his professor of economics, about how to produce and sell wireless data devices. As Smith recalled, "Mike gave me a general introduction to his whole idea. He had a maturity of view that was quite exceptional. One of my earliest impressions of Mike was his commitment to quality for its own sake. He understands that, pragmatically, quality sells. But he has pride in the craftsmanship of an engineer. That's an extremely admirable characteristic, not so common as one might hope."[7]

From his work at CDC, Mike knew he had the skills to make a self-employed living. So he and Doug Fregin agreed to take the entrepreneurial leap, even in the middle of a recession. Mike started off selling a few of their display systems to local stores because, he says, "there were no color laser printers and to typeset display signs was really expensive. Stores would put our signs in their windows to advertise things, or inside the store to attract people to special deals. It was so popular that I even demonstrated it on the television news. That is really what got us started."[8]

At first, he attempted to mix business and school. "I tried," he later related, "bicycling between work and school, studying for my midterms. I even tried to go back a year after, but I couldn't do it. The business kept growing. I realized I had to pick one."[9] So he decided to "take time off," just two months and a few credits shy of a degree in electrical engineering. Doug Fregin also agreed to leave

---

7. Laura Pratt, "Persistence in Motion," *PROFIT* magazine, May 2001.
8. Paul Marks, "Beyond the BlackBerry," *New Scientist*, March 12, 2008. < * >
9. Laura Pratt, "Persistence in Motion," *PROFIT* magazine, May 2001.

the University of Windsor and join him in Waterloo. Their first big break came when General Motors (GM) Canada heard about the wireless message screens they were working on. GM wanted to try them out on the assembly line floor and would be willing to pay for a trial.

⊕　　⊕　　⊕

Mike's parents in Windsor were not entirely happy with his decision and asked him to justify dropping out, but in the end they fully backed his vision. When he was able to rustle up a $15,000 Government of Ontario New Ventures loan, they also came up with some funds for their twenty-three-year-old son. So in February 1985, Mike Lazaridis and Doug Fregin launched Research In Motion (RIM) Inc.

Mike first wanted to call the company "[Something] Research." But all the good names were taken. So Mike flipped the name around and came up with "Research In Motion."

The next step was finding an office. Manfred Conrad, RIM's first landlord, recalls "two young kids coming on a bike who wanted to rent a room in an office building I owned in downtown Waterloo. They needed one room. And they needed a bike rack because it was so hard to tie their bicycles up on the railings. I'll never forget that. They were really nice kids. I didn't know what kind of business they were in. They showed me what they were fiddling around with on the computer, but I had no clue. They were the smallest tenant in the building."[10]

Job number two was to find a good programmer, so they put up a posting on the local Usenet listings. They quickly picked Mike Barnstijn, later RIM vice president, software, who was just finishing his master's degree in computer science. As Barnstijn

---

10. Laura Pratt, "Persistence in Motion," *PROFIT* magazine, May 2001.

recalls, "There was a good personality fit. We were all enthusiastic about technology, had similar educational backgrounds and a big interest in cars. I was hired on the spot as their first full-time permanent employee. I became a partner less than a year later."[11] Those were happy days, biking to work and staying late in their cramped office to finish contracts. They soon had a team of three assistants and secretaries, and had to move into a larger office down the street.

☠   ☠   ☠

The team's first job was a $600,000 contract from General Motors for networked display terminals that could scroll messages and updates across LED signs on GM's assembly lines. Says Lazaridis, "It's kind of noisy to use a phone or walkie-talkies, so most problems are enunciated on large display boards, like giant pagers in the air." RIM sold less than one hundred units. "It probably failed for more than one reason," says Doug Fregin. "We didn't have the funds to properly market it, and there was a lot of competition from the LED sign makers."

Still, they loved the work, in spite of the lack of traction. Says Mike Barnstijn, "We worked long hours back then, but it was what we wanted to do. There's a certain amount of freedom in being part of a very small company, and also a great deal of responsibility. But it was that freedom that all of us really enjoyed. The GM signs were a blast to work on. In the end, we sold the rights to the product to the company that was manufacturing them for us [Corman Technologies], and they installed a whole rack of them at GM's Oshawa plant. I'm not sure whether they're still there, but the way we built them, they could be."[12]

---

11. Laura Pratt, "Persistence in Motion," *PROFIT* magazine, May 2001.
12. Laura Pratt, "Persistence in Motion," *PROFIT* magazine, May 2001. See the Corman Technologies brochure on the Web support site < * >

In 1987, Mike Lazaridis attended a trade show where a company was showing how to use wireless data technology for managing vending machines and delivery trucks for Coca-Cola. The Coke machines could call home when they needed servicing. A light went on in Mike's brain—the demo confirmed that wireless data networking was where RIM should be focusing all its efforts. "I realized that's what I wanted to do, and since then, that's all we've done," he said. "Frankly, we've never looked back."

In the meantime, with their GM profits, RIM hired six new employees to help chase down contract work. They found that Kodak and Canada's National Film Board were teaming up on a tender for a barcode reader for motion picture film. Kodak was pioneering a new film with barcodes every six inches. These were very difficult to read because they were so small and dense.

RIM had just three days to bid on the tender, but they won it, and in 1990 came out with their first DigiSync Film Barcode Reader. The digital footage, frame and time calculator soon became a big hit with film editors and negative cutters in Hollywood—work that used to take a film editor two days now required only 20 minutes. DigiSync earned the company an Emmy Award (1994) and an Academy Award (1998) for technical achievement. Lazaridis attended a pre-Oscar ceremony in 1999, and accepted RIM's Academy Award in person from actress Anne Heche.

The DigiSync was a nice niche product at the time, but Mike soon realized that the company's real future lay elsewhere. "Winning the Academy Award was very exciting," he said. "But I knew that eventually the film technology was going to saturate, and I'd need something new. That's when I came across this wireless digital technology. That was one where we bet the farm."[13]

---

13. Laura Pratt, "Persistence in Motion," *PROFIT* magazine, May 2001.

That technology was Mobitex.

⊕   ⊕   ⊕

*"You have to understand, the BlackBerry didn't happen
overnight; it happened over a decade. It's not like one day
we woke up and said, 'Eureka!'"*

—Mike Lazaridis

By the mid 1980s, Canada's communications king, Ted Rogers, had
finished building his national Cantel cellular phone network. One
day, he was visiting his system supplier LM Ericsson in Sweden and
noticed a wireless data terminal in the cab that the taxi company
was using to dispatch calls to their drivers. Ericsson told him that it
was the next big step in wireless services and showed him their new
Mobitex network technology. Rogers decided to buy into the system,
and in early 1989 he hired Tom Pirner to head up Cantel's new Data
Communications Division. Pirner set about installing what was to
be North America's first public wireless datacom network.*

Mike Lazaridis soon landed a consulting contract from Pirner
to identify potential North American suppliers who could develop
modems to connect wireless devices to computers using Mobitex.
When Rogers found out that Ericsson had no sales demo applications, RIM programmer Mike Barnstijn coded a simple way to send
messages to and from a laptop connected to an Ericsson Mobitex
mobile radio. Barnstijn called it Mobicom.

In late 1989, Pirner brought on board engineering consultant
Robert Fraser, to manage Cantel's Mobitex development program.
Fraser had worked on radio design with Motorola and operated
his own wireless systems integration company. He and Cantel

---

* For documents relating to this network, please see BlackBerry Planet Texts and Documents
  on the Web support site < * >

marketing director David Neale soon saw there were no tools for developers who wanted to write application programs for mobile terminals. And there was no easy way to connect large office computer systems to Mobitex.

So Rob Fraser turned to RIM and had Mike Barnstijn create MobiLib, a toolkit or API (Application Programmers Interface) for developers who wanted to write Mobitex programs. They upgraded Mobicom to Mobitalk, turning it into a PC-based Mobitex e-mail application with file attachments that used the mailbox and "always on" features of Mobitex to let mobile devices talk to office computers.[*]

To jump-start product development, Fraser also pulled together a Mobitex Terminal Specification (MTS), and seeded it along with Mobitalk and MobiLib to Neale's supply channel of system integrators and application developers. Essentially, Cantel gave these specs away free to anybody who wanted to build anything for Mobitex.

At that stage, in early 1990, RAM Mobile Data (later Bell South Mobile) found itself about a year behind Cantel in rolling out its U.S. Mobitex network. So the company eagerly adopted MobiLib, and bought a license from Cantel. Fraser then pulled together a joint R&D funding deal with RAM, and they hired Research In Motion for the next two years. They put forward a set of Mobitex network gateway specifications on how to connect to customer computers, email systems and wireless point of sale terminals. But at that point Mike Lazaridis had a better idea.

Mike said a proper gateway would take a while to develop. To solve the problem in the near term, he proposed a simple Mobitex Protocol Converter (MPC) with a standard modem AT command

---

[*] This was the world's first wireless communications API. It led to all subsequent APOs for all types of smartphones, allowing for developers to create programs for online app stores on various operating systems.

set on the client's computer. RAM and Cantel agreed, and they jointly funded the MPC. RIM, in the meantime, started work on a real gateway, which it would later introduce as RIMGate, the predecessor of the BlackBerry Enterprise Server.*

For David Neale, Cantel needed someone to help figure out how Mobitex really worked and how to take it to market. "I still remember being amazed," he said, "because not only could Mike Lazaridis read this stuff and understand it, but he could actually speak this language. He was one of the very few people in those early days who had the vaguest idea what it was all about."

Neale recalls the Mobitex launch on May 17, 1990, at Toronto's King Edward Hotel. "We rented a whole pile of trees, because we had all these tables with hardware on it and it looked a bit dull. But we put in these trees, and suddenly the basement looked like the Enchanted Forest. There were nearly 300 people there: customers, developers, press. But it bombed. In October of that year, most of us who had been working on the wireless-data project got moved up to the paging network. We were so, so far in advance of the market that nobody was ready."

After building the Cantel Mobitex network over almost two years and burning through about $30 million in capital, Ted Rogers found he had no paying customers except for Rogers Cable service trucks and few prospects. So he downsized the operation only to reignite it again a few years later.

For the rest of 1990 and into 1991, RIM worked on the MPC, enhancing MobiLib, launching the MobiLib Plus API and developing a protocol analyzer called MobiView. This helped Mobitex developers debug applications and gave them a way to install secure end-to-end solutions for wireless credit card transactions on mobile point of sale terminals. RIM also boosted its staffing to

---

* This marked the start of the BES, push email and RIM's hold on the enterprise market.

over 10 employees, adding engineers Herb Little, a recent college grad whose job was to create MobiLib-Plus, and Gary Mousseau, a network expert brought in to quarterback RIMGate. Besides Mike Lazaridis, the pair turned out to be RIM's most prolific patent producers.

Mousseau, a Waterloo graduate, was a tech veteran in his thirties when he joined the kids at RIM in 1991. He had worked with Xicon in Ottawa, then National Semiconductors, building bridges from IBM terminals to mainframes. He was an expert in X.25 and SNA wireless protocols, which were being used to build the fledgling Internet. The global X.25 community had already interconnected over 75 countries by this time.*

David Neale was struck by how much a technology and hardware guy like Lazaridis was dedicated to pure science, and the need to motivate young people to study science and technology. "He would particularly like to see words such as 'geek' and 'nerd' eliminated," Neale said. "It's not because he doesn't like to be called geeky, but why would you dissuade somebody who is young—who has a hunger for this sort of knowledge—by describing this sort of stuff as geeky or nerdy?"[14]

But techies they were, existing on caffeine and pizza and code, like thousands of other eager start-up teams spreading out from Silicon Valley and colonizing the planet with their marvelous toys and tools. As Gary Mousseau, the senior employee and the only dad in the bunch, remembers it:

"In about '94 when RIMGate was going crazy, I used to bring my one-year-old son (last of four kids) to work in a portable rocker. He would sit sleeping in my office while I worked (someone reminded me of this fact recently). This way my wife had a break

---

* X.25 has been largely replaced by the Internet protocol (IP).
14. Laura Pratt, "Persistence in Motion," *PROFIT* magazine, May 2001.

and he always fell asleep on the drive over to work. This was how I managed to work later and later at night. Herb Little, on the other hand, would just work all night, period. Occasionally I caught him building a little bed out of foam inserts and he would sleep there when he got too exhausted. Once when I dared to take a weekend off, Herb decided to re-code my entire Session layer in the MobiLib-Plus product. He felt it just wasn't up to his level of quality and he needed VERY, VERY long module names; he loved names like: *SessionLayerCompressionEncoderDecoderModule* and names that were even longer."

⊕　　⊕　　⊕

The Motorola company had first used the word pager in 1959, when its radio engineers came up with a way to let operators transmit a signal to people such as doctors, alerting them to phone home base to receive a message. Motorola's Pageboy, introduced in 1974, was the first successful consumer pager. But it was one-way only, had no display, and could not store messages.

Fast forward to late 1990. The paging business took a giant evolutionary leap forward when RAM Mobile Data decided to issue a request for proposal (RFP) for a new *two-way* send-acknowledge Mobitex pager, that would behave like the instant messaging (IM) we take for granted today.

Few people could see how evolutionary this device could be. One was Rob Fraser, who had just completed his contract with Cantel. Another was Mike Lazaridis. In February 1991, Fraser agreed to do a presentation of MobiLib for Research in Motion at RAM's network launch in Washington. Fraser came away from the conference frustrated. Everybody was focusing on Mobitex as a simple paging network; nobody saw the great potential of Mobitex as the basis for a true handheld messenger with Personal Digital Assistant (PDA) features. But the Earth was beginning to move.

A year after the Washington launch, the term PDA suddenly came into vogue when Apple CEO John Scully, the former PepsiCo president who ousted Steve Jobs from Apple, used it in a speech at the 1992 Comdex show in Las Vegas. Six months later, in July 1992, Scully told the Mobile '92 conference in San Diego that Apple was readying its own handheld PDA - the Newton.*

Rob Fraser was not impressed. Apple's Newton had no radio transceiver, and thus no mobile communication abilities. It could simply synch to a desktop computer using a cradle and wires. Fraser had already published an article predicting the "wireless" PDA in the July 1991 issue of Communications Magazine.[15] In it, he laid out all the market potential and engineering challenges that had to be met before perfecting what he called the Personal Communicator, a handheld touch-screen Mobitex device with e-mail, computer bulletin board connectivity and a way to manage your calendar, contact list and other personal data.

Not everybody agreed with Fraser about the coming of the wireless PDA. Intel chairman Andrew Grove, for example. Grove knew that the small radios and microprocessors of the day chewed up power, far more than current batteries could provide. He scoffed at the idea of a wireless personal communicator in every pocket, calling it "a pipe dream driven by greed"[16] Ironically, within a few short years, Intel's low-power processors became the heart of RIM's product line.

Rob Fraser is still baffled how Mike Lazaridis led the way forward. "He had Motorola, Apple and General Magic, Bell South,

---

* Scully later predicted that the personal communicator would be "the mother of all markets."

15. *Communications Magazine*, July 1991 < * >

16. Peter Lewis, "The Executive Computer; 'Mother of All Markets' or a 'Pipe Dream Driven by Greed'?"New York Times, July 19, 1992 < * >

AT&T, Palm and a host of other heavyweights trying to accomplish the same thing." Later, when he asked RIM's chief radio engineer Dr. Peter Edmonson to speculate, Edmonson laughed and said, "everyone else was trying to add a radio to a PDA, whereas Mike's mindset was how to add a PDA to a radio."

Mobitex, in the words of Jim Balsillie, was "RIM's sandbox." The platform let Research In Motion tinker with, master and incubate a whole range of new technologies before its BlackBerry breakout.

During these pioneering years, few knew that our planet was on the cusp of a colossal cultural change brought about by the Internet. Mike Lazaridis was one, as was British computer scientist Tim Berners-Lee, who was playing around with a way to unify and interlink private network servers using hypertext, a browser and the global domain name system.

"My bottom line about Mike Lazaridis," says Fraser, "is that he's always at the right place, at the right time, with the right solution. In the mid '90s, when the World Wide Web dropped out of the sky onto millions of PCs, dragging POP email with it, Mike Lazaridis was ready—with compression, encryption, synchronization, a thumbwheel, context ribbons, thumbpad, dual destination email, always on, push BES and enough bright minds and capital to get the job done."

⊕　　⊕　　⊕

"Jim Balsillie and Mike Lazaridis are a very tenacious team."

—David Neale, Rogers Cantel

Suzy Brown, a founder of RadioMail Corp. in San Mateo, California, led the first company to provide wireless e-mail services to pagers and laptops, and she had dealings with Mike Lazaridis. "Early on," she recalls, "RIM had the engineering talent but no business sophistication. All of the discussions centered around develop-ment, and it was clear that they weren't going to develop into a long-lasting company."

Mike Lazaridis and his financial backers also knew that RIM desperately needed an energetic and skilled manager who could shore up the company's patent portfolio, negotiate supply deals, stickhandle around competitors and build new markets. In 1992, he found the leader he wanted in Jim Balsillie, CFO of a small technolo-gy firm and RIM customer Sutherland-Schultz in Kitchener, Ontario. Balsillie was hired and immediately put in charge of business devel-opment and strategy, with a mandate to find investment capital, take RIM's technologies to market and build sound client relations.

Jim Balsillie was born on February 3, 1961, in Seaforth, north of London, Ontario. His father, Raymond, worked as an electronics technician at Ontario Hydro's Darlington nuclear reactor on Lake Huron, and mother Laurel raised a family of two boys and a girl. In 1966, Jim's family moved to Peterborough, Ontario, where the boy grew up playing hockey, basketball, badminton, and track and field.

Jim showed an early talent for business, selling greeting cards door to door at age seven and handling several paper routes at the same time. As a teenager, he helped out with a Big Brothers camp, ran a ski tow, managed a student painting franchise, and did main-tenance jobs at a local trailer park. According to Balsillie's mother, "He just never let any opportunity pass up where he could learn or investigate something."[17]

After graduation from high school, Jim studied commerce at the University of Toronto. His Trinity College roommates recall that he kept his hockey interest strong, playing at Varsity Arena and budgeting breaks from studying to watch the National Hockey League playoffs.

---

17. "Jim Balsillie" by Simon Avery and Paul Waldie, Globe and Mail, February 20, 2006.

In 1984, Balsillie got his chartered accountant (CA) certificate and joined the old Toronto firm of Clarkson Gordon, now part of Ernst & Young. Three years later, he headed off to Harvard to do an MBA with new partner Heidi.

A dedicated golfer, hockey player, and triathlete, Balsillie was an aggressive, high-energy business competitor. He came on board RIM at a crucial time, and much of RIM's success in the late 1990s came from the new marketing focus engineered by Jim Balsillie.

When he joined RIM, Balsillie recalls, "There was great technology and great people at RIM, but the commercial situation was in clear need of attention. There were a lot of contracts where the ownership was unclear, the deliverables were unclear, and what it takes to get paid was unclear. That stuff is very non-trivial. That's where most companies with good technology fall down."

According to Lazaridis, Balsillie was "as creative on the business side as our team was on the science side ... RIM had been looking for a business partner like Jim for a long time. It didn't take me long to realize Jim had the talent and experience we needed to get to the next level. We could read each other's minds on a lot of things ... We're both aggressive about opportunities and going after them, and making sure we don't do things half-hearted. We make sure we have all the resources to get the job done and don't quit. But we're different in that Jim likes the business and financial ends a lot more than I do."

So while Lazaridis remained cautious about "marketing dumbing down innovation," a lesson he had learned at CDC, he trusted that Balsillie's marketing focus would not impact on RIM's technological thrusts. Like a team of horses, they knew they had to pull together toward a common goal or go careening into the ditch.

As co-CEOs of RIM, Lazaridis and Balsillie became the odd couple of the wireless business. But Balsillie knew his role. "In a few areas, Mike and I are alike," said Balsillie. "In a few areas, we're very different. Mike's the visionary, I'm the parrot.

I communicate the things he dreams up . . .. Whether I was the motor on the boat, or the one that plugged the hole on the boat, is an angel-on-the-head-of-a-pin question. Good boats don't go with holes or without motors. When I met Mike, I thought he had big expectations and ambitious dreams. And he struck me as unconventional. Sometimes his stuff made sense, and sometimes it seemed overly ambitious. I'm a pretty systematic person when it comes to commercial development: step by step by step."

"This is what impressed me about Jim," said Lazaridis. "With all the other people I'd interviewed, it was more of, 'What are you willing to give me?' Jim came in and said, 'I want to invest. I know we can make this thing work. Let's figure out what I can bring to this company.' That made a huge positive impression on me."

Inspired by what he saw at RIM, Balsillie confidently mortgaged the family house and poured $250,000—most of his life savings—into shares in Lazaridis's fledgling operation. "My wife believed I knew what I was doing," he says, "even though I'm a single breadwinner, and we'd just had a new baby, and I took a 60% cut in pay. I was thinking, this should be fun. I had had enough experience growing companies and making money that I felt I was plenty capable."[18]

> *"Mike is one of the most tenacious people I've ever met. Keeps grinding toward his goal until he gets there. There were eight or nine failures before BlackBerry. He took lots of at-bats before he hit his home run."*
>
> —*Bill Frezza, ex Ericsson*

Like Rogers, the Swedish telco Ericsson was also struck by the quality of RIM's work. Bill Frezza, director of marketing and business

---

18. Laura Pratt, "Persistence in Motion," *PROFIT* magazine, May 2001.

development, was trying to push Ericsson to move into new horizontal markets just opening up, in particular with mobile PDAs and laptops. Growth was starting to stagnate in the classical vertical markets of dispatch, utilities, police/fire/ambulance, and parcel delivery.

At the time, says Frezza, Ericsson had set up a joint venture with General Electric to develop the world's first portable wireless data modem, the Mobidem. "It ran at 8,000 baud and operated over the Mobitex data network being built by RAM Mobile Data. It weighed a pound. It lasted maybe eight hours on a full charge. The battery was about the size of today's cell phones .... One little problem. We lacked a killer app. Wireless e-mail, that's the ticket! Where can I get some? Fortunately I found this geek named Mike up in Canada who shared our vision, and then some."

Frezza and Ericsson GE Mobile Data product manager Tim Meyer created an entire development environment for RIM so they could adapt the Mobidem to communicate with PDAs and laptops using the standard Hayes AT modem command set. RAM Mobile Data had set up a Mobitex base station in Corvallis, Oregon, to test mobile PDAs such as the ultra-cool Hewlett-Packard HP-95 palm-top computer, a kind of glorified calculator with a radio that had a beautiful groundbreaking feature—it ran MS-DOS.

Frezza lobbied Ericsson to come up with an initial $50,000 loan for RIM. He also hired another company called Anterior Technology (RadioMail) to back up the system with a service bureau. Anterior was led by Geoff Goodfellow, the California techie who came up with the whole idea of wireless e-mail in 1982.[19]

By late 1991, Lazaridis and his RIM team had cranked out some decent software—their Mobitex Protocol Converter (MPC) was the critical link that created the world's first commercial

---

19. See Real World Services for the Technological Elite on the *BlackBerry Planet* Web Support site. See also Chapter 3, Lawsuits in Motion.

wireless e-mail program. It worked very well with both Microsoft Mail and Lotus cc: Mail, and Ericsson were delighted with the quality of Mike and his team's work. According to Tim Meyer, "Ericsson needed the AT commands built into the Mobidem and he delivered beautifully on a very complex assignment."*

So Ericsson GE agreed to license RIM's technology. "That was a very big early highlight," recalls Lazaridis. "That was a very large wireless company adopting our technology. The first payment was for $250,000."

⊕　　⊕　　⊕

In January 1992, Ericsson launched the Viking Express, the world's first commercial wireless e-mail solution. Enveloped in a sleek black leather case, it featured the Ericsson Mobidem, Velcroed together with an HP-95 palmtop and bundled with RIM's MobiLib-Plus application programming interface (API) to work with Goodfellow's gateway to major e-mail systems.

By the time Viking Express shipped, there was a major falling out between RIM and RadioMail. Goodfellow and his group refused to work with the RIM mobile client application and demanded Ericsson use its RadioMail-developed client. Ericsson caved in.

According to Tim Meyer, "Goodfellow had this vision of an e-mail system that had a client and a server and he built both. Frezza liked RIM and pushed Mike to build a client application for the HP95 PDA, which he did. However, Mike was not happy with the situation and I suspect neither was Goodfellow, so at the eve of the launch of the Viking Express we decided to go with RadioMail. I was not in the meeting where there was a shouting match between Goodfellow and Lazaridis, but Goodfellow won that one."

---

* Meyer says, "The protocols being converted (from one to the other) were the Hayes AT commands (the de facto standard for landline modems) and the Mobitex packet protocol. This enabled Lotus cc:Mail to run pretty much unmodified on a HP95LX."

Meyer felt that the sensible thing was to go with RadioMail, since RIM didn't yet have a workable client and server.

The Viking Express didn't go anywhere in particular. According to Frezza, "The concept was a smash even though Viking Express was a cumbersome kludge . . . Finally, we landed an OEM [Original Equipment Manufacturer] to take our product into the channels because Ericsson sure didn't have a clue." The OEM was Intel. "Behold, the Intel wireless modem. This 500-pound gorilla of the PC industry geared up for a nationwide launch. We had Intel training. We had Intel collateral. We had Intel support at the highest levels. Until a week before the launch date when they pulled the plug and everyone disappeared. Poof."[20]

Frezza was not particularly shocked. He knew by experience how tough it could be to work on the bleeding edge, ten years in advance of the market. In those early days, everybody was focused on voice, not data. Says Jim Hobbs, wireless strategist with BellSouth:

It was late 1991, and RIM was wanting to build Mobitex radios. In those days, vendor support for Mobitex was just starting. Everybody was thinking cellular, not Mobitex.
You needed all the friends you could get in those days. When you had a bunch of smart guys who had studied your technology, who had some ideas, then you were naturally drawn together. I thought Mike Lazaridis was brilliant because of his vision for the technology, his appreciation that it was about functionality and not speeds and feeds, and his willingness to innovate.

Mike Lazaridis was forced to back off, but he and his team did get from their work with Ericsson the tech savvy and core knowledge

---

20. Laura Pratt, "Persistence in Motion," *PROFIT* magazine, May 2001.

of complex radio design that eventually led to the far more functional BlackBerry platform. He also learned from his experience
with Ericsson that he needed a tough management sidekick, and
that was when Jim Balsillie entered the picture. He and Jim quickly
developed a complex code of shrugs and twitches to send signals
to each other during contract meetings.

Says Tim Meyer:

> Jim was smooth, but they brilliantly did the good cop/bad
> cop on us after he joined. Jim would literally scream over
> the phone at the Swedes for not supporting the "Mobidem
> AT" effort, which was what Ericsson paid a considerable
> sum to RIM for.
>
> The arc of deciding to build radios, then PC cards, then
> the "two-way pager" was internal to RIM. We just speeded
> things up by showing them the guts of the Mobidem OS,
> design, and development tools. Really handing them on a
> plate! So RIM danced with the elephant quite well and just
> left Ericsson in the dust in the Mobitex device business.
> Really, Ericsson was focused on a bigger nut, GSM mobile
> phones.

Meyer feels that Ericsson gave RIM a plum job, but there was no
expectation of further business. Still, he admired RIM for wanting to make everything work together in one device. "RIM could
easily have gotten locked into RAM's orbit and kept supplying
them with software drivers, adapters (The Mobitex Protocol
Converter), and other bits and pieces. In other words, become
RAM's system integrator, but they did have the foresight of
doing their own thing and charting their own course. Nowadays,
it is fashionable to talk about tight integration of hardware and
software, and that seamless integration is what it's all about.

Apple is offered as the prime example, and Microsoft as the failure with Windows Mobile. But RIM practiced this back in the 1990s!"

While Balsillie made sure the company stayed hard-nosed, Lazaridis and his team kept their eye on the ball, and RIM soon rolled out its software developer's kit (SDK) for adding wireless connectivity to Windows 3.x applications. This let software developers and programmers use RIM's code to build links between Windows programs and Mobitex.

Mobitex also let RIM compete in other emerging markets. In 1992, the team started adapting the Mobitex Protocol Converter for use in point-of-sale products such as restaurant credit card readers. Two years later, RIM introduced the first Mobitex Mobile Point of Sale Terminal (MPT) at a football game in Toronto's SkyDome [now Rogers Centre]. It was the world's first handheld point of sale card reader, with all the features vendors needed to sell beer and popcorn right in the stands. It could verify and handle debit and credit transactions directly to the bank host, in this case, Rogers' bank, CIBC.

The MPT depended on Gary Mousseau's new RIMGate system, the first general purpose Mobitex X.25 gateway. Launched in 1993, it was a whole new way to "push" packets of information across wireless networks. It could link mobile applications to services such as bank computers, AT&T Easylink (a large mail solution), Compuserve (a forerunner to AOL), and INet2000, a directory of network services, in real time.

When Jim Balsillie came on board, one of his first goals was to leverage the RIMGate advantage. He sold major site licenses to RAM Mobile Data (US), Bell South (World Site License for UK, Australia and other installations they owned) and AT&T Easylink. These site licenses amounted to over $1 million at a time when RIM was cash strapped and subsisting on contract work. Suddenly,

RIM could start leveraging its technologies and muscling its way forward.

⊕　　⊕　　⊕

At this time, RIM also helped launch two wireless modems, the Ericsson Mobidem AT and the competing Intel Wireless Modem containing RIM modem firmware.* Ericsson engineers had just launched the world's first modem card - a Type III PCMCIA radio modem that worked with laptops with Type III slots (two Type II slots, the thin ones, stacked). An impressive feat, but Mike Lazaridis knew that RIM could improve on the Ericsson product.

Their experience with Ericsson and RadioMail had also soured Lazaridis and Balsillie on working with the giant Swede, and the two sides gradually stopped talking. They soon started competing with each other.

In fact, by the mid-1990s, Lazaridis and his team were getting more and more frustrated doing wireless point-of-sale integration with another company's radios, so they started tinkering with building a RIM-only device. As Bill Frezza saw it, Mike "beavered away in obscurity, deciding to build his own hardware rather than rely on Ericsson. The Ericsson engineers laughed at this Canadian upstart who thought he could build a better radio."

Says Lazaridis, "I remember thinking, 'Hey, we can build a better radio than this.' And we did. That got us into paging, and we turned ourselves into experts in terms of the specifications of the paging network. We soon realized that, even though it was designed for one-way communication, you could incorporate a back

---

* In Canada, Mobitex is still handled by Rogers, and by Velocita Wireless in the US. The network is used for mission-critical dispatch, telemetry, POS, DB-access, Internet access, e-mail and interactive messaging. The system operates on 900 MHz frequency bands and covers major urban areas all across North America.

channel so messages could go both ways."[21] It was another in a series of corporate Eureka moments for Research in Motion.

As for Ericsson, they were hurt by RIM's go-it-alone attitude. Says Tim Meyer, Ericsson's PC card "was the first PCMCIA radio modem in existence. It was a technological tour de force and required extreme precision assembly and miniaturization. So imagine our surprise when RIM outdid us with a thinner PCMCIA card (a Type II versus ours, a Type III, double the thickness, and requiring two stacked slots).

"Also we were shocked when RIM landed a private label deal for their PC Card modem with a modem company called Megahertz.* Things rapidly deteriorated when RIM launched a competitor OEM module to ours. We knew it was over .... RIM was a partner and then a competitor, and it is interesting how we did not know how to deal with this situation."

Ericsson was slowly coming to realize that Lazaridis and Balsillie wanted to "control the whole value chain: making the radio, OS, software libraries, applications (client and server), and it is true Ericsson (especially the Mobitex product management team in Stockholm) didn't think they could do all that."

Meyer feels that in the end, Ericsson missed the boat with RIM: "I eventually did get a peek at the BlackBerry software under a tight NDA (non-disclosure agreement), and I told my boss we should buy RIM and he laughed and said the Swedes don't have a clue. So true!"

⊕　　⊕　　⊕

By this point, Lazaridis and his engineers in "the pit" were running hot, determined to squeeze what was a big old alarm clock

---

21. Industry Canada. Innovation Secretariat. Case 7. Research In Motion Limited.
* Now part of 3Com.

radio into the fine dimensions of a Swiss watch, with a battery life to match. "Have you saved a milliwatt today?" became RIM's unofficial in-house mantra. By 1995, Team Lazaridis had succeeded in building their own tiny radio modem, smaller than Ericsson's, that enabled wireless e-mail, and putting it on a PC card. The RIM Freedom radio modem was the world's first Type II PCMCIA card for wireless.

The Freedom card was a major evolutionary leap in terms of size. Janet Boudris, vice president of RAM Mobile Data, recalls that when she joined RAM in 1993, "a modem was the size of a brick and cost $1,875. The key was to identify a company that could produce smaller devices and less-expensive modems." RIM fit the bill perfectly.

Says Tim Meyer, "When RIM came out with the Freedom radio modem, RAM promptly plugged it into the Type II slot of the HP95LX (tossing out the Mobidem) and it worked fine as a demo. Unfortunately, it had horrible battery life."

After RIM brought out the Freedom radio modem, Lazaridis paid a visit to Bill Lenahan, then-CEO of RAM Mobile Data, bringing him a wooden model of what was to be the Inter@ctive Pager 900, a wireless handheld that was the prototype of the BlackBerry. Mike chuckled and said to Bill, "Wouldn't it be great if we could figure out how to put all of this technology into a small footprint, like a pager, and be able to put the processing power of a computer into that kind of form factor?"[22] Lenahan and the RAM Mobile people thought it would be a great idea. Mike shot back with the news that the first 900s were already being tested.

RIM relied on Intel Corporation support to build the first Inter@ctive pager prototype. It was designed with a 16-bit operating system along with built-in contact manager, scheduler, and

---

22. Laura Pratt, "Persistence in Motion," *PROFIT* magazine, May 2001.

forms-based messaging applications. It sported a QWERTY keyboard and a small, text-only display screen that showed four lines of text. Network service was provided by RAM Mobile Data and Ardis Co. The Inter@ctive pager could send and receive messages and had its own Internet address. It could store 100 kilobytes of data and had some pre-programmed responses, such as "I'll be late."

Research In Motion released its RIM 900 OEM radio modem and the RIM 900 Inter@ctive Pager in 1996. They marked the last step before the first BlackBerry.

⊕　⊕　⊕

"We have a saying here at RIM. It is 'do your math.' Our culture is to double-check, check twice, and ask customers before we undertake changes. If we work long enough, we know users will find value in our products."

—*Mike Lazaridis*

Bob Crow, now RIM's director of government and industry relations, says that RIM's graceful, simple designs masked incredibly complex engineering. Lazaridis and his RIM engineers found themselves bashing against a very formidable wall. Unlike Moore's Law, which states that the number of transistors on a semiconductor chip will double every year, neither battery power nor available radio spectrum can be expanded quite so easily. So RIM had to pioneer the rational use of battery power. This meant finding clever uses of bandwidth that wouldn't drain the batteries so quickly.

The first BlackBerrys were speedy, even though they operated on about the equivalent of 28.8 kilobytes per second. "This really was rocket science," says Crow. RIM also developed engineering that let the early BlackBerrys run for three weeks or more on a single AA battery feeding a lithium-ion internal battery, using an old 32-bit Intel 386 processor in a way that the chip was only used about 1 percent of the time. Where possible, software replaced hardware.

Gary Mousseau points out another RIM adage from those days: "RIM built *everything* themselves (except the wireless network itself) and we fine-tuned every piece to make it work fantastically. With Mobitex, our first wireless network, RIM suggested key changes and improvements to allow it to work better (power saving mode improvements, mostly). Then we educated the wireless network carriers and fine-tuned everything to work even better."

In early 1996, RIM's engineers had pulled together a usable two-way flip-top Mobitex pager, about the size of a large bar of soap. It was given to employees to use at work, but Mike Lazaridis soon noticed that people loved to be able to stay in touch outside work hours, at the shopping mall, or as they picked up their kids from soccer games. According to Lazaridis, "Our employees were embarrassed to admit they were taking them home to use. It was pretty big back then. People called it the hamburger."[23]

"The more we interviewed them, we noticed that, even when the battery life was only a few hours and the device was the size of a hamburger and had wires sticking out of it, they still carried it everywhere. When you see something no one else is doing that your employees find that addictive, you jump on it."[24]

Lazaridis believed that his potential customers craved solutions in the way of small, user-friendly handhelds with a secure and reliable system of transmission—a technology that would keep everyone in the loop, no matter where they were or what access they had to standard computer servers. All of RIM's nearly one hundred employees were soon totally focused on getting their

23. Alan Reiter, review, *Infoworld*, February 27, 2002.
24. David Fielding, "Leaps of Faith," *Globe and Mail*, April 25, 2008. < * >

pager technology to market, and by the autumn of 1996, RIM was ready to show the 900 to the world.

⊕   ⊕   ⊕

"The BlackBerry is really the culmination of more than ten years of investigating and researching and trying to get wireless e-mail to work. We always knew the experience was addictive. We had to make it practical."

—Mike Lazaridis

Lazaridis launched the RIM 900 Inter@ctive Pager in September 1996 at the PCS '96 trade show in San Francisco. The list price was a hefty $675, not including service fees. It was one of the world's first wireless data devices, and the world's first pocket-sized, two-way pager. A flip-open clamshell that fit on your belt, it sported a small keyboard for sending and receiving messages wirelessly. The network service had all the features of a traditional one-way paging system, but also added two-way features such as peer-to-peer delivery and read receipts. It could also send faxes and leave voice messages on a telephone. The 900 could communicate with the Internet, peer users, and the phone network via a gateway, which also served as the store and forward mailbox for the wireless user.

RAM Mobile Data was sold and renamed BellSouth Wireless Data in 1995 and later became Cingular Interactive when BellSouth and SBC formed Cingular Wireless (now renamed AT&T). Operator of the Mobitex network in the US, they brought the Inter@ctive Pager service to market in 1997. *Corporate User* Magazine named it Top Wireless Product of the year. But not everybody liked the device. Alan A. Reiter, writing in the *Wireless Internet & Mobile Computer Newsletter*,[25] said, "The RIM Inter@ctive Pager is a good

---

25. February 26, 1997.

device, but it's a bit too heavy, bulky and expensive to attract many mobile professionals."

There were also some hardware glitches with the 900, and as Gary Mousseau says, "it didn't exactly go as expected. The failure rate on the clam-shell component was nasty and the 'contract-ed' number of devices were about all RIM sold." No time to sit around and fret about that. Said RIM production team leader Dale Brubacher-Cressman, they were running hot, and already moving onto the next devices, "quickly evolving from the 900 to the 950 and beyond, iterating handhelds from generation to generation as we honed our hardware (handheld) design and manufacturing skills." He calls the 900 "the most successful product RIM had ever produced, but was quickly surpassed by subsequent generations of product."

     ◉   ◉   ◉

"Mike Lazaridis has nine lives. He came through one scrape after another. Because each time he built another product that solved one problem but not all, the product failed. He had to dust himself off and move to the next one. I like to describe wireless data as a safe with a ten-combo lock. A bunch of us were walking around with six of the numbers. Over the years, we would go to the lock and try to open it. Mike went to it again and again. When he came up with all ten numbers, the BlackBerry popped out."

—*Bill Frezza*

Lazaridis and his team worked tirelessly in those days to optimize the network performance of the early RIM 900. But it was still a large and cumbersome brick by today's standards. He was determined to produce a cheaper, friendlier, and even smaller device that could be the basis of what he knew Ericsson, Rogers, and

BellSouth really needed—a true two-way Star Trek–type communicator for business and consumers.

The company was already steaming flat out on the successor to the 900, code named "LeapFrog." "How we just did business just accelerated for me, at least in software," Gary Mousseau says. "I got my answers so much faster; the roadblocks were just cleared quicker; I could just make decisions faster in '98." Richard Donnelly, vice president, network operations, at Velocita Wireless (formerly a division of BellSouth), was astounded by Mike Lazaridis's pace. "I've always thought of Mike as a compulsive, relentless innovator," says Donnelly. "His technical mind seems to run day and night."

One of Mike's great innovations had come earlier, in 1997, during a writing blitz on his basement computer after nursing his baby son to sleep. In a midnight to 3 am marathon, he had a brain wave, and e-mailed to his office a white paper called "Success Lies in Paradox." In it he asked his team, "When is a tiny keyboard more efficient than a large one?" His answer - "When you use your thumbs."

Lazaridis had hit on a way of messaging using the one big physical factor we share with monkeys and apes—opposable thumbs. The resulting e-mail device, optimized for thumb computing, he still calls RIM's "secret sauce." The RIM team filed for a patent for the device in June 1998.

Another great innovation by Lazaridis and Gary Mousseau was the "Two Mailbox Solution." In those days, mobile users had to have a special, separate wireless mailbox—apart from their corporate e-mail—for e-mail, fax and text-to-voice services. Says Mousseau, "People didn't know whether to reach users by sending e-mail to their desktop computers or wireless devices."

They first tried jury-rigging email by forwarding their work e-mail inboxes to their RIM950 devices. "We discovered that we liked the experience of getting e-mail to our belts. But we were unable to reply to the messages, since the 'from' address was our desktop address and not the original sender. This messed up the reply path. Our IT Director, Wade Brown, was 'extremely concerned' about the security of forwarding all our communications outside the corporate firewall."

Eventually, they had to stop the practice, says Mousseau, but "one day Mike just called me into his office and said, 'Gary, we're going to solve this two-mailbox problem once and for all,' and we just started hashing it out."* They brainstormed all the work that Herb Little had done in compression and encryption, the many wireless transport layers RIM had built over the years, and the work on Microsoft and Lotus connectivity.

They hit on an integrated, single-mailbox, end-to-end wireless data solution. It mirrored a user's e-mail account, making RIM's handheld an extension of their PC desktop inbox, with the same e-mail address doing double duty. They also perfected a continuously connected "push model" of e-mail delivery that automatically found the user. Lazaridis gave Mousseau the job of "putting together the first definition and design for the product and began drafting the first 'single mailbox' patent using the ideas Mike and I had come up with." The patent was filed on May 29, 1998.[†]

Toward the end of the summer of 1997, Mousseau assembled his software team and told them that they had a new job. From that

---

* Comment from Steve Carkner, former director of product development at RIM; Matt Walcoff, Memories of BlackBerry still vivid 10 years later, *The Record*, January 31, 2009 < * >
† US Patent 6,219,694, Filed May 29, 1998 < * >

time forward, they would develop a RIM-only version of the client software parallel to the one they had agreed to build for RAM. "At that time," says Mousseau, "the RAM client was almost shipped, and we had been using it in Beta for some time with their gateway." He "assigned them roles to build the necessary user interface (UI) and personal information manager (PIM) components, plus the Network Operations Center (NOC), the Enterprise Server and the Desktop Redirector elements."

The Network Operations Center in Waterloo was the brains of the whole process. When the client company's desktop redirector (later called the BlackBerry Enterprise Server or BES) pushed out data or a message, it went to a virtual device on the NOC. The NOC then pushed the message to the real handheld on behalf of the BES.*

RIM also patented a way to compress and re-envelope the message so it was completely secure and opaque as it moved through the NOC to the destination device. Waterloo grad student Hugh Hind, now a VP in the radio protocol team, figured out a way to generate a two-to-one compression ratio on small bursts of data, then encrypt the data, which saved lots of bandwidth. Hind developed the compression and encryption technology working closely with Herb Little.

"At this same time," says Mousseau, "David Castell, David Werezak and Mark Guilbert starting doing focus groups, considering names and putting the marketing touches together. We called the project PocketLink ..."†

A few months later, all the late nights finally paid off in the form of a smaller, more efficient machine, the RIM Inter@ctive pager 950.** The 950 measured 3.5 inches by 2.5 inches by 0.93 inches— about half the size of today's Bold. It weighed in at 3.95 ounces

---

* See the Web Support Site for a diagram.
† At the same time they worked with Puma Software, makers of Intellisync, to get a PIM (instant messaging) synchronization into BlackBerry before launch.
** See the Web Support Site for images.

without the battery. It sported a monochrome LCD with backlighting, 2W transmitter, and 32-bit Intel 386 processor with 1Mb of flash memory plus 204 kilobytes of SRAM.

The 950 had Mike's 31-key PC-style angled keyboard and a thumb-operated clickable roller wheel that worked like a PC mouse. Plus it came with an address book that could store up to 1,000 entries, selectable alerts, and an intuitive menu-driven interface. The team filed for a patent for the device in June 1998. Besides Mike Lazaridis, the patent holders were Jason Griffin, John Holmes, Herb Little, and Harry Major.

The killer app of the new 950 was its ability to replace a heavy PC or laptop for e-mail. With its "PocketLink" software, it could receive a response in an astounding twenty seconds. With the PocketLink (later BlackBerry) service, e-mail was always on. You didn't need to retrieve your e-mail. Your e-mail found you and discretely notified you it had arrived. But there was a bit of smoke and mirrors involved. Tim Meyer says that "One of the key insights that Mike had about wireless e-mail was that by only giving an alert (beep) to the user after the e-mail was received gave the sense of instantaneous reception. No one knew that it took twenty to thirty seconds to receive the e-mail. In comparison, using dialup modems you were waiting and staring at a screen after you had hit the Get Mail button. So the slow speed of the network was removed as a factor in the user experience."

The 950 had other advantages for connectivity freaks. You didn't have to dial in and make the connection. You didn't have to raise an antenna. You could move in and out of coverage areas without the fear of losing messages. As soon as you entered a coverage area, the 950 would start pulling or sending mail automatically. With the RAMFirst solution, you could also send faxes, alphanumeric pages, and even messages to a phone using the service's text-to-voice translation software.

The 950 could run about three weeks on a single AA alkaline battery, depending on usage. (Some cynics have quipped that things have gone downhill ever since.) One RIM veteran told me that "It was a decent device. For years, RIM left massive boxes of Duracell AA batteries around for workers who still used the 950 and 850. Every Christmas, the batteries used to disappear rapidly. RIM probably saved a bundle when they finally replaced all of the older devices with ones that would charge."

Wireless projects weren't that unusual for telecom companies at the time, says Lazaridis, but the business was "a consulting industry, not a product industry. A customer had to take products from tens to hundreds of different companies and weave them into a solution."[26] The 950 changed all that.

BellSouth Wireless Data was a true believer in RIM's solution. In August 1998, it replaced the older RIM 900 with the RIM 950 and started marketing the service as BellSouth Interactive Paging, to compete against the inferior SkyTel two-way paging network and Motorola's PageWriter 2000, as well as Motorola's Synapse Pager Card for the PalmPilot.[27]

Bill Lenahan, CEO of RAM/Bell South, was delighted with the new trimmer design for the 950: "We committed to hundreds of thousands of these devices so they could get their manufacturing set up and their costs down. Without that, I don't think RIM would have been able to develop the products and manufacture them at the price point they did."[*]

---

26. Erick Schonfeld, BlackBerry Season, *Business* 2.0, Oct. 1, 2004. < * >
27. Rebecca Day, "Pagers Get Smart," *Popular Mechanics*, February 1999. Paging became known as Interactive Messaging Plus(sm) when BellSouth and SBC formed Cingular Wireless. < * >
* At time of writing, RIM still supports the old Mobitex devices, including the only Java-based device they created for the Mobitex network, the data-only 5790. See the RIM Archives. < * >

Suddenly, RIM had traction. By early 1998, Balsillie had inked a contract to supply IBM with Inter@ctive pagers for use by its field service representatives across North America. Other customers included Panasonic Corp., Mobile Integrated Technologies, and Telxon Corp.

The new RIM Inter@ctive Pager 950 got rave reviews, and won the C|Net Editors' Choice award: "The updated version, the Inter@ctive Pager 950, is even better. It's more compact (you don't have to fold it out), a brand-new interface makes it much easier to use, and a jog-dial switch takes you through the menus quickly and intuitively. And it still boasts nearly instantaneous send and receive times and excellent service prices."

Pricing for the RIM Inter@ctive Pager 950 started at $249 with a flat monthly fee of $24.95. Companies who wanted RIM's enterprise server (later the BlackBerry Enterprise Server or BES) to manage company e-mail, had to fork over $2,999 for a twenty-user license and $490 for every ten additional users.

Back at RIM, many people were getting frustrated that the company's customers were not taking full advantage of the 950's power. They were hooking it up to old servers and weak networks, using it mostly for paging, rather than email. Maybe the name was the problem.

⊕　　⊕　　⊕

"As soon as I saw 'BlackBerry,' for some unknown reason . . . .
It's like when you first fall in love you know right away."
　　　　　　　　　　　　　　　　　　　—Mike Lazaridis

Mike Lazaridis had a hunch his new baby needed a proper name, instead of calling it the RIM 950, RIM 960, RIM 970 . . . and so on. RIM marketing had come up with the name "PocketLink," but that didn't turn too many cranks. Mike decided to talk to some professionals, and in 1998 he contacted Lexicon Branding, the Sausalito, California, marketing firm that had crafted such brands as the Apple PowerBook laptop and Intel Pentium processor.

Lexicon president David Placek remembers being very impressed with the RIM 950, code-named "LeapFrog". He told Mike the device deserved a name and personality of its own. "We wanted to give them a great name, which could really help them. At that time, they were going up against the pagers, and everybody had a pager .... You need to have a really distinctive name. And let the operating companies, like AT&T, let them have the more conservative and descriptive names. But I had a sense that this was going to be a really good product."[28]

"We looked at the form," says Placek, "and, with all the little buttons on there, began to create metaphors. We looked at the world of fruit because it does, from a distance, look like it could be some kind of fruit. Also, BlackBerry is a very friendly, approachable name. And it must have worked for RIM, because I keep seeing these things everywhere."[29]

Some of the Lexicon team were struck by the little keyboard buttons, which resembled nothing so much as the tiny seeds covering a strawberry. Several suggested "Strawberry." "No, 'straw-' is a slowww syllable," said Stanford University professor Will Leben, director of linguistics at Lexicon. "That's just the opposite of the zippy connotation Research In Motion wants. But '-berry' is good."

"Lexicon research had shown that people associated the b sound with reliability," said David Placek, "while the short e evoked speed.

---

28. Thomas Wailgum, "Meet Tech's Product Name Guru," *The Industry Standard*, November 11, 2008. < * >
29. Laura Pratt, "Persistence in Motion," *PROFIT* magazine, May 2001.

Another syllable with a short vowel would nail it." Within seconds the Lexicon team had picked its fruit, and it was BlackBerry.*

Lazaridis paid a visit to Lexicon in Sausalito, and he remembers the occasion well.† The Lexicon team came in with "boxes of white cardboard sheets, forty of them, each one had a single word. They set them up on an easel." As Lazaridis remembers, "after about twenty-five of them I thought, Gosh, I've made a big mistake ... they put up name after name ... there were some strange ones ... you might have heard of the HipTop."

"At that point," he says, "I knew I was being set up because the last one was so much better than all the others ... What I decided to do was have some fun with them. I leaned back in my chair, crossed my arms, and told them, 'I don't like any of them!'—You should have seen the look on their faces." And then he paused for effect ... "' except the last one.' And we all burst out laughing."

Back home, the RIM engineers weren't sure they liked their baby being named after a fruit. Gary Mousseau was "just floored" by the choice of the California marketing pros. "But we didn't have the branding, marketing and sales experience of these guys. We just couldn't appreciate their skill set."

Mike liked it. The name stuck.

RIM's timing was just about perfect. According to Balsillie, if the BlackBerry had come out a couple of years earlier, it may not have been very interesting because e-mail wasn't as popular yet. "It was the right time for us to do that because the offering and the market opportunity and the value proposition and the uniqueness stood

---

* Words such as BlackBerry, MySpace, YouTube, and LinkedIn are all examples of CamelCase, or forming compound words by capitalizing each chunk to preserve its identity. This produces "camel" words with a range of "humps." CamelCase has been around since the 1950s in a few brand names, such as CinemaScope.

† See the accompanying video on the *BlackBerry Planet* Web Support site.

on its own merit. We did it at that time and we certainly have no regrets. It appears, in hindsight, to have been a very wise strategy," he says with a grin.*

RIM launched its BlackBerry wireless e-mail service across North America in January 1999 through partners Rogers Cantel and BellSouth. The package included the RIM 386-based wireless handheld device with typical PDA organizer software (calendar, address book, task list), along with a docking cradle and synchronizing software to connect with a PC. E-mail was encrypted using Triple DES and remained encrypted at all points between the desktop PC and the handheld device. RIM's first relay server was located in a crowded office under the desk of software developer Matthias Wandel. Soon RIM had a server farm that filled an air-conditioned cement block warehouse.

The BlackBerry was the first wireless device that synchronized with company mail systems so that users did not need a different e-mail address when traveling. This was a very big selling point. Initially set up for Microsoft Exchange, RIM later added Lotus Domino and Novell GroupWise synchronization. The 950 cost more than $500 (including activation fee) or could be rented for $25/month plus a one-time $69 activation fee. Cost for the service was an additional $50/month, of which half was rebated monthly for the first twelve months. There was also a thirty-day full-refund guarantee.

Recalls Lazaridis:

The period leading up to the launch was frenetic. It was very, very exciting because the early response to the product was overwhelming. We were seeding it in a number of target companies who took to the product immensely quickly.

---

* Industry Canada. Innovation Secretariat. Case 7. Research In Motion Limited.

When you seed products, you expect a return rate of maybe half. Our putback rate was zero. That's staggering. At that point, we sit there and go, "This sticks. This sticks big."

We had a lot of partners lined up: Intel and their senior execs, Microsoft and their senior execs. We had the carriers lined up, like Rogers and BellSouth. We did it over the Web, and there were hundreds dialed in. And here we are, with it really being one of the top one or two pre-eminent brands in handhelds, and certainly the No. 1 brand in wireless data, so far. The senior executives at Intel use it, so do the senior executives at Microsoft. And very well-known people like Mike Dell, Gerald Levin and Al Gore love it.

But the most exciting thing has been the holistic success of it. That we nailed it. That it was pulling through. That it was compelling. That it was going to be a big market, and everybody liked it.[30]

RIM marketing went into overdrive. Balsillie was so sure that it would just take a few days for business users to get hooked on the BlackBerry that he hired evangelists to seed thousands of devices to influential professionals on Wall Street and on Capitol Hill. In no time flat it became a must-have tool for leading journalists, lawyers, political aides, members of the U.S. Congress, and big banking and brokerage firms. "You immediately saw everyone get it," says Leonard G. Rosen, a former technology banker at Lehman Brothers.

The 950 became a huge commercial hit when it was rebranded as the BlackBerry, and the successful launch and publicity boosted RIM's sales that year by 80 percent, to US$85 million. In 2000, RIM revenue leapt another 160 percent, to US$221 million. By February,

30. Laura Pratt, "Persistence in Motion," *PROFIT* magazine, May 2001.

2000, and even before entering Europe, RIM was boasting 164,000 BlackBerry subscribers in 7,800 companies. The payoff was spectacular: suddenly Research in Motion was earning 65 percent-plus margins on the service from the telcos and 35 percent-plus margins on the hardware.*

🌐   🌐   🌐

"The BlackBerry is a synch engine because it synchronizes data across a mobile work force."

—*Mike Lazaridis*

According to Jim Balsillie, RIM's original entry strategy into the marketplace was to build great handheld devices and offer them to alliance partners, such as Bell South, to integrate into their own operations. But they soon found they were at the point where a lot of technologies were converging—wireless handhelds, behind-the-firewall enterprise servers, and infrastructure to relay between wireless networks and the Internet. The BlackBerry platform was set up precisely to make wireless easy for network providers and software developers. Balsillie says:

> That was definitely a spectacular step forward. The company got into the business of creating wireless software protocol stacks and application interfaces, and that's what BlackBerry is—a very sophisticated distributed set of wireless protocol stacks and application interfaces. It's just all the suite you need and all the distribution you need to connect what you need connected. So, in a sense, that sort of redefined the value proposition and really catapulted us forward in terms of a very, very valuable market and a very, very defined brand ...

---

* According to National Bank Financial analyst Deepak Chopra.

But we still got that market through alliances with great technology companies like Microsoft, Lotus, IBM and Sun, and outstanding wireless carriers like Rogers, Bell Mobility, Cingular, T-Mobile, Motient and AT&T.*

The BlackBerry name itself soon had a profound impact, and the word quickly embedded itself into the popular consciousness, much like Windows, Macintosh, or Nokia. As British advertising genius Maurice Saatchi wrote, such "one-word equity" is a new business model for marketing, appropriate to the digital age. "In this model, companies compete for global ownership of one word in the public mind. In this new business model, companies seek to build one-word equity—to define the characteristic they most want instantly associated with their brand around the world, and then own it."**

On April 11, 2000, RIM released the first BlackBerry with a full length brick-sized shape—the RIM 957 Wireless Handheld, code named "Proton." RIM billed it as a "palm-sized wireless hand-held with integrated support for wireless email, Internet, paging and organizer features." It measured 4.6 inches by 3.1 inches by 0.70 inches and weighed 5.3 ounces. It came with a crisper backlit screen, a 32-bit Intel 386 processor, 5 MB flash memory, a thumb-friendly QWERTY keyboard, and an embedded wireless modem. It was priced at $499.

With the 957, RIM took a giant step beyond the pager. It was a real "synch machine," with full support for BlackBerry wireless e-mail. RIM's "Always On, Always Connected" campaign boasted

---

* Industry Canada. Innovation Secretariat. Case 7. Research In Motion Limited.
** M&C Saatchi < * >

that the BlackBerry 957 was much more than a two-way pager. It could operate 24/7 while staying connected to the Mobitex network for incoming e-mail and other functions such as paging and stock alerts.

The 957's built-in organizer software also gave users access to their own calendar, address book, task list, memo pad, calculator, and alarm. Users could synchronize the 957 with their office PC using a docking cradle and Puma Technology's Intellisync software.* It used the trusty thumb-operated trackwheel for navigation and multiple notification alerts, including tone, vibrate, on-screen or LED indicator. It housed an internal rechargeable lithium battery and came with a docking/charging cradle.

The 957 did not have Web access in the early days for lack of a browser, although Internet-based services were available via WolfeTech PocketGenie, which supported limited HTML access. The browser was slow as molasses, but it worked. Sort of.

According to one RIM veteran:

> I really enjoyed using my RIM 957 via the Mobitex network, but the network never supported decent speeds or could handle a lot of traffic. The bonus to Mobitex was the distance you could be from a base station and still get signal strength. I heard a story years ago about some high end U.S. politician who used his 957 to help get a plane down. The radio had failed and the flight crew were screwed, so the pol and his 957 came to the rescue by opening a line of communication with the tower. I remember taking a flight to Florida in 2002 with my 957 and having signal strength while airborne in places. My GPRS, EDGE, and 3G devices

---

* RIM eventually developed its own synching software and started competing directly with Intellisync. The company was acquired by Nokia in 2006.

can't do that because you have to be within a few kilometers of a node to get a signal.*

⊕   ⊕   ⊕

"My job is to get the money, Mike's job is to spend it."
                                        —*Jim Balsillie*

Research In Motion was financed at the start by a Government of Ontario New Ventures loan, with matching funding from Lazaridis's parents in Windsor. By 1992, the company had sales of about $500,000 a year and three or four different business lines. Jim Balsillie also brought his own $250,000 investment into RIM. In 1994, the University of Waterloo helped RIM land a $100,000 grant from the Industrial Research Assistance Program. More funding came forward from the Business Development Bank of Canada (then the Federal Business Development Bank), and the Innovations Ontario Program provided them with a grant of close to $300,000.

Lazaridis negotiated an early $300,000 R&D investment from Ericsson, the Swedish telecom giant, and Balsillie helped attract almost $2 million in financing from COM DEV, a local Waterloo technology company. In 1996, when it was clear RIM had a winner with the BlackBerry handheld, it pulled in another $36 million from a special warrant (like a private IPO) before going public, an amount that helped RIM employees invest in the company as well. RIM raised an additional $115 million when it listed on the Toronto Stock Exchange in October 1997 (TSX: RIM). The fresh capital infusion paid for sales, marketing, and patent protection, and helped ramp up R&D and manufacturing of the RIM 950 Wireless Handheld and future machines.

Jack Barse of the Mobitex Operators Association was at a meeting in Singapore when news came of RIM's listing. "I remember

---

* See Fraser's Mobitex report on the Web Support Site

RIM's Don McMurtry opening his presentation by saying, 'I'm very pleased to be here today representing a company that is now worth $140 million.' It was more money than anybody was worth in the business at that point, except for the Ericssons and the BellSouths. It was quite a dramatic moment, to think back to little RIM."

The Canadian and Ontario governments helped out as well, and RIM obtained $4.7 million from the Ontario Technology Fund and, in 1998, a $5.7 million loan from Industry Canada's Technology Partnerships Canada, which provides investments repayable out of future profits, to develop the next generation of handhelds. This was followed by another $33.9 million in 2000. RIM also made use of the Government of Canada's Scientific Research and Experimental Development investment tax credits, which amounted to almost $12 million in 2002 alone.

RIM listed on the NASDAQ (RIMM) in late 1999 and raised another $250 million in capital, which the company followed up with a huge $900 million share issue in November 2000.

"We are very systematic in how we fund the company, just like in how we develop our technology and build our markets," says Balsillie. "You must be ready to get money ... there is a readiness process of networking and having people aware of your company, and having a plan ready and a cash flow driven by assumptions. It's not just 'Gosh, let's go get a check.' It isn't like that. It's a very systematic exercise. We are active in keeping the capital markets up-to-date and aware, and are always talking to the analysts."*

The investment community liked what it heard. Balsillie had boosted the strength of the company by negotiating strategic alliances with BellSouth Wireless Data and Sybase. He also had in his pocket signed wireless handheld supply contracts with American Mobile (now Motient), IBM, Rogers Cantel (Rogers AT&T), and BellSouth

---

* Industry Canada. Innovation Secretariat. Case 7. Research In Motion.

Wireless Data (Cingular); plus wireless radio modem supply contracts with Telxon, Panasonic, GMSI Fleet Management Systems, Itronix Ruggedized Notebooks, and DataWave and Gooitech.

⊕　　⊕　　⊕

In spite of burgeoning revenue and the hundreds of millions of dollars raised going public, RIM had been steadily burning through capital and went into the red in 2000.

For 2001, RIM's revenue more than doubled to US$221.3 million, but growing operating expenses led to an overall net loss of US$7.6 million.

True to form, Lazaridis and Balsillie had gone ahead of the market and bet everything on the Java-based 5800 series. Prior to these devices, RIM sold direct. This let them pocket a greater percentage of the revenue. Once they switched to Java-based devices with cell phones, they had to sell through carriers.

The carriers were proving to be laggards in selling such high-end devices, and RIM's major investors were concerned that revenue growth was dipping and costs had spiraled almost out of control. So in 2002, the company had to undergo what is still called "The 10% Purge." They culled staff and cut back expenses to get into the black, then focused on developing even better devices and helping carriers learn how to sell them.

The slim-down was useful, and as the new century took shape, RIM emerged stronger than ever, with enough capital to execute its R&D and marketing plans and fully able to keep up with skyrocketing demand for its flagship product, the BlackBerry.

What Mike Lazaridis and Jim Balsillie didn't realize was that as their company grew big and bold, and as they mastered key technologies and crossed major technical hurdles, an evil troll was waiting for them under the very next bridge.

3

Lawsuits in Motion

Patent trolls are a relatively new event. Folks have figured out the patent loopholes and how to exploit them, and this case highlights how the Patent Office needs to be reformed to address the modern needs of the patent system. We're testing the boundaries of a lot of the concepts of patent law, and we're on the cutting edge, although I'm sure the client, RIM, would want somebody else on the cutting edge."

—RIM lead attorney David Long

A patent troll is a patent owner who never makes his property into products but rather lies in wait for unwary companies, scares them with the threat of costly court action, and tries to squeeze them for royalties or licensing fees.

Most of us know about trolls from *Three Billy Goats Gruff*, an old Norse fairy tale. Three goat brothers want to cross a river to graze in the lush green meadow on the other side. But a big hungry troll lurks under the bridge, with eyes as big as saucers and a nose as long as a poker. The two younger brothers each escape by telling the troll that a bigger goat is coming along behind. The last billy goat is the biggest brother, and he butts the troll into the river. End of story.

In real life, Research In Motion was not a smart billy goat as it started to ramp up real revenue in the U.S. marketplace in 2001.

While basking in the lavish praise the BlackBerry was attracting, the company got careless and ran head-on into an ugly but highly effective patent troll who quickly tied up RIM in a ball of sticky patent claims, then put it through a five-year legal wringer.

RIM was fortunate to escape from the nightmarish troll, but only by paying him a king's ransom. The main reason RIM survived at all was that the BlackBerry was so *good*. The device was so essential and so beloved by Washington insiders—even by the lawyers who were suing RIM—that the U.S. Justice Department eventually went to bat for the company, forcing a settlement just in time to stop a complete shutdown of RIM's BlackBerry service.

⊕　　⊕　　⊕

Today's technology companies are built on owning and licensing patents and intellectual property (IP). Patenting is a large and growing business, with nearly 200,000 patents issued every year in the United States and 500,000 more in other countries, with 6.1 million patents in effect worldwide.

IBM earns at least $1 billion a year from a portfolio of almost 50,000 U.S. and more than 30,000 European patents and is stockpiling more than 3,000 IP awards every year. Xerox is another giant that has emerged as a major patent owner. There is now a brisk marketplace in patents and claims, with trolls abounding. Some even claim the trolls have a beneficial effect, creating a market for inventors and developers, monetizing patents that would otherwise not stand a chance, and forcing patent clarity.

Many tech firms like RIM are on a constant patent war footing. They regularly have to unleash teams of legal experts to research filings, bolster patents, clarify claims, defend brands, box in enemies or interlopers, chase off trolls, or force other parties into mediation. Since some patent disputes have more twists and turns than a John Grisham plot, if a company decides to go to court, it can lead one day and lose the next, depending on the whim of a judge or jury. At worst, these disputes end up like gunfights at the O.K. Corral, with the winner the last man standing. At best, they lead to Mexican standoffs with other patent holders, so both sides can move forward, sometimes together, sometimes apart.

Companies that live by the patent can also die by the patent. For a time, RIM had created a climate of uncertainty around itself with its various patent disputes, which did not help boost investor confidence. Only RIM's aggressive defense of its patent rights left it ultimately in a far stronger position to survive, and avoid being gobbled up by a larger competitor.

Research In Motion had become known as a company that would fiercely defend its patent turf and do right by customers, even if it meant short-term loss and pain. But, unfortunately for RIM as it entered a high R&D phase, the United States Patents and Trademark Office (USPTO) was then groaning under a 600,000 patent backlog and reeling under sharp criticism and sarcastic rage from inventors, lawyers, and politicians.

Much of this patent pandemonium arose from the U.S. Supreme Court's 1998 State Street Bank decision, where patents for business *methods* had become allowable in U.S. patent law. Tech companies like RIM now had to scramble to patent their processes and swallow higher costs to ensure that not just their inventions but also their methodologies could not be hijacked.

A torrent of "method" patent applications flooded into the USPTO. Many were from trolls, but others showed a marked sense of humor and a desire to put one over on the patent office. One early methodology award, U.S. Patent 5,443,036, "Method of exercising a cat," covered having a cat chase the beam from a laser pointer. It was widely criticized as an inappropriate patentable invention.

Another award, by an enterprising U.S. inventor named Steve Olsen, covered an improved method for a child to swing on a swing. The USPTO actually awarded him U.S. Patent 6,368,227, entitled "Method of Swinging on a Swing."

The swing award was roundly ridiculed and the patent was later rejected. But Olsen's exercise showed that it could be easy to be awarded near-bogus patents. And it soon became clear to RIM's legal department that they would have to play by the new rules, and if necessary go to bat against nuisance patents covering obvious or common sense business methods.

⊕ ⊕ ⊕

RIM had its first run-in with a patent troll in November 2000, when Luxembourg-based patent holder InPro II Licensing filed a U.S. suit claiming that RIM and T-Mobile USA were infringing its wireless e-mail patents. InPro II called for damages "in no event less than a reasonable royalty."

RIM accused InPro of "threatening and grasping behavior" and filed suit for a ruling that the European firm's patents were invalid. InPro backed off after it lost an appeal.[1]

InPro also lost an action against RIM in 2003 related to its thumbwheel input. InPro subsequently appealed but was finally chased away in 2006.[*]

RIM's propensity to litigate elicited the moniker "Lawsuits in Motion" from the British webzine *The Register*. From 2001 to 2004,

---

1. See *InPro II Licensing vs. T-Mobile USA and Research In Motion* at: www.cafc.uscourts.gov/opinions/05-1233.pdf. < * >

* *Research In Motion Ltd. 6-K for 12/21/04* at: www.secinfo.com/dsVsj.12vn.htm. *RIM Provides Update on InPro Patent Litigation in the United States* at: www.rim.com/news/press/2006/pr-11_05_2006-02.shtml. < * >

the company had several overlapping patent cases on the boil with technology companies Glenayre Electronics, Good Technology, and Xerox that tested both the quality of RIM's patents, its resolve in defending them, and its ability to either win or settle these challenges and move ahead with its game plan.

But RIM's fate was starting to hang in the balance as big companies such as Xerox were also claiming RIM infringed on some of its patents. And now Nokia and PalmOne were holding back from offering RIM software on their new devices in the United States, citing the uncertainty brought about by RIM's patent battles.

⊕　⊕　⊕

In July 2001, Research In Motion filed a forty-five-page application with the USPTO for a "Handheld e-mail device with a keyboard optimized for use with the thumbs." At this time, other manufacturers were coming out with stylus-based keyboards. RIM's saw the thumb-operated keyboard as a more efficient method for capturing user data.

The RIM filing went into great detail about the geometry of the keyboard: "In order to operate within the limited space available on a handheld electronic device," RIM said, "the present invention optimizes the placement and shape of the keys, preferably using keys that are oval or oblong in shape, and that are placed at angles designed to facilitate thumb-typing. The angles at which keys on either side of the keyboard are placed are complementary."

On September 17, 2002, the USPTO awarded RIM United States Patent: 6452588, A handheld electronic device with a keyboard optimized for use with the thumbs, for a new keyboard design on handheld e-mail devices. Forty-eight hours after receiving the patent, RIM filed suit in Delaware court against

PDA maker Handspring,* of Mountain View, California, alleging that the company's Treo organizers were infringing on the RIM patent.

The RIM complaint charged that the keyboards on Handspring's Treo Communicator k180, 270, and 300 models infringed on a RIM patent. These Treos featured a small keyboard like the BlackBerry's, angled so that it could be typed on with one's thumbs.

In the suit, RIM noted that "many experts and those knowledgeable in the industry have commented that the keyboard of the Treo series of products is remarkably similar to the keyboard in RIM's BlackBerry Wireless Handheld devices."

RIM asked the court for a cash settlement, a declaration that Handspring did infringe on RIM's patent, and an injunction barring further infringement.

Handspring eventually agreed to license RIM's keyboard design and avoid further litigation in November 2002. As Handspring co-founder Donna Dubinsky said bravely in her news release, "Wireless device users are finding that integrated QWERTY keyboards are a fast, easy and familiar method of data input. We are pleased to come to this agreement with RIM so that we can focus our resources on product innovation and expanding the market for our Treo communicators."

RIM chairman Jim Balsillie crowed about the decision and told reporters that BlackBerry technology must have the leading edge if companies such as Handspring were now working with RIM. His good mood also stemmed from the fact that Nokia, waiting for the outcome of the Treo case, had also agreed to join RIM as a licensing partner. He was also delighted that RIM could make money off the patent and avoid costly litigation.

---

* Handspring was created by the original inventors of the Palm Pilot: Jeff Hawkins, Donna Dubinsky, and Ed Colligan. When 3Com bought Palm Computing in 1997, the founders grew unhappy with the new managers, left, and founded Handspring in June 1998.

Handspring's partners had lost heart over the keyboard case and had neither the desire nor the means to keep fighting the battle. In August 2003, the partners returned home, merging Handspring with Palm Inc.'s hardware division to form PalmOne. Their Treo 600 was the last product to use the Handspring name. The two companies merged fully in September 2007.

The worst of all these patent cases, and the one that could have brought RIM to its knees, was a seemingly nuisance lawsuit that snowballed into a major battle involving America's two largest IP law firms, which ultimately led to the largest technology patent payout in U.S. history.

The plaintiff was an obscure IP firm named NTP Inc.—the initials stood for New Technologies Products—which held several wireless e-mail patents but had never practiced its inventions. NTP's attorney Donald Stout quietly filed suit in Richmond, Virginia, on November 13, 2001, alleging that RIM had infringed its patents. NTP declared it was the sole licensee of eight patents issued since 1995 for transmission of e-mail messages over a radio frequency signal, and "a wireless mobile e-mail unit and the infrastructure necessary in the e-mail system to update the user's e-mail messages."

On the announcement, Research In Motion shares fell $1.45, or 6.1 percent, to $22.34.

A few months after Donald Stout filed his lawsuit, he engaged Washington lawyer James Wallace of the major DC firm Wiley, Rein & Fielding to research the case and litigate for NTP. One of Wallace's first jobs was to fly to Prague, Czech Republic. His mission was to talk to an expatriate American bar owner by the name of Geoff Goodfellow.

Geoff Goodfellow had bought the tavern four years earlier with proceeds from a failed Silicon Valley start-up and contract work on Mobitex with Ericsson and RIM. He was attracted to Prague by the low prices and high hopes of a new country emerging from the nightmare of communist rule.

A California high-school dropout with a love of grassroots technology, Goodfellow had one interesting item on his résumé—he was the first person to come up with the idea of sending Internet e-mail messages to pagers.

As a teenager in 1974, Goodfellow loved hanging around the Augmentation Research Center (ARC) at Stanford Research Institute (SRI), a think tank developed by Douglas C. Englebart, who eventually hired him an assistant computer operator.

Englebart was a Silicon Valley legend, an engineering inventor who pioneered many of the technologies we use today, from personal computing to social networking. A radar and radio technician during the Second World War, Englebart had been deeply influenced by Vannevar Bush's 1945 essay "As We May Think." He began to "envision people sitting in front of displays and 'flying around' in an information space where they could formulate and organize their ideas with incredible speed and flexibility." He came to believe in using computers to communicate and collaborate, as a way of solving humanity's most crucial challenges. To turn these visions into reality, he got a research job at SRI and threw himself into computer R&D.

On December 9, 1968, Englebart gave a groundbreaking ninety-minute multimedia demo to the Joint Computer Conference in San Francisco. It was nothing less than *the world premiere of personal and interactive computing.*

For the first time, people saw a computer "mouse" control a networked computer system to demonstrate hypertext linking, real-time text editing, multiple GUI (graphical user interface) windows with flexible view control, cathode display tubes, and shared-screen teleconferencing. What particularly blew the participants away was the live videoconference Englebart held with SRI staff members back in his lab thirty miles away.

To this day, Englebart's show is still known as "the mother of all demos." It was so far ahead of the time that some people in the audience thought the whole thing was a hoax. Paul Saffo of the Institute for the Future said, "It was like a UFO landing on the White House lawn."

Englebart had more up his sleeve. A year later, on October 29, 1969, his lab at SRI brought into being the world's first electronic computer network, the ARPANET, connecting with a node at Leonard Kleinrock's lab at UCLA. Interface Message Processors at both sites served as *the backbone of the first Internet.*

By the 1980s, thousands of academics, scientists, and military officers were using the ARPANET, but so were lowly techies such as Geoff Goodfellow and students such as Mike Lazaridis at the University of Waterloo.

⊕   ⊕   ⊕

One day in 1982, Geoff Goodfellow was brainstorming when he suddenly realized it was possible to relay a mail message from the network to Millicom's new Metagram alphanumeric mobile pager, made in nearby Sunnyvale. This was in 1982, at the same time as Mike Lazaridis was entering his second year at the University of Waterloo.

Goodfellow published his idea for e-mailing from computers to pagers on a widely read ARPANET mailing list called Telecom Digest, in a note titled "Electronic Mail for People on the Move." "The service," wrote Goodfellow, "allows ARPANET users to send messages to people on the MetaNet without having to run and find a terminal with a modem on it or go through the human dispatcher, i.e., so you can now do fun things like be driving down the road and have a message appear that says: [YOU HAVE NEW MAIL]."*

Today, the Internet assigns different addresses, known as ports, to different services such as e-mail or the World Wide Web. Port 99 is reserved for Geoff Goodfellow's brainwave—pushing an e-mail message to a pager.

Goodfellow eventually got $3 million in backing from Motorola and others for his pioneering RadioMail concept in 1986, but his company, Anterior Technology, went under in the early 1990s.

As we have seen, Ericsson at that time was launching the Mobidem, the first portable wireless data modem, and Viking Express, which packaged the Mobidem with a HP-95 pocket computer. The Swedish firm approached both Goodfellow and Mike Lazaridis to do some consulting work. But by the time Viking Express shipped, there was a major falling-out between RIM and RadioMail. Goodfellow and his group refused to work with the RIM mobile client application and demanded their own RadioMail-developed client.

Mike Lazaridis backed off, but he did get from his RadioMail work the savvy that eventually led to the BlackBerry platform. As for Goodfellow, he eventually grew restless and bored. Three years later, disgusted with the dot.com boom then raging, he left off consulting for Ericsson and bought his bar in Prague.

So it was that in the late winter of 2002, Geoff Goodfellow was paid a visit by NTP lawyer James Wallace. Goodfellow was delighted: "I kind of had a big grin on my face that someone had dug deep enough to find the person where it all began. He basically wanted to hear my story."

Wallace told the bar owner that he represented a company that was defending its wireless e-mail patents in a lawsuit against

---

* See Geoffrey S. Goodfellow, "Real World Services for the Technological Elite", on the BlackBerry Planet Web Support site

Research In Motion. He also confessed straight up that NTP was worried Goodfellow's work might undermine NTP's patent claims, and his client was going to great lengths to fortify those claims.

Wallace needed the whole narrative from Goodfellow. He needed to establish whether Goodfellow's work represented what is known in patent law as "prior art"—whether the discoveries and work Goodfellow made public before the NTP patents were filed could let RIM attack NTP's claims of originality. If an invention has been described in prior art, a patent on that invention is not valid.

Wallace offered Goodfellow a consulting fee of $4,000 a day, and he accepted, all the while suspecting that NTP might want to neutralize him in its patent case and in effect buy his silence. Part of his consulting deal was a nondisclosure agreement that prohibited him from "revealing any information or consulting with any other parties during the period of the lawsuit." Wallace paid him for several days' work, including two trips to Washington.

Goodfellow was amazed at the pains Wallace took. He later recalled that at one Washington meeting, when he was outlining his technology on a white board, Wallace insisted that the other lawyers not take handwritten notes for fear of leaving a paper trail. At another session, the legal team focused on "which claims in NTP's patents were least likely to be compromised by Mr. Goodfellow's prior work."

Goodfellow was flattered when Wallace introduced him to a travel companion by saying, "Geoff's the inventor of wireless e-mail. My client patented some of its implementation workings."

Four years later, in April 2006, *New York Times* reporter John Markoff caught up with Goodfellow back in Silicon Valley, where he was working for his brother's open source high-tech venture and hanging out as a DJ at the Stanford University radio station KZSU, doing a show called *beat.net*.

Chapter Three

When Markoff asked him about the NTP patents, Goodfellow was scornful about the whole process and told the *Times* reporter, "You don't patent the obvious. The way you compete is to build something that is faster, better, cheaper. You don't lock your ideas up in a patent and rest on your laurels."[1]

The co-owner of NTP, and originator of the patents, was Chicago engineer and inventor Thomas Campana Jr. Like Mike Lazaridis, Campana had a passion for all things electronic, fixing transistor radios, and building stereos and TV sets from kits. At age twenty-four, he started his own contract engineering company, Electronic Services Associates, later ESA Telecom Systems. One of his first patents, developed with a young Virginia lawyer named Donald Stout, was a national paging system that could be used on different frequencies using radio waves.

Donald Stout had spent four years as an examiner in the U.S. Patent and Trademark Office. Once he learned the ins and outs of the system, he left the USPTO and opened his own patent practice across the Potomac.

In 1985, Stout joined Campana and others in starting a new marketing company called Telefind Corp. in Coral Gables, Florida. ESA was folded into Telefind as its engineering arm, and Campana and crew worked on building a better paging system.

In 1987, five years after Geoff Goodfellow's RadioMail, ESA brought out a primitive form of wireless e-mail that could send 500-character messages from computers to pagerlike devices, but it was not a two-way system and they could not transmit messages back. Two employees of ESA, Michael Ponschke and Gary Thelen, wrote the software.

---

1. John Markoff, "In Silicon Valley, a Man Without a Patent", *The New York Times*, April 16, 2006 < * >

In 1990, Campana's work in wireless e-mail caught the eye of AT&T executive Murali Narayanan, who signed up Telefind to help build a system to send e-mails to the telco's experimental Safari laptop computer via a wireless paging system. He described Campana as "an absolute entrepreneur—a kid at heart." Telefind pulled together a working demo at AT&T headquarters in New Jersey on October 26, and AT&T showed it off at the huge Comdex show in Las Vegas. But there wasn't much interest, and the system didn't yet work very well. Narayanan then decided to drop Telefind and keep looking. He later hooked up AT&T with a larger wireless partner—Skytel.

Donald Stout and Thomas Campana were devastated by the loss of the AT&T account, which put Telefind over the edge into bankruptcy. Campana was left with debts of nearly $500,000 and the rights to much of Telefind's paging technology, which nobody wanted. So he and Stout took stock and decided they might as well salvage some of the work ESA had done, plus some new ideas Ponschke and Thelen were developing, and file for patents.

The pair worked hard pulling the documents, claims, and technical drawings together and, on May 20, 1991, filed a patent application for a method to merge existing e-mail systems with radio-frequency (RF) wireless networks. It was titled "Electronic mail system with RF communications to mobile processors and method of operation thereof."

The method showed a system to receive e-mail outside the office without needing a computer connected to a landline. The patent office granted Campana the first patent—#5,436,960—on July 25, 1995, and four others: #5,625,670, #5,819,172, #6,067,451, and #6,317,592, each with a similar title; they are considered continuations of the first. The Campana patents were quite bulky, with from 62 to 665 claims each, and they were densely interrelated.

Campana's patents described a system where "a message originating in an electronic mail system may be transmitted not only by wireline but also via RF, in which case it is received by the user and stored on his or her mobile RF receiver. The user can view the message on the RF receiver and, at some later point, connect the RF receiver to a fixed destination processor, i.e., his or her personal desktop computer, and transfer the stored message."

Murali Narayanan, who later ended up testifying on behalf of RIM, was surprised Campana got the patents in the first place. "As a computer guy, putting e-mail and paging together seemed obvious to me." However, many early patents only seem obvious after the fact. But to the USPTO in 1991, the Campana patents hardly seemed obvious, as very few people were in the field of wireless e-mail.

For Stout, the important thing was to file. In 1992, he and Campana decided to partner in a new "virtual company," NTP Inc., to patent and license more of Campana's inventions and methods and sit on the e-mail patents until the market warmed to the technology.

Stout was able to attract twenty-two investors to cover litigation expenses. Most were former Telefind shareholders who had just seen the company go under.

One of Campana's fifty patents was for a wireless locater technology that helped parents find their kids within a one-mile radius—his wireless child finder won first prize at the 1996 Consumer Electronics Show.

The idea with emerging patent holding companies such as NTP—the so-called patent trolls—was to focus their license demands on the smallest companies in a sector and overwhelm them with claims. Some of Campana's individual patents were quite elaborate and held more than 2,000 claims. Even if many of these claims were quite obvious, the point was to pack as many of them as possible into a patent.

Stout knew that in most cases, even if only one of their 2,000 infringement claims could withstand a validity challenge, NTP would win in court. Most small companies lacked the resources for a court battle, nitpicking over countless claims, and were happier settling out of court, regarding the NTP demands as rent or a tax on doing business. Stout used the income from those early licenses to build a war chest for challenging richer, more established players in future, when the potential payoff could be much, much higher.

The beauty of the patent troll approach was that because NTP was not producing any product or service, it was not infringing on anyone else's patents, and there were not many areas where it could be countersued. The only effective way to fight back was to get the Patent Office to do a re-examination and throw the *all* the patent claims out.

⊕　　⊕　　⊕

"In the world of patents, you're not going to get any traction unless you're willing to enforce them."

—*Donald Stout*

At the end of the 1990s, wireless e-mail was starting to emerge as a viable business, and NTP started finding and targeting emerging wireless e-mail providers and software and equipment makers, citing the Campana patents and offering to license the technology.

Research In Motion was one of the companies targeted, and on January 27, 2000, NTP sent RIM a letter placing the company on notice regarding six of its patents and inviting them to negotiate a licensing agreement. Charles Meyer, RIM's in-house attorney, talked with his staff and they concluded that RIM was not infringing on the NTP patents.

For the time being, RIM ignored NTP. Stout for his part still kept one radar eye on RIM. The BlackBerry was gaining serious traction as a must-have toy for busy executives, politicians, and lawyers. Their business was exploding, and RIM, which had patents of its own, was starting to flex its muscles in the legal arena. Stout suspected that it was only a matter of time before the two companies came to blows.

On the morning of May 18, 2001, Stout was leafing through *The Wall Street Journal* in his eighteenth-floor Arlington office, with its splendid view of the Washington Monument and the Capitol dome. Suddenly his eye caught a headline that made him start: "Pager Maker Gets Patent for E-Mail Delivery." The story related how Research In Motion Ltd. was suing Glenayre Electronics Inc. to enforce a newly awarded patent on its BlackBerry wireless device.

The story quoted RIM's Jim Balsillie warning that "BlackBerry knockoffs will now need a license from us. The amateurs out there have to stop."

The patent in question was U.S. Patent #6,291,694, newly awarded to Michael Lazaridis, RIM's president, and RIM software VP Gary Mousseau. It was for a single synchronizing e-mail box integrated between a desktop PC and server and mobile communications device.

According to Balsillie, RIM's software was a "redirector program." Any trigger—an incoming e-mail message, a calendar alarm or timer, a screensaver or keyboard timeout—made the computer automatically and continuously send e-mail messages to a mobile device, instead of waiting to respond to a command like existing systems. The patent described this as "pushing" e-mail instead of allowing it to accumulate and "pulling" it in periodically.

"When e-mail comes in and out of an existing host computer system, office PC or server, it is concurrently redirected in and out to a mobile communications device," Balsillie said. "It's not forwarded to another device, but it's continuously synchronized between the BlackBerry and the e-mail account. As you send e-mail from the BlackBerry, it shows up as 'sent' on your PC. The recipient can't tell where it was sent from."

Balsillie also told financial analysts that the RIM patent was "a bedrock aspect of BlackBerry functionality. We think this technology is very, very critical technology, and we definitely intend to license single-integration technology to develop a market for the consumer. We think the market shows signs of being a very big market."

That was just the news Stout was waiting for, and he quickly dialed up Tom Campana. The two agreed to check out the RIM patents in detail and start planning a lawsuit.

Six months later, in November 2001, Donald Stout filed the NTP suit in the U.S. District Court for the Eastern District of Virginia in Richmond, claiming that RIM's wireless e-mail service infringed on eight NTP patents relating to an "electronic mail system with RF communications to mobile processors."[*]

Stout knew the Richmond court, just down the highway from his office, was the perfect place to attack RIM because its proceedings were efficient and speedy. Sure enough, the case went to trial less than one year later.

For the Eastern District of Virginia, home of the "rocket docket," this was standard fare. The cases that went to trial were usually off the docket within a matter of months.

---

[*] *35 U.S.C. 271 Infringement of patent.* (a) Except as otherwise provided in this title, whoever without authority makes, uses, offers to sell, or sells any patented invention, within the United States, or imports into the United States any patented invention during the term of the patent therefor, infringes the patent.

A former district judge, Albert V. Bryan Jr., set the tone back in the 1960s. It's said he could try an entire case in an afternoon. Judge Bryan was so speedy that, according to local defense lawyer Edward B. MacMahon Jr., "the only grounds for a delay were a death in the family—your own."

Quick trials normally favored plaintiffs such as NTP by cutting their legal costs, while it worked against defendants such as RIM, forced to spend billable time untangling complex technical issues. However, in this case Stout knew RIM was a big billy goat, with relatively deep pockets. He wanted quick proceedings so RIM would not have time to assemble an airtight case, research prior art, and get all NTP's patents re-examined by the U.S. Patent and Trademarks Office.

RIM responded to the suit in a short news release, saying NTP's claim was "unsubstantiated" and sniffing that NTP's earlier licensing demand was simply "a collection of seemingly random marketing materials printed from RIM's website." Lazaridis for one was totally convinced that there was a body of "prior art" that made NTP's patents invalid.

To chase away the troll, RIM engaged the large, 2,000-partner Cleveland-based megafirm Jones Day Reavis and Pogue. Jones Day had a track record for wearing down opponents with paper filings and delays.

⊕   ⊕   ⊕

"Frankly, I never thought this case would make it to trial."
— *Judge James Spencer, 2003*

On the Virginia court's "rocket docket," things moved rapidly, and Judge James Spencer was picked to hear the case. Despite numerous motions filed by Jones Day, a jury was impaneled by mid-2002.

Judge Spencer was a fifteen-year veteran of the Virginia court, with a reputation for blunt talk and fair treatment. The son of an auto mechanic, he became a Baptist minister before deciding to go to law school. An honors graduate of the Harvard Law School, he served as an Army lawyer before being appointed to the bench by Ronald Reagan. He was the first African American to serve as a federal judge in Virginia.

Spencer was surprised to see the NTP-RIM case on his docket since cases such as this were usually settled out of court or at the last minute on the courtroom steps.

Judge Spencer called the trial to order on November 4, 2002, in Richmond, Virginia, the original capital of the Confederacy. The oldest part of the court complex, situated across from the State House, once served as the Treasury building of the Confederate States of America, and Jefferson Davis had had his office on the third floor.

Mike Lazaridis came face to face with Tom Campana on that day. The two inventors—one a beefy Greek, the other a rail-thin Italian—listened intently as counsel droned on in their opening statements about the facts of the case.

Campana came to the trial with a chip on his shoulder. He felt that Lazaridis was underestimating his work by daring to go to trial. As he told his father, "I made up my mind that if they didn't co-operate I was going to close them down." For his part, Donald Stout played the folksy country lawyer, arguing that RIM wasn't taking the patents of a small inventor such as Campana seriously.

When RIM's legal team started to present its case, they were clearly rushed, and made an initial slip up—a taste of things to come. They insisted that Research In Motion had written a letter to NTP telling them they weren't infringing on their patents. But when Stout asked to see the letter, RIM's team was unable to produce any evidence to show that RIM had ever acknowledged

NTP's inquiries. The judge and jury were clearly swayed toward NTP by the courtroom drama.

RIM's lead lawyer soldiered on, suggesting that Campana's patents were not valid because there was indeed "prior art," that other people had already invented wireless e-mail well before Campana had applied for his patents in 1991. To prove this point, he called to the box RIM's star witness, David Keeney, founder of TeckNow. Keeney had developed and sold a workable e-mail process called SAM (System for Automated Messages) fifteen years earlier, in 1987. This was four years before Campana's filing. If RIM could show that TekNow's technology worked, that would clearly invalidate NTP's patents.

But RIM's legal team had again been overconfident. In their scramble to provide evidence of prior art, they presented what appeared to be a flawed demo to court.

To prove his point, the RIM lawyer had Mr. Keeney do a demo for the jury with two old laptops and a pager. First Keeney told them how he could send an e-mail message using SAM, and then he typed "Tommy, the deal is closed." The phrase then popped up on the pager.

Donald Stout smelled something fishy, and when his team looked carefully at the demo they noticed the file directory's size was far too large to be from 1988 SAM software. He challenged Keeney to admit that he was using software from 1993 to do the demo, instead of his original code. Keeney got rattled, then started flubbing his lines and went on the defensive.

Stout immediately moved to strike the TekNow demo, arguing that the date on the file directory for the demo software was two years after 1991.

An increasingly furious Judge Spencer, thinking he had been duped, angrily left the courtroom to compose himself. When he returned, he instructed the jury to leave the room. He then glared at RIM's lawyer and told him, "I'll count to twenty. I don't want to yell at you." After chewing out the legal team, he summarily ruled that RIM had infringed four claims across three patents. He then called the jury back in, told them to disregard the whole RIM demo, and asked them to come up with a verdict.

The jurors filed out of the courtroom with the impression that RIM's lawyers had tried to pull a fast one with fabricated evidence. They took just four hours to reach a verdict. It was bad news for Research In Motion. They found that RIM had infringed in fourteen claims on the remaining five NTP patents and, worse, that its conduct had been "willful."

On November 21, 2002, after thirteen days of trial, Judge Spencer declared that RIM's case was not even close. He assessed damages of $23 million, a royalty based on the number of BlackBerrys sold in the United States, and then slammed down his gavel to end the trial.

RIM said it would appeal the decision. "We do not believe these patents are valid. We do not believe we infringe on them. And we are willing and prepared to do whatever is necessary to ensure that we prevail," RIM co-chief executive Jim Balsillie said in a conference call.

But RIM's trial wasn't over yet. NTP then applied to Judge Spencer to have the damages "enhanced" because of RIM's "fraudulent" demo during the trial. The judge agreed and said RIM had "consistently engaged in a variety of questionable litigation tactics throughout the course of this action." He then boosted the damages to $53 million, plus about $4.5 million in legal fees, and jacked the royalty rate to 8.55 percent.

But there was more bad news to come. On August 5, 2003, Judge Spencer issued a surprise injunction barring the sale of BlackBerrys in the United States until NTP's patents expired on May 20, 2012. He only agreed to stay the injunction if RIM would put an amount equal to the damage award in escrow. His ruling was stayed when RIM filed an appeal.

Stout had easily skewered RIM's hastily prepared demo, even though the company was in the right. Two years later, RIM's lead replacement lawyer David Long argued at appeal that Judge Spencer's decision to throw out the demonstration was "an abuse of discretion" since TekNow clearly had software for SAM from the 1980s and that the post-1991 directory dates of the demo software "occurred merely because TekNow's license-protection software automatically updates the directory dates with each new installation of the SAM software." He said there was "nothing fraudulent, and it was simply a mistake in copying over the file." His team successfully ran the demonstration after the trial with 1980s software to provide evidence of prior art.

By mid-2003, things were looking grim for RIM. The company found itself dug into a deep financial and legal hole, with very few avenues of escape. Lazaridis and Balsillie had expected to walk away from the trial leaving behind a few million dollars in change. But then the sum had ballooned to $60 million in damages at trial, and they had to set aside at least $200 million in escrow for a potential royalty payment. And now they had to fight the threat of an injunction, which could shut down the whole BlackBerry system in the United States. Lazaridis and Balsillie had been naive, but they were now fully aware that a foxy patent troll had entrapped their company in a tangled skein of patent claims.

RIM's lawyers told them the odds were very good that the U.S. Patent Office would re-examine the patents, but they also feared that the odds were against them. It was hardly possible that the USPTO would strike down *all* of the hundreds of NTP claims. So to fight off an injunction, sooner or later they would have to come to a settlement.

The lights burned late at RIM as Lazaridis and Balsillie debated proceeding further. Lazaridis was clearly bent on going the distance. RIM company lore—not verified—tells of major shouting matches with Jim Balsillie over settling with NTP, with Mike arguing that they were HIS patents and damned if he was going to settle. Certainly, it was clear that whatever the outcome of the case, it was going to cost the company far more than they had bargained for. How much more was the moot point.

Mike was determined to hold fast and fight the ruling with all the resources at their command, so a new legal team was assembled to appeal the Virginia verdict or to get a new trial.

Mike Lazaridis's old friend at Ericsson, Bill Frezza, was not surprised that RIM didn't settle with NTP and stayed on to fight. "Mike is the kind of guy who doesn't make business compromises. You know how people plead guilty, even when they know they're innocent, just to get a reduced sentence—Mike wouldn't do that."

Lazaridis remained defiant. And the more he learned about the inner workings of the patent system, the more he was appalled. "There's a tremendous amount of innovation and hard work that goes into taking an idea and realizing it and then making it into a product," he said. "There are 16 million lines of code in BlackBerry. Sixteen million. It's hard to imagine 16 million lines of code. They all have to work in harmony and perfection to make this thing do its job. Are you trying to tell me that one little concept is more important than another little concept, and that it didn't take man-years and man-years of effort to make all that stuff work?"[2]

---

2. Barrie McKenna, Paul Waldie, and Simon Avery, "Patently Absurd: The Inside Story of RIM's Wireless War," *Globe and Mail*, February 21, 2006.

Jim Balsillie came around to the same uncompromising position. A dedicated and tenacious hockey player, he was not afraid of some rough grinding stuff on the end boards. For the two of them, RIM had been wronged, and the fight against patent troll NTP was now something of a righteous crusade.

Word of Donald Stout's quick and convincing jury trial victory in Virginia soon spread, which brought out the big Beltway barracudas, attracted by the smell of RIM's blood in the water. One of the best patent lawyers in Washington, James H. Wallace Jr., readily agreed to take on NTP's case with little persuading.

A diligent patent and trademark litigator, Wallace had won multiple actions against seventeen Japanese and Korean electronics giants for infringing rights to use the charge coupling device (CCD) technology at the heart of digital camcorders and cameras. He had also emerged the victor in several high-profile pharmaceutical patent cases for Claritin, Prilosec, and Ditropan.

Wallace's megafirm, Wiley Rein & Fielding (now Wiley Rein LLP), are a highly plugged-in partnership, with almost 300 lawyers on tap. One of the senior partners, Richard E. Wiley, was former chairman of the Federal Communications Commission. Another, Fred Fielding, was appointed George W. Bush's White House counsel in January 2007. Fielding had already served as associate counsel for President Richard Nixon from 1970 to 1972, and served as counsel to President Ronald Reagan from 1981 to 1986. He was also a member of the National Commission on Terrorist Attacks Upon the United States (the 9/11 Commission).

In the 1970s, Fred Fielding had a ringside seat during the Watergate scandal as John Dean's deputy. Long before FBI official Mark Felt was finally unveiled as "Deep Throat," Fielding was widely fingered, even by President Nixon and his staffer H.R. Haldeman, as the man who leaked the Watergate break-in to *Washington Post* reporters Bob Woodward and Carl Bernstein.

One official told *Time* that Fred Fielding was "the ultimate Washington lawyer-insider—he's the man to see …. He's the guy who helps you defend your position, stick to your principles, but tries to work out a reasonable compromise. He's highly partisan, but he's highly regarded by everyone."[3]

RIM had already engaged its own heavyweight firm, Howrey LLP, another global behemoth with more than 600 attorneys focusing on complex litigation, antitrust, and IP cases. Pegged as the number-one U.S. IP firm in 2006 by *Managing Intellectual Property*, Howrey was also a perennial top-ten firm in the *National Law Journal*'s "Who Defends Corporate America" ranking of the Fortune 250 companies. Howrey put two IP experts on the NTP case: Henry C. Bunsow of the San Francisco office and lead attorney David W. Long in Washington, D.C.

Henry Bunsow was a Silicon Valley veteran. David Long, like Mike Lazaridis, was an electrical engineer, with more than five years of experience in telecom, control systems, guided rockets, and radar systems. In the 1990s, he changed careers, getting a degree in intellectual property law and graduating magna cum laude from the University of Alabama.

The RIM case was meat to the tiger for Long, who specialized in complex patent cases. Apart from RIM, his client list included Verizon (interactive voice communication systems), Toshiba (memory circuits), Xybernaut Corp. (wearable computers), and chipmaker Qualcomm (wireless communication equipment).

To stave off an injunction against BlackBerry sales in the United States, Long immediately filed requests with the USTPO for re-examination of the NTP patents and moved to stay all court

---

3. Mike Allen, "Bush Picks a Replacement for Harriet Miers," *Time, January* 8, 2007.

proceedings while this was under way. He also asked for a new trial and filed a request to the Court of Appeals for the Federal Circuit in Washington.

Long also went to work on several fronts to salvage as much as possible from the Virginia disaster. His motion for a new trial didn't work; neither did his request to stay pending re-examination. But for the time being, RIM was safe from an injunction, since a three-judge appeal court panel was in the process of reviewing the rulings and verdict.

Long then did some damage control with Judge Spencer in Virginia, especially regarding the finding of willful infringement, which could triple the jury's $34.4-million damage award and force RIM to pay NTP's attorney fees.

Long convinced Judge Spencer that RIM had a good faith belief it hadn't infringed the patents, so treble damages weren't warranted. His diligent work bore fruit, and Spencer boosted the $33.4-million award to only $47 million, instead of the expected $100 million.

But Judge Spencer stuck to his decision to award NTP its legal fees. Long got him to cut 20 percent from the $5.25 million in costs, for a total of $4.2 million. NTP had originally filed suit claiming infringement of eight patents having a combined total of more than 2,400 claims, then later asserted only five patents and sixteen claims at trial, which lowered costs.

On December 14, 2004, the three-judge appeal court panel allowed RIM to go ahead and appeal by striking down the injunction and the verdict. But they also delivered some bad news—their finding that RIM had violated eleven NTP patent claims. The panel also said that part of the lower-court ruling was flawed and ordered that five full patents should be reargued in Judge Spencer's court for a closer look at infringement and damages.

David Long, realizing that the game was far from over, suggested to Lazaridis and Balsillie that, after a year of wrangling, perhaps it was time to raise the white flag and get a settlement. Otherwise they would be in for a long, drawn-out legal fight and an inherently risky trial.

The pair agreed and instructed Long to start negotiations. NTP's patent claims were starting to unravel, and besides, Lazaridis and Balsillie were starting to feel a tad generous. Research In Motion had celebrated its twentieth anniversary that year, and its BlackBerry was now reaching more than 2 million subscribers worldwide.

By the time Judge Spencer had issued his first Virginia ruling, Tom Campana was battling esophageal cancer. A heavy smoker all his life, Campana underwent radiation treatment and surgery that removed much of his esophagus. He died on June 8, 2004, at age fifty-seven, the day after an appeal got under way in NTP's patent infringement case against RIM.

"I've been practicing for thirty-five years and I've never seen anything like it. Most companies don't have this amount of fight in them."

—Donald Stout

The year 2005 began with Jim Balsillie's demand for a face-to-face meeting with the head of the U.S. Patent and Trademarks Office.

On Saturday, January 1, 2005, Theodore Kassinger, the deputy secretary of the Department of Commerce, wrote an e-mail to Jon Dudas, head of the USPTO, to arrange the get-together. On Monday, he sent a "High Importance" e-mail with a laundry list of demands:

- Identification of the various outstanding patents (by number and owner), and whether they are *inter partes* re-exams (IPRs) or director-ordered re-exams (DORs);
- Current status of each;

- Procedural history of each IPR and DOR;
- Information on the volume of new materials being reviewed and the number of USPTO employees reviewing materials;
- Summary of the litigation history; and
- Outstanding issues before the USPTO.

That Tuesday at 4 p.m., Balsillie and Don Cameron, RIM's Canadian counsel, arrived at the USPTO for the meeting. Their lead U.S. lawyer, David Long, did not attend, since it was purely an information meeting. Ten USPTO officials sat around the table, including Dudas, Steve Pinkos, deputy under secretary of commerce and deputy director of the USPTO, and Eleanor K. Meltzer, an attorney-advisor in the office of legislative and international affairs of the USPTO. There is no record of the meeting available, but one official later complained about "the propriety of industry leaders seeking an audience with the Director."

The meeting was perfectly legal and proper, as long as "the merits of the proceeding" were not discussed. For David Long, it was as much a data gathering meeting as an attempt to keep the USPTO's feet to the fire and leverage with NTP, as he was meeting with them to discuss a settlement.

While Balsillie and Cameron were paying their courtesy visit to the USPTO, and David Long was meeting with the NTP legal team, Long's co-attorney Henry Bunsow was in appeals court trying to get some leverage over NTP and let RIM escape the legal stranglehold.

His argument was essentially this—RIM was not based in the United States, and therefore NTP's U.S. patents did not apply to the BlackBerry system. Plus NTP did not hold any wireless e-mail patents in Canada. Bunsow had a point—a U.S. patent could not be enforced outside the country's borders. Because RIM's relay server farm, through which all BlackBerry e-mails passed, was in Waterloo, Ontario, the software was beyond the reach of American patents.

"We don't care if one part of the system is run in Canada," Donald Stout rejoined. "The beneficial use of the system is in the United States."

At Jim Balsillie's personal urging, Canada's Department of Foreign Affairs and International Trade also filed a brief requesting a hearing on the cross-border issues. Spokesman André Lemay said his government was concerned that the Virginia court might be extending United States law into Canada.

"We're not defending, endorsing or criticizing RIM's position in this case," Lemay said. "We're simply acting to protect the interests of Canadian businesses."

On the surface, all this intense lobbying seemed to be having an effect on Donald Stout and NTP's big legal armada, but the end game was just beginning.

On March 16, 2005, David Long finally struck a deal, or so he thought, with NTP. He had in his hands a half-page term sheet signed by both parties, whereby RIM would pay NTP $450 million to sublicense certain NTP patents that "interface, interact or combine with RIM's products, services or infrastructure."

RIM boldly announced a contract settlement to the public: "The resolution permits RIM and its partners to sell its products, services and infrastructure completely free and clear of any claim by NTP, including any claims that NTP may have against wireless carriers, ISV partners or against third party products that use RIM's BlackBerry Connect/BlackBerry Built-In technology."

The $450 million in settlement money included $152 million in judgment money less $15 million in other litigation related fees.

RIM said a large chunk of the $313 million, which was the balance of the settlement amount, would be expensed in its next quarterly financial statement.

RIM's stock jumped $14 a share, or 17 percent, on the announcement. But the news was premature. Talks broke down on June 9 over some details of the contract, and NTP demanded a return to the bargaining table. RIM's stock price tanked again. A frustrated David Long then asked Judge Spencer to enforce the terms of the March deal, but on November 30, Spencer ruled that "the parties do not have a valid and enforceable settlement." Rather than improving its offer, Long played for time and launched yet another appeal, this time to the U.S. Supreme Court. He decided to ask for a stay pending that body's decision on whether it would hear the appeal of the Federal Circuit's stand; but he did not expect a positive decision. Long also recommended that RIM mount a major charm offensive, since tens of thousands of BlackBerry users inside the Washington beltway were howling for a settlement so they could keep their beloved devices buzzing away.

While David Long and Henry Bunsow were working the courts, RIM also ramped up a lobbying and public relations push in Washington and set to work to convince policy-makers that it was the victim of a dysfunctional patent system that had to be reformed and to urge members of Congress to save their beloved BlackBerry.

RIM hired two Americans who knew Canada well—former U.S. ambassadors James Blanchard and Gordon Giffin. Blanchard, a Michigan Democrat and former governor of the state, had written the legislation saving Chrysler from bankruptcy. A Clinton appointee, he served as ambassador to Canada from 1993–96 and then joined Washington-based DLA Piper Rudnick Gray Cary in Washington.

Giffin, also a Democrat, was born in Springfield, Massachusetts, but grew up in Montreal and Toronto. He earned a J.D. from Emory University School of Law in Atlanta, Georgia, and went into practice there, heading the public policy and regulatory practice of Atlanta-based law firm McKenna Long & Aldridge. He was ambassador to Canada from 1997 to 2001.

Giffin's job was to offer RIM a bit of "strategic advice on the Washington environment." Jim Blanchard's role was more active—to push the cause of patent reform in Congress and get the USPTO to speed up its review of NTP's disputed patents. This was a key goal, and the lobbyists reckoned that Judge Spencer would never leave millions of BlackBerry users in the dark to protect a batch of near-worthless patents.

RIM supporters in Congress also lobbied hard in committee hearings, warning that shutting off their BlackBerry devices threatened national security in the event of terrorist attack. Several members brought up the fact that their BlackBerrys had not failed on 9/11 while cell phones everywhere went dead. Among the testimonials submitted for RIM's court case, a former Homeland Security official said the BlackBerry worked brilliantly when Hurricane Katrina struck the Gulf Coast when cell phones failed. A New England health group warned that BlackBerrys were integral to its response plans in the event of an avian flu outbreak. Even House Speaker Dennis Hastert, the top Republican in Congress, backed RIM's case while freely admitting he was a BlackBerry addict.

RIM also engaged Orlando attorney David Stewart, who had once served as a USPTO examiner, as well as a judge at the Board of Patent Appeals and Interferences (BPAI). Stewart's job was to file RIM's requests for re-examination that eventually led to the invalidation of some of NTP's patents on wireless e-mail technology.

This unrelenting pressure stoked the fire under the USPTO and may have nudged the office to move its review of NTP patents to the head of the line. The first ruling appeared on April 19, declaring a major NTP patent invalid and rejecting all 89 claims used to support it. That made a total of 612 NTP patent claims dismissed by the USPTO to date. Even veteran Washington IP lawyers were amazed at the speed at which the USPTO was now moving.

⊕　　⊕　　⊕

More good news came from Howrey patent consultant Thomas Pavelko, who with RIM software developer Gary Mousseau had unearthed prior art in Norway that further diminished NTP's claims.

In June 2005, RIM attorney David Long turned up the heat on his adversaries by writing to NTP: "I bring to your attention information that is highly material to the patentability of those NTP patents so that you properly may fulfill your and NTP's duty of candor and good faith in dealing with the Patent Office with the NTP patents and related patent applications."

Long then described six technical books published by the big Norwegian telco Telenor in 1986 and 1989, which describe a wireless e-mail messaging system. The Telenor books, said Long, talked about an integrated system combining a "Message Data Network" with a "Message Handling System" to transfer e-mail messages on a store-and-forward basis via radio frequency transmission. The system was quite similar to the way RIM's BlackBerry network worked.

"The Telenor publications openly disclosed and described to the public the mobile e-mail system sought to be claimed years later in NTP patents. Indeed, the Telenor publications openly disclosed that e-mail system long before NTP claims that its system was even conceived."

Long's letter concluded by citing a sworn NTP statement saying its patent was first dreamed up a year or two later, in July 1990.

Other good tidings for RIM came in late June, when the USPTO found that U.S. patent #5,159,592 by inventor Charles E. Perkins, assigned to IBM, also anticipated many claims in the NTP patents and was filed earlier than any of them.

The USPTO then found that U.S. patent #5,278,955 dealt with e-mail processing and cited a 1989 IEEE article by Richard Verjinski called "PHASE, a portable host access system environment," that anticipated many NTP patent claims.

NTP was now on the defensive. Forced to investigate and answer the Telenor prior art claim, counsel James Wallace complained to Judge Spencer that he couldn't root out missing reports from Telenor's library in Trondheim, Norway, because "RIM checked out the documents and refused to return them."

Outside court, David Long told the press that NTP was sent hard copies of the exact technical treatise from Telenor that Wallace referred to. "It's just disturbing," he said of NTP and the Telenor footnote. "They'll use charged words like that and they are misleading. It sounds like we're up to no good and we're hiding something, and that couldn't be any further from the truth." No matter that patent consultant Thomas Pavelko had taken several weeks to get the documents copied for NTP.

Long also argued in so many words that NTP was nothing but a patent troll: "NTP's request for an injunction is about money, not equity. Unlike RIM, NTP is not in the business of selling wireless products or services, or serving the public. Instead NTP is, and always has been, a patent licensing company." RIM had "made the investments, put its energies into the business and bore the risk that ultimately resulted in the commercial success of the BlackBerry system."

Stirring words aside, the press and BlackBerry users were getting tired of the whole patent charade. "I wish they'd settle and get it over with," snarled one frustrated CIO who had 500 workers relying on BlackBerrys and asked not to be named.

RIM could afford to be confident about a good settlement. Over the past year, its share price had been hammered—an unavoidable consequence of the trials—but sales were healthy and profit had climbed nearly 400 percent, to $90.4 million on revenues of $365.9 million.

⊕　　⊕　　⊕

"NTP has improperly tried to claim for itself what RIM and others independently developed."
                                    —Howrey lawyer David Long

The Federal Circuit issued a second decision on August 2, 2005, concluding that RIM didn't infringe NTP's six "method" claims but did infringe seven "system" claims. They stated that Spencer needed to reinterpret his 2004 ruling on system-type claims and re-manded the case back to him to determine whether RIM infringed three other similar NTP claims.

They suggested that while BlackBerry devices are sold in the United States, RIM and its relay station for sending e-mail wire-lessly were both located in Canada. NTP's patents only covered complete systems and methods for wireless e-mail in the United States; not the BlackBerry device itself, which was only a compo-nent of the system.

The judges held that RIM had put the patented system into use in the United States, but not the method, since the relaying didn't occur in the States. Patent infringement takes place when a prod-uct is imported into, or sold in, the United States. But what if the invention were a method? How do you import or sell it?

In late September 2005, the USPTO issued a first look at U.S. patent #6,317,592 and came out in RIM's favor. NTP's claim gov-erning a digital mailbox feature was found by the patent office to have been invented before NTP made its filing.

"All 665 claims in this NTP patent were unanimously rejected by a panel of three senior patent examiners in the initial ruling," RIM crowed in a news release. "The U.S. Patent and Trademark Office has now issued initial rulings in the reexaminations of all eight NTP patents relating to the NTP vs. RIM litigation and has rejected 100% of the 1,921 claims contained in those patents, including the 16 claims asserted against RIM." But the courts were not moved by the news. The USPTO still had to make final rulings, and NTP was expected to appeal.

On October 7, the Court of Appeals for the Federal Circuit denied RIM's request for a complete rehearing by all twelve of its judges. The appeals court had previously upheld a lower court ruling that RIM had infringed on seven patents held by NTP.

Wiley Rein lawyer Kevin Anderson said that NTP would now ask the court to apply the injunction to the patent claims that were no longer under review. Those patents, he added, were broad enough to prevent RIM from continuing service in the United States, which accounted for almost 75 percent of its revenue. "The case is pretty much over," said Anderson.

In a release, RIM said that, with the backing of the Canadian government, it was requesting the Federal Circuit Court of Appeals to hold off on any action while it asked the Supreme Court for a review. "RIM continues to believe this case raises significant national and international issues warranting further appellate review." On October 10, the Court of Appeals turned down RIM's request to hold off on any action.

On October 25, newly appointed U.S. Chief Justice John Roberts simply denied RIM's request to delay proceedings, with no explanation. But that did not mean the high court had refused to take up the case, and RIM had ninety days to file an appeal on the appeals court decision.

The case was now proceeding on two tracks, one at the Supreme Court level and one back in Judge Spencer's district court, which could reinstate the injunction.

Even though Justice Roberts had turned down the request for delay, RIM maintained its stance that "an injunction is inappropriate given the facts of the case and substantial doubts raised subsequent to trial as to the validity of the patents in question." But the company also acknowledged that "it ultimately will be up to the courts to decide these matters and there can never be an assurance of a favorable outcome in any litigation."

In the meantime, the case had sent RIM's stock reeling. Since the appeals court's initial ruling in December 2004, the company's stock had fallen 47 percent.

RIM's charm/terror offensive was now starting to bear some heavy fruit, and the prospect of a BlackBerry shutdown was the talk of Washington. But not everybody was concerned. One Washington staffer laughed: "It might be a nice change. Instead of looking at my BlackBerry the first thing in the morning, I might actually be able to take a shower without work on my mind."

Finally, the U.S. government began to rouse itself, and one early November morning in 2005, Uncle Sam himself ambled into Judge Spencer's modest courthouse in sleepy Richmond, Virginia, and put his very large red-and-white-striped hat on the courtroom table. An injunction, said Justice Department lawyer Paul McNulty, "would literally prevent RIM from providing the services that would be essential for the federal government, as well as state and local governments, to continue their use of the BlackBerry devices."

The government, McNulty said, was concerned "there may be a substantial public interest that may be impaired" by shutting down the BlackBerry e-mail service. It might not be feasible to shut it down for consumers and not for federal employees, he warned, and "there does not appear to be a simple manner in which RIM can identify which users of BlackBerrys are part of the federal government."

At this, NTP attorney James Wallace scoffed that McNulty's claim was "highly misleading and inappropriate." NTP had promised numerous times that an injunction would not apply to any government or emergency personnel, and that it would not be difficult to identify such users. He would also request to the court that users be given ninety days to find an alternative e-mail service before their BlackBerry wireless service was shut down.

McNulty drawled that it wouldn't be so simple. The government would need to build a database or "white list." This could be costly and time-consuming, but "it is imperative that some mechanism be incorporated that permits continuity of the federal government's use of BlackBerry devices."

McNulty could only guesstimate, but there were at least 200,000 federal employees and another 100,000 state employees using BlackBerry devices to retrieve their "essential government" e-mails wirelessly. He requested, on behalf of various government agencies, a stay of ninety days to put together a white list. The Justice Department also wanted non-governmental organizations added to the white list, including the regional Federal Reserve banks that used BlackBerrys to communicate with the Federal Reserve. Access to BlackBerrys was crucial for ensuring a stable economy, and the devices were "important for monetary supply, particularly in a time of crisis."[4]

The bottom line was Judge Spencer should delay even thinking about bringing down an injunction for at least ninety days, given the potential expense and complexity involved in inventorying all those little machines.

---

4. Simon Avery, "The BlackBerry Conundrum," *Globe and Mail*, March 1, 2006.

Christopher Null, reporting for *Mobile* magazine, only half-jokingly said that if the BlackBerry service were no longer available, even temporarily, "you'd have all these Type-A personalities unable to stay in touch with the office. It'd be mass hysteria."

⊕　⊕　⊕

*"Bureaucrats are like amoeba. They respond to heat, light,
and nourishment, but especially heat."*

—Anon

Members of Congress from both parties were growing increasingly enraged that the USPTO had let this state of affairs come to pass in the first place, threatening their freedoms and their constitutional right to bear BlackBerrys. The fire of this rage was starting to scorch the USPTO's tail, accelerating the final review (and dumping) of all the disputed NTP patent claims.

The fire was reaching right into Judge Spencer's courtroom. Public anger grew when he refused to force NTP to accept the proposed $450-million settlement with RIM and then denied RIM's request to throw out the case entirely. And now Citibank's Daryl Armstrong was estimating that RIM's cost of settlement had risen to between $650 million and $1 billion. If true, it was a heavy penalty that RIM shareholders would have to swallow.

But RIM was also putting forward an alternate lifeline: it could rework its operating system and download new non-infringing software to its installed base of customers. If Judge Spencer agreed to the work-around idea, then the possibility of a shutdown went away for the near future.

On December 7, NTP waved a peace flag, saying it was willing to drop its demands and settle the case in exchange for a royalty rate of 5.7 percent over the life of the patents, until 2012.

All this left poor Judge Spencer in a bit of a box. A jury trial had already ruled against RIM. And without a new trial, he had to act inside his trial judge role until final ruling after the inevitable appeals. Until that happened, the NTP patents were assumed valid and he had to rule that way. His job was not to decide whether NTP's patent claims were really valid.

Strictly speaking, the onus was still on RIM to prove with clear and convincing evidence that NTP's claims, most of them still presumed by law to be valid, were in fact not. But in real life this could still take years. NTP also had the right to appeal any final rejection notice to a three-judge panel at the USPTO and could file further appeals at the Federal Court level. And Donald Stout and James Wallace were automatically appealing each USPTO decision as it came down. The company stood a good chance of having at least some of the claims reinstated.

If RIM could not satisfy the standard, all Judge Spencer was supposed to do was find that RIM had failed to meet its burden. As for NTP's patent claims, all he could do was find they were not invalid.

Judge Spencer was a fair and honorable man, and he wanted to minimize damage and deliver some kind of rough justice that would let both sides walk away with their heads held high. If he dropped the injunction bomb, RIM would pay the damages it owed to NTP. But the situation was becoming absurd and even dangerous. What if RIM appealed again and lost? RIM would have to shut down the BlackBerry system. If NTP's patents were later eradicated either in court or by the USPTO and NTP lost all appeals, the injunction against RIM might still not be lifted, and the company might not get its money back. Then anyone but RIM could offer a BlackBerry-type service without fear of infringing NTP's patents.

All in all there was too much uncertainty because of the density of the case and the issues, not to mention public safety considerations.

Judge Spencer made a decision. He had to convince the two warring parties that if he dropped the 100-kiloton bomb—and they were forcing him to do this—both of them took the risk of losing very, very big. RIM could throw away all the considerable business and loyal clientele it was now growing. As for NTP, time was running out. With its Campana patents in tatters, and facing an onerous appeal process, it could potentially walk away with nothing, unable to sue anybody else for the rights. So he proposed a timetable for decision, appointed a court mediator, and asked the two sides to file briefs by February 1.

Judge Spencer was weary of the whole affair and rapidly losing patience. His docket report was now showing 426 separate entries in the BlackBerry litigation, and clearly, a new trial was not in the cards. In late 2005, he quipped to a reporter, "I intend to move swiftly on this case. I've spent enough of my life and my time on NTP and RIM."

On January 23, 2006, the Supreme Court refused to hear RIM's appeal, as expected. But it bought RIM a bit more time. For the next six weeks, the end game played out at a majestic pace, with one good news day for RIM following another good one for NTP. The two sides were still talking to the mediator. Judge Spencer's February 1 deadline passed without incident. On February 9, RIM said it had successfully tested software work-around designs for BlackBerry service in the U.S. market, if needed. A week later, on February 17, RIM said it remained open to a "reasonable" settlement with NTP.

On February 22, the USPTO issued a final rejection of one of the five disputed patents owned by NTP Inc. But NTP lawyer James Wallace then put a damper on any happy feelings that NTP was willing to walk away from appealing. He declared that he thought the patents would be upheld on appeal. Wallace said the USPTO examiners, in rejecting the patents, used an overly broad construction of the patents' specific claims. The narrower construction was upheld in the infringement suit, and he was confident it would be upheld again if and when the patents reached the federal Appeals Court. This was a clear signal to RIM that NTP was willing to continue the patent tournament, which was now causing RIM to lose potential business.

The two RIM CEOs—the press were now calling them "the BlackBerry Boys"—were finally coming around to that conclusion as well. On February 23, Jim Balsillie told a technology conference in Whistler, B.C., that the company had developed and tested a workable system to allow BlackBerry service to continue in the United States, if the judge ordered an injunction. But he also said the company would be willing to boost its payment to NTP to settle the dispute. Jim Wallace was also conciliatory, saying that "We are more than willing to license RIM on a reasonable royalty-paid-up basis—RIM has the keys to its own jail."

On February 24, Judge Spencer, suspecting that the end was near, turned up the heat on RIM, repeating his mantra that it was clear RIM had infringed on NTP patents. He said he would decide on damages and whether to eventually issue an injunction "as soon as reasonably possible," but he was upset that the two parties had not resolved the dispute on their own. Spencer chastised the two for not having settled and warned that any court-imposed decision would be "imperfect."

NTP had a strong incentive to settle, since with every week that passed without a deal, they were passing up the rewards of the case. While Judge Spencer was sticking to the original jury decision, there was always the threat of a new trial hanging over their heads.

For a hockey player such as Jim Balsillie, RIM's game situation was getting grim, like being down three goals in the third period of the last game of the playoffs. But on the bright side, there were other more important games to play and a new season coming up. RIM was rolling out great new products and now had 4 million users paying $25 a month. Who wanted to walk away from $100 million a month in revenue?

Balsillie wanted a clean hit, and he and Don Cameron and David Long discussed how to turn the pending settlement to their advantage. An obvious talking point was, if they were going to benefit NTP, how could they at the same time help their business allies and put the stick to their other competitors? Paying go-away money to NTP might have some advantages.

Spectators at the RIM-NTP tournament were eager to know, would NTP blink first or would RIM? Would RIM blink, not daring to take a chance on Judge Spencer imposing the injunction? Or would NTP blink, believing that RIM's game plan was to go all the way, essentially daring the judge to shut down BlackBerry service?

Some commentators suggested that a shutdown would be a terrific thing to do. It would cause a firestorm of outrage against a flawed justice system. It was pathetic that a single judge in a remote city could single-handedly shut down a great and even essential service for a bunch of now worthless claims held by a greedy patent troll. It would shake up a patent system badly in need of reform and modernity.

Other RIM watchers were sure this would never be allowed to happen. They were convinced a settlement was at hand, and many felt NTP would walk away with cash in the neighborhood of $1 billion to $1.5 billion. Others felt that RIM should hang in longer, and wait for another year or two or three until NTP's appeals to the USPTO were finally exhausted. Still others predicted that the Department of Justice would have to intervene and stop the trial entirely, on the grounds of national security.

All speculation went out the window when on March 3, 2006, Research In Motion and NTP suddenly announced a settlement of their long-running patent dispute. For RIM and its customers, the uncertainty was now over. Their beloved BlackBerry service would not be shut off. RIM agreed to pay NTP $612.5 million to settle all claims and for a "perpetual, paid-up license going forward." Under terms of the deal, NTP gave RIM the "unfettered right" to continue all of its BlackBerry services. The deal let RIM sell all its products and services without the need to pay further royalty payments to NTP. RIM's wireless carriers, partners, suppliers, and customers were also protected from being "trolled" by NTP. They would never have to pay licensing or royalty fees to NTP.

So what could have been a potential disaster ended with a whimper. The market shrugged off the $612.5 million and RIM's stock surged 16 percent the next trading day.

Judge Spencer immediately approved the settlement, dismissed all NTP litigation against RIM, and kicked the parties out of his courthouse. Then he went back to his usual docket of drug cases, domestic scraps, and armed robberies with violence.

Was RIM's punishment for violating a bunch of worthless patents and spending five grueling years being jerked around in court all that bad?

Research In Motion had already put aside $450 million to account for a possible settlement. The additional $162.5 million would be reflected as a charge in the fourth quarter. A few bucks would have to come off the next dividend.

RIM grumbled in public that the number of new subscribers to its BlackBerry service was going to fall short of expectations by as much as 120,000 subscribers in the fourth quarter. The uncertainty caused by the dispute with NTP was evidently causing many potential customers to either put off their BlackBerry purchases or choose a competing wireless product, such as Palm's Treo.

The case seemed to be taking its toll on RIM, whose market share of wireless e-mail had slid from 81 percent in 2004 to 70 percent in early 2006. RIM's share price also plunged 25 percent in 2005, compared to a 5 percent drop in the tech-heavy NASDAQ composite index.

RIM worried that the uncertainty had knocked $40 million to $70 million off sales revenue for the current quarter, which was now expected to be around $550 million, rather than the previous forecast range of $590 million to $620 million.

Jim Balsillie complained, "It's not a good feeling to write this kind of check." But the truth was that while many other companies had entered the wireless e-mail market, none of them had such a brilliant product. And the number of BlackBerry subscribers was in fact doubling every year, leaving RIM with about $1.8 billion in the kitty. In truth, RIM was rolling in dough.

Predictably, Balsillie put the craziness of the outcome in sporting terms, downplaying the loss, telling reporters RIM was "taking it for the team."

⊕　　⊕　　⊕

"Patent law and case law do not intersect until the very end."

—*Peter Misek, Canaccord Adams*

So NTP finally blinked. The troll agreed to walk away forever and never bother RIM again, for far less money than expected—$612.5 million.

Still, not a bad payday for the tenacious Donald Stout, who emerged with about $200 million. The Wiley Rein take was also in the neighborhood of $200 million—normally the firm gener-ated about $140 million a year in total. The balance went to the Campana family and NTP investors who had hung in for five long years.

Balsillie had the last word in this maddening case, publicly dumping on the U.S. patent system, accusing it of issuing too many "bogus" patents. He called for a sweeping overhaul of the present broken regime so "no other company" faced the legal nightmare that RIM had endured. And he quoted inventor and venture capitalist Greg Blonder, writing in *Business Week*, that "protecting intellectual property (IP) with today's patents is virtu-ally worthless .... Wasteful court cases, like the recent BlackBerry imbroglio, occur because patents are granted for narrow, redun-dant concepts that courts find difficult to unravel, and so are open to interpretation. We need to invent ourselves out of this mess."[5]

Turning on Judge Spencer's actions after the jury trial, Balsillie said he was baffled that the judge ignored USPTO findings that NTP's patents were invalid. He then quoted a *Newsweek* article saying the court's treatment of RIM was like "a judge in a murder case pondering execution while ignoring DNA evidence that exon-erates the accused."

⊕　　⊕　　⊕

Sour grapes. Both RIM and NTP were victors in the biggest patent fight in technology history.

NTP walked away with a bundle of cash that it could use to target other unfortunate tech firms. Palm Computing was quickly in NTP's sights, potentially the first of a long line of victims of a cash-flush NTP. Stout also filed for infringement on the same

---

5. Greg Blonder, "Cutting Through the Patent Thicket, *Business Week*, December 20, 2005.

patents in the Eastern District of Virginia against T-Mobile USA Inc., Verizon Wireless, AT&T Mobility, and Sprint-Nextel Corp. But this round of suits didn't get very far. All were quickly stayed by Judge Spencer, pending the resolution of the re-exam appeals.

As for RIM and partners, they were now completely off the hook. RIM walked away with its head high and with a well-earned reputation as a grinder and a scrapper—maybe a bit bull-headed, but a company that would not be pushed around. The NTP case was no longer a distraction for RIM, plus the troll was now going after RIM's competition.

RIM also emerged from the case blessed with a boosted public awareness of the qualities of its flagship BlackBerry device. The lawsuit created a media profile about the BlackBerry's security features and its use by high-powered U.S. politicians that would have cost millions to build through advertising.

Said analyst Kevin Burden of IDC, "This is probably money well spent. It's a boatload of money for patents that may not be worth anything, but it's worth it if it removes the cloud over RIM's future."

To conclude: RIM's payout to NTP was worth every penny. It ramped up brand awareness, turned the tables on the competition, and induced smart cell phone makers with shaky patents to adopt RIM software if they wanted to avoid the troll lurking under the bridge.

⊕　⊕　⊕

While the U.S. Patent and Trademark Office approved the junk patents at the heart of RIM's legal battle with NTP, it soon recognized its mistake and started to invalidate them, but not in time to save RIM from having to pay out $612.5 million.

Negative publicity over the RIM case forced some rethinking on patent quality, and several software-related applications were turned down in Federal Circuit Court.*

In early 2008, the Board of Patent Appeals and Interferences (which is above the USPTO but below the Federal Circuit in the appeals process) rejected patents on simulating physical processes using mathematical models. The court ruled that they involved only the manipulation of abstract mathematical formulas and were not tied to a specific machine or physical process. One patent succeeded on appeal because it was tied to the real world—it described a specific machine—a computer with two processors instead of one.

The U.S. Supreme Court has always held firm that abstract concepts and mathematical algorithms are not patentable and has increasingly smacked down the Federal Circuit Court in recent years. The high court has never endorsed software patents, and justices have voiced concerns about the patenting of software.[6]

Ironically, a few months after the RIM/NTP settlement, the Supreme Court unanimously ruled in MercExchange LLC vs eBay against an appeals court decision saying injunctions must be generally issued against companies found guilty of infringing patents. Judge Spencer's threat of an injunction stopping BlackBerry sales would not have been allowed.

RIM's battle with NTP clearly demonstrated how a dedicated patent strategy, and a willingness to defend intellectual property,

---

* In the *In Re Nuijten* case, the court did not invalidate the claims relating to a watermarking algorithm itself, but focused on whether a digital signal could be the subject of a patent claim. The court said no.

6. Timothy B. Lee, "Patent Office Finds Voice, Calls for Software Patent Sanity," *Ars Technica*, July 28, 2008.

can be key factor in the growth and survival of any technology company.

Lazaridis and Balsillie now integrate patent building into the whole corporate R&D process at RIM. "If you are not patenting everything you are working on, someone else might patent what you are working on," says Lazaridis. "Patenting should be a standard operating procedure for your company, a standard operating procedure for your researchers and engineers. If they come up with an idea to solve a difficult problem, then they should immediately apply for a patent."*

* Industry Canada. Innovation Secretariat. Case 7. Research In Motion Limited.

From Brand to Icon: Seven Years in Motion

"Our approach was to create very marketable products—something that could really solve problems today. We made the right bets. You don't see them with certainty, but, with foresight, you are always playing this positioning game, this execution game, this sensing game, this adapting game, and this adoption game for affinity. It's all about systematically improving yourself in your position in a sector that you think is going to be important."

—Jim Balsillie

The early years of the twenty-first century were good for RIM, as its devices went from strength to strength, growing in power and sophistication, and morphing into true MPCs—mobile personal computers—also known as smartphones. Revenues and profits also skyrocketed. From revenue of $85 million in 2000, RIM was generating $595 million in 2004 and a colossal $6 billion in 2008.*

---

* For a detailed review of the evolution of the BlackBerry in these years, see BlackBerry Planet Device History and RIM Financials on the *BlackBerry Planet* Web Support site.

Right from the start of their relationship, "twin CEOS" Jim Balsillie and Mike Lazaridis shared the same wavelength—that people would want constant access to e-mail and that wireless datacom was the one technology that would have the greatest impact on the business world. And Balsillie shared Mike's conviction that the keys to ongoing success were simplicity and security. RIM needed to focus on simple and secure wireless access to corporate e-mail instead of bombarding users with unnecessary bells and whistles.

For a while, the pair shared an office as well and joked that they invented the BlackBerry so they could talk to each other after hours without their wives knowing. "Now we have our own offices," says Balsillie. "So, success has its privileges." "Jim had one more luxury than I did," quips Lazaridis. "He had a cell phone. I was jealous."

The two don't socialize much outside of work. Says Balsillie, "I already spend more time with Mike than I do my wife. By the end of the day, we've pretty much had enough of each other. That's been a strength: that we haven't endeavored to mix our private lives too much. I just think, when your days are that intense, and the work is so excitingly consuming, you can't help but want to talk about it, and giving yourself a social break from it is probably not a bad thing."

Says Lazaridis about his tandem understanding with Balsillie, "It's all about timing. We know where we're both going, we both agree on that. It's just a matter of when situations will be beneficial for product launches and market entry. I'm always pushing for it to happen faster. But then, I'm always overly optimistic. He reins me in." For Balsillie's part, he has "no memory of ever having an argument with Mike. At the end of the day, you have to trust the other guy ... I think the biggest way our job has changed us is that Mike has more white hair and I just have less of it."

⊕　⊕　⊕

As Team Lazaridis worked away in the labs and assembly shops of Waterloo, they were constantly evaluating new technology, with feedback from Team Balsillie's customers out in the marketplace. If need be, Mike's hardware ninjas invented and patented tech solutions on the fly. Driven by customer demand and competition from older companies such as Palm and newer catch-up devices from Asia, the team worked on packing more and better hardware into their prototype BlackBerrys, evaluating and testing smaller and more powerful radios and embedded antennas, or finer screens and speakers, or new battery technology, USB chargers or easier-to-use keyboards and peripheral ports.

Over a seven-year period, from 2002 to 2008, Team Lazaridis bolted on to the BlackBerry a dazzling array of new hardware features:

- 2002—cell phone service with international roaming; rechargeable lithium battery
- 2003—color display and Bluetooth
- 2004—the SureType compacted keyboard
- 2005—high-speed EDGE network access and camera
- 2006—MicroSD card expansion slot and trackball
- 2007—stereo headphone jack; speakerphone; Media Manager
- 2008—Wi-Fi; internal GPS; 3G; Click-Through touch screen

Driven by Turing's dictum that software always replaces hardware, RIM's code warriors constantly tweaked the little machines to deliver more and better computing power, to match advances in the memory and processors used in newer BlackBerrys, all the while maintaining the same obsession with battery life.

In most cases they serviced a growing demand from BlackBerry customers and wireless partners for a finer and more feature-packed product line. But they also had to drive down costs. New hardware platforms such as today's BlackBerry Bold, and new network options such as 3G, have higher costs that can't always be passed on to the customers.

The company takes open bull sessions seriously. Balsillie says, "We make a point of getting together nearly every week and throwing around ideas about where we go next, what can we do. We've never had trouble recruiting bright people, and keeping bright people. Our turnover rate is less than one percent. That's unheard of. So that tells you that there's always a sense of challenge to do new things in a new way in the air, or we wouldn't keep these people. They'd get bored."

RIM invests about 6 percent of sales on research and development, and more than 600 people work in its new state-of-the-art R&D facility, with testing and certification labs to push new product development and speed up time to market. "You don't just do research for the sake of 'Gee, it's intriguing,'" says Balsillie. "It's got to have some market context. If it's got some core technical benefit that is disruptive, can fit within the product, and allow us to enhance or redefine the value proposition, that is totally cool."

In the front office, Balsillie and COO Doug Fregin match the work in the labs by building the business and meeting rising demand. The pair manage BlackBerry production, negotiate with parts suppliers, invest in marketing programs, analyze market share and trends, control production costs, and get the devices to market through rapidly changing channels, even some big box ones such as Wal-Mart and Best Buy.

They also have to respond quickly to competition. According to Bob Crow, RIM's director of government and industry relations, "Both Mike and Jim have a healthy respect for their competitors. You aren't going to beat everybody in every category, so we decided that focus would be one of the keys to RIM's competitive success," a focus on the wireless end of the business, playing on the convergence of mobility and digital data.[1]

Jim Balsillie is a fitness fanatic and ferocious competitor, and he is particularly passionate about the game of hockey. He coaches his son's team and loves to take in Toronto Maple Leafs hockey games when he can. He's been fighting with the National Hockey League (NHL) for years to scoop up a franchise and move it into southern Ontario, and some in the NHL hate his brashness. Maybe he suspects they'd rather put a team into Las Vegas!

Balsillie happily takes his philosophy of sport into the arena of business. He lives and breathes the knowledge that you should never lose sight of the fact that you are in business to beat your competitors. Balsillie is especially fond of Wayne Gretzky's greatest quotations, that "I skate to where the puck is going to be, not to where it has been," and "You'll always miss 100 percent of the shots you never take."

Now in his late forties, Balsillie still plays in a nighttime senior league that has not abolished bone-crushing rushes into the boards, nor hard checks in the corners. Some of his fellow players worked for Research In Motion, and Balsillie recently joked to the press that he quit playing with RIM employees after he noticed they weren't hitting him as hard as others. "Who enjoys that? asked Balsillie. "The guys I play with are brutal."

---

1. Industry Canada Innovation Secretariat. Case 7. Research In Motion Limited. Feb. 15, 2005

He also brought his love of hockey into the executive suites at RIM. Meeting rooms near his office are named after hockey greats, including Rocket Richard, Wayne Gretzky, and Bobby Orr. Another love is heavy metal rock: two electric guitars hang on the wall of his office. One is signed by heavy metal king Eddie Van Halen, who played at a November 2007 company party in Toronto's Rogers Centre.

⊕　　⊕　　⊕

Apart from being his tenth anniversary with the company, 2002 was a transitional year for Jim Balsillie. The hardest decision he had to make was to prune 10 percent of the company's workforce, because RIM's first Java device, the 5810, was not selling well. The device was flawed, and besides, RIM was moving from direct sales to carrier sales, and the telcos had little experience marketing such a high-end device.

RIM's major project that year was to open a new 18,300-square-metre plant in Waterloo, with the capacity to produce 6 million BlackBerrys a year. While RIM now manufactures in several countries, analysts questioned why RIM would locate its major manufacturing in Waterloo, close to its R&D facility, instead of out-sourcing and building devices offshore. Balsillie and Lazaridis both stressed that this gave RIM a strong advantage in getting innova-tion to market faster than other companies. More design control over the product line meant RIM could quickly refine its devices in face of changing market needs, leading to a fatter bottom line. It also let RIM quickly tailor machines for specific carriers' needs, as most of the world's telcos now wanted to distribute custom BlackBerrys.

RIM initially relied on its BlackBerry Web Client for non-corporate BlackBerry users getting service from a carrier, but now BlackBerry users are assigned to a BlackBerry Internet Server

(BIS), a stripped-down version of the BES that serves only e-mail and Web access. Service goes either on the carrier's network or RIM's network.

With strong carrier interest outside North America, RIM also went global in 2002, adding General Packet Radio Service (GPRS) wireless handhelds to their product portfolio. BlackBerrys could now use the GPRS protocol—which, like EDGE, sits on top of the GSM network—for cellular phones in about 140 countries, including all of Europe.

Business soon boomed in the United Kingdom, the Netherlands, Germany, Ireland, and Italy, as Team Balsillie built new strategic alliances with companies such as Nextel Communications, Telecom Italia Mobile in Italy, T-Mobile in Germany, and Vodafone in the United Kingdom, and also built carrier relationships in Hong Kong and Australia.

To seed BlackBerry developers, RIM made its Java Development Environment available at no charge, so 3 million Java developers worldwide could build apps or games to work on the BlackBerry. At the JavaOne conference in San Francisco in June 2002, the company handed out more than 4,700 free Java developer kits on CD. According to Lazaridis, RIM can't create everything for the BlackBerry. "We couldn't possibly figure all this out," he said. "There are a thousand niches out there, and they're going to have to be developed by other people."

RIM sales started to explode in 2002, increasing by 33 percent over 2001, and RIM soon had a debt-free balance sheet, with new products that leapfrogged the competition and critical endorsements from blue chip corporations. To feed such a fanatical following, says Balsillie, "there are a huge number of execution issues to keep up and accelerate the growth." RIM uses the "ERP [Enterprise Resource Planning] system for production and engineering, expanding the plant, the sales and marketing, and the customer care, and getting the technology on time ... there are marketing programs to get done .... There is a lot to do."

Lazaridis insists that since RIM was turning out new technology every day, he wasn't worried about bigger competitors snuffing out RIM's marketplace advantages. "Competing companies keep coming at us," he said, "but we've done a lot of the heavy lifting, and that counts for a lot. They'll have to do at least some of their share of the lifting, and, in the meantime, we're moving on."

RIM was also benefiting from its unique market situation: As Mark Guibert, RIM's vice president of corporate marketing, says, "As the world converges, there will be increasing alternatives from phone companies and handheld manufacturers. But because of the way we've brought BlackBerry to market—as a whole solution, with servers, handhelds, software and service—it's very difficult to compare ourselves directly."[2] RIM is also able to offload local marketing to its telecom partners, freeing itself to focus on R&D. "Instead of having to learn about each global market," says York University marketing professor Alan Middleton, "they're using the people who have the deepest level of market knowledge to do it for them."[3]

In 2002, InfoWorld named the BlackBerry 5810 gadget of the year and best wireless product of the year, and the RIM 957 product of the year and best handheld of the year. The BlackBerry wireless solution received 2002's MIT Sloan eBusiness Award in the disruptive technology of the year category—an award that recognizes technology that has begun to, or has the potential to, positively disrupt our daily lives. (ROB is national) *Report on Business Magazine* poll placed RIM first in innovation as one of Canada's most respected companies. The year 2002 also saw Mike Lazaridis

2. Charles Finlay, "Research in Commotion". Canadian Business, (75)16, Sept. 2, 2002; 61-62
3. Rebecca Harris, "Homegrown icon: 2006 marketers that mattered", Marketing Magazine, November 20, 2006

voted Canada's Top Nation Builder in a (Globe is national) *Globe and Mail* poll, beating out hockey player Wayne Gretzky. "This is progress," he quipped, on learning of the award.

For Mike Lazaridis, tech is a bit like hockey: "Innovation and entrepreneurship is a process, a discipline. It's one you either want to do or you don't. It doesn't just happen. You don't have a eureka moment. It's like any art—you have to train for it and you have to get experience for it. You have to discipline yourself. It's hard work, and it pays off if you stick to it. It took RIM a long time. We started in 1984 and took a long time to get success, but all along we were innovative. It's a journey."

Starting in 2004, RIM ramped up marketing of its new consumer-friendly devices such as the Pearl and adopted a whole new *People* magazine–type spin, linked to the public's fascination with celebrities.

RIM market evangelists, aided by PR firms and telco partners, targeted TV and Hollywood, and their efforts soon started to bear fruit, as fans emulated their heroes. Soon the BlackBerry became known as the feel-good device of the stars. In November 2005, Oprah Winfrey featured the BlackBerry 7105t on her pre-Christmas "Oprah's Favorite Things" segment, and the hyperexcited guests on her annual giveaway show won free T-Mobile BlackBerrys. According to eBay Marketplace Research, in the two weeks following the show, the 7105t enjoyed a 26 percent increase in sales, compared to the previous two weeks before Oprah's big giveaway.

Soon an endless selection of celebrities were snapped carrying around their BlackBerry, and a website, Celebrity BlackBerry Sightings (http://celebrityblackberrysightings.com/), became a popular way for amateur paparazzi to share images. Even megastars like Madonna were caught admitting CrackBerry addiction. Madonna, who recently turned fifty, confessed she "cannot bear to be without her BlackBerry—and even sleeps with it under her pillow."

In a 2007 interview with *Elle* magazine, she said that her then-husband, film director Guy Ritchie, was similarly attached to his gadget. "We lie right next to each other with our BlackBerrys under our pillows. It's not unromantic. It's practical. I'm sure loads of couples have their BlackBerrys in bed with them .... I have to sleep with my BlackBerry because I often wake up in the middle of the night and remember that I've forgotten something, so I jump up and make notes. Guy's always waiting for me to come to bed, so he plays Brick on his BlackBerry until I'm ready."

Unfortunately, Madonna's marriage crashed in 2008, and some blamed her BlackBerry use. Psychologist Fiona Travis says that people who think the device helps them find time are really fooling themselves. "It is just another way of avoiding being intimate."[4]

RIM marketers also looked for business-friendly ways to showcase BlackBerry smartphones. On December 11, 2007, RIM and Yahoo sponsored the launch of JetBlue's free in-flight Internet service.

JetBlue's Wi-Fi service relies on about one hundred cell towers across the United States that communicate with radios onboard the planes. Once the airplane reached an altitude of 10,000 feet, customers were able to turn on their laptops and Wi-Fi-enabled BlackBerrys and connect through Yahoo's e-mail and instant messaging services.

All this marketing glitz helped boost RIM's profits in 2007, and on October 24, Research In Motion Ltd. reached a brilliant milestone, edging out the Royal Bank of Canada (RBC) and energy

---

4. Oliver Burkeman and Bobbie Johnson, "From backbenches to the bedroom, the BlackBerry is taking over.". The Guardian, Saturday June 23 2007 < * >

giant Encana to become the largest company in Canada in terms of market capitalization. Listed on NASDAQ and the TSX, RIM's share value reached $69.2 billion by the close of trading.*

Nomura analyst Richard Windsor commented that the company's regularly updated products had helped make RIM "the most profitable device maker in the industry." But Windsor also warned dryly that "You have to remember what Research In Motion is. It's primarily a handset maker, and it should be valued as such."**

RIM took the top spot thanks to a hectic 150 percent run-up in its share price in 2007, healthy profit margins of more than 30 percent of revenues, and a more than twenty-fold growth over the previous five years. The latest uptick came the day after the market learned that the company was partnering with Paris-based Alcatel-Lucent to put BlackBerrys on store shelves in China, starting with the older 8700 model. For a few glorious months, Wall Street analysts went bananas over RIM.

Jim Balsillie seems satisfied as he leans back in his office chair, smiling at the stuffed beaver on his desk as he ponders a point. He feels obsessing on the stock price is not useful—it was Balsillie who invented RIM's rule that if he caught anyone checking the stock price, he or she would have to buy doughnuts for everyone else. He's caught two people in the act, and got them to pay up. Balsillie has no illusions about the immense task facing Research In Motion as it aims to be a major player in the world marketplace. He doesn't believe you can create opportunities but rather capitalize on them. "Our job is to fully capitalize on the opportunity before us," he says.

As for Mike Lazaridis, he has unbounded enthusiasm for RIM's upcoming software and hardware, He says RIM's moves are purely

---

* IN 2008, RIM slipped to third place behind RBC and Manulife Financial
** This of course begs the question, how can a simple handset cause Oprah's studio audience to scream with delight?

demand-driven and not a product of corporate fantasy. The Pearl is "not a consumer product, but consumers want it." The BlackBerry is like a Porsche. "It's a sports car, but people drive it in the city and they wouldn't drive anything else. [The Pearl] was like adding a trunk and a couple of cup-holders to our Porsche."

Lazaridis usually declines to talk about the competition, saying simply, "You call it competition—it's our challenge!"[5]

RIM has been part of the Deloitte's North American Technology Fast 500 for ten consecutive years, more times than any other company, and for good reason.

First, Mike Lazaridis has always insisted on progressive evolution for BlackBerry devices, from the two-way pager to the first BlackBerry with an integrated cell phone, to the Storm touch-screen model. All major changes had to be incremental, with thoroughly tried-and-tested solutions to meet the growing needs of its messaging loyalists, especially in the business world.

Lazaridis also sees the key to the BlackBerry's success in the fact that RIM employees use the device to collaborate, swap ideas, get client feedback, and generally keep the operations running in sync. "There are two types of companies," he says. "There's one company that makes products that other people use, but they don't actually use them themselves. Then there are companies that make things they actually use and depend on. We fall squarely in that space—we build things that we use every day.

"We have people making sure we choose the right technologies three years out, four years out, and so on."[6]

Lazaridis is driven to innovate and perfect. He once invited a group of Zurich watch designers to RIM headquarters in Waterloo

5. Jane Martinson interview in The Guardian, Friday March 2, 2007 < * >
6. David Fielding, Leaps of Faith, Globe and Mail, April 25, 2008 < * >

to consult on building miniature devices. His goal as always was to craft elegant smartphones built like Swiss watches. Perhaps a voice-activated Dick Tracy–style BlackBerry Watch is in the cards.

⊕ ⊕ ⊕

During the first five or six years of the BlackBerry, this corporate attitude kept RIM running hot and competing at a very high level, packing in new features and turning out an increasingly sophisticated series of smartphones, until by 2007, RIM stood at the pinnacle of the wireless world, making the best smartphones and providing the best e-mail services bar none.

As 2007 began, RIM's future looked dazzling, and some analysts were expecting the BlackBerry business to grow exponentially. Nomura Securities estimated that only 1.2 percent of a total number of 600 to 700 million corporate e-mail accounts had been "mobilized" so far.

The only major distraction came in March 2007, when securities regulators on both sides of the border, trying to make the granting of corporate stock options more transparent, turned the spotlight on companies like Apple and RIM. On the advice of its accountants, Research In Motion had granted employee stock options under new options backdating rules, but when questions arose, an internal investigation showed RIM it had to change its methods. In response, Balsillie stepped aside temporarily as chairman until the needed changes were made. RIM also agreed to restate financial results since 2004 and deducted US$250 million from recent earnings, and top RIM execs later agreed to pay penalties to U.S. and Canadian securities regulators.

Meanwhile, back in the battlefield, competitors were sharpening their axes, attracted by the margins RIM enjoyed by blending its hardware with software and service solutions. There is a saying that success breeds not just envy but demand, and other hardware companies soon rushed in to tap into the growing demand for smartphones equipped with Web access and push e-mail.

In May 2007, just as Balsillie and Lazaridis were sitting back and enjoying their perch at the top of the smartphone food chain, suddenly their whole field of vision was blurred by the arrival of an upstart from Silicon Valley—Steve Jobs of Apple and his game-changing device, the Apple iPhone.

⊕ ⊕ ⊕

"I wouldn't underestimate the amount of research we've done on user interfaces and technologies. We are not afraid to reinvent ourselves."

—*Mike Lazaridis*

Apple CEO Steve Jobs launched the eagerly awaited iPhone at Apple's WorldWide Developers conference in San Francisco. Reporters quickly dubbed the device the "Jesus Phone"—why? because it's so *good*, said one developer—because it was hyped more than the second coming of Christ, said another.

What was so spectacular about the iPhone? Forgetting the cool factor,

- Apple had created perhaps the world's first true mobile PC, cramming its dazzling Leopard UNIX-based operating system into a smartphone, which was a native iPod to boot.
- The iPhone came with Apple's superb Safari Web browser, providing an experience that rivaled a laptop.
- Apple gave a new definition to usability on a touch screen, with a full QWERTY (virtual) keyboard and Wi-Fi support.
- The iPhone existed in its own mobile ecosystem, with its own business model, seemingly in another universe above the world of locked-down, carrier-centric devices. This was

not true, of course, but such was the effect of Steve Jobs's well-known "reality distortion field."

The iPhone was not your normal Nokia, and it earned Apple a coveted spot in the top ranks of handset makers, grabbing 13 percent of the smartphone market in its first year alone. It boosted the bar for Balsillie and Lazaridis, who were already facing growing competition at the high end of the market from a posse of other touch-screen phones—Sprint's Instinct, the HTC Touch Diamond, and Sony Ericsson's XPERIA X1. But none were as intuitive and beautifully crafted as Apple's phone.

Jobs's first version lacked many of BlackBerry's key business features—true push e-mail or links to Exchange, Lotus Notes, and Novell GroupWise. It didn't have RIM's stingy use of bandwidth and superior security. But Lazaridis and Balsillie were not complacent about the threat from Silicon Valley. The two devices weren't yet competitive, but there was some overlap that would only get tighter. In public, Lazaridis was quick to differentiate the two devices, calling them "two very different tools"—the BlackBerry an enterprise-class phone for business power users and the iPhone a "multimedia machine." But clearly the trend was toward unified devices that could be used seamlessly in both markets.

While Apple was clearly a formidable challenger to RIM, the battle between the two companies had an element of unreality. It's not a stretch to say that these two corporations were so far ahead of the game with their superb devices that the laggards in the industry were simply flogging commodities.

The media adored the BlackBerry versus Apple story angle, and reporters swarmed to Waterloo to get Mike Lazaridis to comment on the new iPhone. Lazaridis, a secret Apple admirer, told the media that most BlackBerry e-mail devotees demanded the tactile feedback of a physical keyboard. He sniffed that he didn't like the iPhone's glass pad. "I couldn't type on it and I still can't type on it, and a lot of my friends can't type on it," he scoffed. "It's hard to type on a piece of glass."

Meanwhile, deep inside the bowels of RIM, Team Lazaridis engineers in white lab coats were prepping their own touch-screen device for release. Rumors emerged from Waterloo that RIM's version of the touch phone—code named "Thunder"—had a touch keyboard that was far superior to Apple's. RIM engineers privately referred to it as the A.K.—the "Apple Killer."

Down in Cupertino, Steve Jobs replied to the RIM challenge, quipping to reporters that he didn't like trying to type on "little tic-tactile plastic keys." Apple fanboys with big thumbs took up the master's call, complaining about the BlackBerry's "cramped little QWERTY."

⊕　　⊕　　⊕

In a market littered with ugly brick communicators and me-too plastic devices with all the quality of a cheap pink water pistol, the BlackBerry stands out as the standard against which all others measure themselves. Except for the iPhone.

When Steve Jobs launched his iconic device, there was a lot of poo-pooing at RIM headquarters in Waterloo and from BlackBerry fanboys in the press. And the critics were right. With its dazzling design and superb mobile browser, Jobs's first device sported the clunky EDGE network, and if you wanted your e-mail, you had to ask for it.

But behind the scenes, the iPhone had RIM concerned. It was flying off the shelves of Apple's elegant stores and AT&T's

warehouses. And a 3G version with better security was on the way.

Waterloo heard the iPhone ringing, and it was a wakeup call.

RIM's initial response to the coming of the iPhone was long overdue. Beginning with the Curve and Pearl, it took the clunky MS-DOS–style fonts and crafted them into smooth and modern typefaces. At the same time, the company boosted the screen resolution to handle them. And it worked to produce radios and software optimized for the new 3G networks on the horizon from Verizon and AT&T.

The clear demand for new touch screens and different form factors had RIM designers, programmers, and engineers working late into the night. The Pearl 8220 Flip phone (like Captain Kirk's communicator), the Curve 8900, and the Storm touch phone were soon coming down the pipe.

Apple's major advantage—the superb Safari browser and ease of Web access—would prove a more difficult nut to crack. The Internet data deluge had many wireless warriors panting for such a device. Some corporate cowboys were still firing off e-mails on their corporate BlackBerry, but keeping an iPhone in the other holster, for after-hours Web browsing.

RIM's first reply to the Apple challenge was bold—the BlackBerry Bold.

RIM launched the feature-packed BlackBerry Bold 9000 with a great deal of fanfare on May 12, 2008, beating Apple's iPhone 3G to market by a month. The Bold was the first 3G BlackBerry device, bringing a level of faster data downloads to BlackBerry owners in North America and around the world over UMTS (Universal Mobile Telecommunications System) networks, with download speeds almost three times faster than EDGE.*

The Bold also came with Wi-Fi (802.11 a/b/g), Bluetooth 2.0 (including the stereo headset profile), and built-in GPS for AT&T Navigator to go along with BlackBerry Maps. It featured 128 megabytes of flash memory, with 1 gigabyte of on-board memory. Bold fans loved the fact they could quickly swap memory cards up to 16 gigabytes in a new side loading slot, moved out from behind the battery case. Bold's "personal" applications included a music player that could be used with Media Sync, as well as a 2.0-MP digital camera (with 5x digital zoom, flash, and video recording functions) and a video player.

RIM loaded the Bold with a sleeker and faster BlackBerry operating system, which shone on its 480 x 320 high-res display. The Boy Genius blog called it "the most vibrant, color-rich, sharp screen we've ever seen on a mobile device."

The Bold's 624-MHz CPU gave the device far peppier performance, twice as fast as on previous BlackBerrys. Best of all, the Bold blew away the competition in downloading media files, loading movies twice as quickly as the iPhone 3G.**

The major con that bugged reviewers was the BlackBerry Web browser, which was still not ready to go head to head with iPhone's or Google's G1, which uses WebKit, the open-source cousin of Apple's Safari. eWeek reviewer Andrew Garcia complained about the icon-only display and the lack of a helpful zoom feature:

---

* The BlackBerry 8707 with CDMA by Qualcomm has had 3G capacity since 2006, for use I nGSM countries and Korea and Japan.

** EE Times reported that RIM's use of the Cypress Semiconductor West Bridge peripheral controller, found in the previous BlackBerry 8120 Pearl, provides "a direct connection of peripherals and creating fast transfer tunnels without loading the main processor. Instead of routing files from the computer through the phone processor to the storage device, it sets up a tunnel directly from the computer to the storage device. < * >

"Simply put, the Bold's zoom controls stink when compared with the iPhone's touch-screen-based pinch and spread motions or the G1 with Google's on-screen action buttons."[7]

RIM's approach to Wi-Fi was also problematic for some, but the company had to retain a proper level of paranoia about corporate security. The Bold and other BlackBerrys with Wi-Fi have a browser setting called "HotSpot Browser," which gives users direct Wi-Fi network access to the Internet without having to go through a secure BlackBerry Internet Service or a BlackBerry Enterprise Server. This is by far the fastest browsing experience on a BlackBerry since it is just you and the Internet. However, corporate BES administrators can remove the HotSpot Browser, for compliance and/or security reasons, leaving you with just the BlackBerry Browser, or no browser at all.

Out of the gate, the Bold got high praise and rave reviews in Australia, Canada, and Malaysia but was delayed in Europe when France Telecom's Orange service temporarily pulled the Bold from its shelves for unspecified "software issues." AT&T also delayed launch in the United States, partly because RIM and the carrier were both wary of running into the same 3G reception problems that plagued Apple's iPhone 3G on launch. This was due in part to overenthusiastic users glutting the new AT&T 3G network, but also to the fact that the iPhone lacked any data compression technology and was turning out to be a resource hog on AT&T's infrastructure. According to Canaccord Adams analyst Peter Misek, AT&T pushed back the launch of the Bold to build out and repair its networks. He said that for every iPhone without compression technology, the network could equivalently support up to twenty BlackBerry

7. Andrew Garcia, RIM's BlackBerry Bold Comes Up a Little Short," *eWeek*, Dec. 8, 2008 < * >

devices and that AT&T would need to spend up to $1 billion to make things right.[8]

With most kinks out of the system, AT&T finally released the Bold to salivating U.S. buyers on Election Day, November 4, 2008. While voters lined up around the block to elect a new president, there were also respectable lineups outside some AT&T stores, and many sold out by noon, at a price of $299 for a two-year contract. Wal-Mart soon offered a free $199 Bold with a service plan and after a rebate.

🌐   🌐   🌐

While BlackBerrys are still slower than iPhones in rendering Web pages or executing JavaScript, RIM was making big browser strides. The Bold's enhanced HTML helped the device better mimic or emulate desktop viewing. Users could pick whether they wanted to view sites in full desktop-style HTML or in the older mobile version.

Users found texting and e-mailing a breeze on the Bold. Reviewers liked the revamped keyboard and sculpted keys with metal dividers like guitar frets that separated the keys and helped to minimize finger slippage. The device came with built-in spell checking for apps that could use it—a first for BlackBerry.

The Bold also came standard with the usual BlackBerry applications, software suites, and iPod quality AV features. You could now edit Microsoft Office files using the Documents to Go[*] suite by DataViz. And you could use the new BlackBerry Media Sync applications to pull your Apple iTunes digital music into the Bold. The device supported streaming video through real-time streaming protocol (RTSP). To round out the menu, the Bold came with BlackBerry's premium phone features, including Speaker Independent Voice Recognition for Voice Activated Dialing (VAD). It

---

8. Matt Hartley, "U.S. iPhone traffic clogs RIM's Bold plans," Globe and Mail. Sept. 17, 2008 < * >

* See www.dataviz.com/products/documentstogo/index.html.

also had dedicated send, end, and mute keys; smart dialing; speed dialing; conference calling; call forwarding; noise cancellation technology to offset background noise; speaker phone; and support for polyphonic, mp3, and MIDI ring tones.

Meanwhile, down in Cupertino, California, the engineers at Apple had RIM squarely in their sights. Sure enough, on June 9, 2008, Steve Jobs popped the champagne cork on iPhone version 2.0, for 3G wireless networks. It confirmed RIM's worst concerns. The device was a truly smart phone—some even said a *superphone*. Jobs argued that it had enough security to satisfy all but the most paranoid IT manager. At the same time, he also launched Apple's iPhone software development kit (SDK) and an online applications store in iTunes where developers could sell software. But what really had developers salivating was Jobs's final goodie—a $100-million applications fund set up by valley venture capital wizards Kleiner Perkins.

Apple fanboys soon dubbed the iPhone 3G a "BlackBerry Killer." Granted, it was faster, slicker, and cheaper than the old entry device. Plus it had better integration with iTunes and the new App Store for programs and freebies. Apple also added true GPS to the iPhone, and dropped the entry price to just $199 plus plan, $299 for the 16 GB version. Cult followers and newbies flocked to Apple's retail cathedrals and bought like gangbusters—U.S. orders in 2008 totaled 10 million units.

Apple also launched a new cloud computing sync setup called MobileMe, with push e-mail into the cloud and quick delivery down to all blessed devices. It provided sync and storage for anybody. And Apple was rolling it out to the world for $100 a year.

In one year, Apple had addressed most of the criticism head-on and come up with some superb solutions. Plus, the accelerometer and finger-swiping gestures in the devices opened up a whole new territory for smartphones, from gaming—where the handheld itself is the steering wheel—to medical diagnosis. In the three days after launch, Apple sold 1 million iPhone 3Gs in twenty-one countries. Happy users downloaded 10 million programs from the newly launched App Store on iTunes over that first weekend. In all, the iPhone gobbled up 17.3 percent of the world's fast-growing smart-phone market in 2008, up from just 3.6 percent a year earlier.

Now RIM seemed slightly dowdy, and risked becoming another Palm, or being seen as the John Hodgman character in the "I'm a Mac, I'm a PC" commercials. In the month following the iPhone 3G launch, the bad news bears drove RIM stock down 31 percent, from a record $148.13 in June. The whole world wondered, Could RIM compete in the smartphone arms race? Could RIM come up with a killer response to stem the bleeding and retain a BlackBerry flock thinking of defecting to the iPhone?

"What distinguishes the BlackBerry from the iPhone is the back-end support."

—Roger Kay, Endpoint Technologies

When the iPhone 3G hype died down, people started putting the Apple and RIM devices side by side and a different picture emerged. They found that, unlike RIM's Bold, Jobs's new baby didn't have stereo Bluetooth for wireless listening. It didn't do video recording. It lacked multitasking, or even copy and paste. It didn't yet work as a tethered modem. It still didn't have office level security. Users got frustrated by not being able to swap SD memory cards or carry along an extra power supply, causing that well-known psychological condition called "battery anxiety." On balance it was a Mexican standoff, with RIM's business features and open slots easily matching Apple's touch screen and browser.

To a tech media eager for angry RIM reaction, Jim Balsillie—ever the hockey jock—simply replied that RIM "welcomed the competition." This wasn't a throwaway line. RIM's engineers respected what Apple was doing, but they knew they had many superior goodies, plus the bandwidth economy and super-security needed by paranoid corporations and their wireless road warriors. Also, as Balsillie suspected, the iPhone's entry into the market raised awareness about what smartphones could do and got people salivating for more. Steve Jobs had simply whetted the market's appetite for BlackBerrys.

When the first rumors of the iPhone 2 surfaced, jittery investors sold RIM short, assuming the company would get pasted by Apple. But not so fast—RIM actually experienced a big bump in U.S. sales, with its share of the smartphone market swelling from 35 percent in the fourth quarter of 2007 to 45 percent in the first quarter of 2008. In the twelve months since the original iPhone launch, retail sales of the BlackBerry rocketed 38 percent.

Wrote Pablo Perez-Fernandez, an analyst with Global Crown Capital, "There were a lot of BlackBerrys in those stores where iPhones were selling, and there were people who may not have thought about a smartphone before, wanted the iPhone, thought it was too expensive, and bought a BlackBerry instead."

Clearly there was plenty of business for both companies. "What the iPhone did was make it cool to use smartphones," said Ramon Llamas, an analyst with IDC. "Before, you had the BlackBerry, which mostly just resonated with enterprise users or business people. Now, there's a whole new market of smartphone consumers. Before the phone came out, I actually asked guys from companies like Nokia and RIM how they were going to respond, and the answer was unanimous—it was, 'Welcome to the party, hop in the pool, the water's fine.'"[9]

---

9. "What's Good for Apple is Better for Everyone Else," by Betsy Schiffman for Wired.com Jun 9 2008 < * >

Mike Lazaridis took the long view about the entry of Apple: "I think that BlackBerry was the first and best integrated and most secure smartphone solution in the world a decade ago. And it continues to be today. But I think what happened was the amount of marketing and the attention [Apple] generated in the market—the customers are now coming to the store and saying I didn't know you could do all that with a phone. And when they get there they realize there's a selection—there's not just one device. And so what it's actually done is increased our sales."[10]

Jim Balsillie said his product strategy wasn't swayed by the iPhone, and RIM didn't need to copy Apple. RIM's plans, he said, included boosting advertising spending, hiring more engineers, and accelerating product introductions, starting with the BlackBerry Bold. Balsillie said companies would pick the BlackBerry over the iPhone because the e-mail service was more reliable and the keyboard better for business users.

"We know where we're heading," he said. "We've got all the growth we can handle."

Balsillie told reporters he'd rather take the lead, not follow. "I play offense," he said. "There's no glory in defense."

The Windows world has always had a prejudice against Apple. Perhaps it was the 1984 Super Bowl ad, which portrayed IBMers as automatons, that started things. Then there was Cupertino's "computer for the rest of us" attitude. Recently it has been the "I'm a Mac, I'm a PC" ads that have stoked the fires of envy. Windows fanboys also don't like Apple's walled-garden approach to computing—users can't even swap the iPhone's battery. No

---

10. Natasha Lomas, "RIM's Lazaridis on why Qwerty's still working", ZDNet News: May 16, 2008 < * >

wonder corporate IT, which loves to get under the hood of devices, has so enthusiastically adopted the RIM platform on top of Windows.

But now Apple's universe of UNIX-based Intel Macs can run Windows, and iPhone 2.0 is making Apple a serious corporate contender, helped by Vista's rough launch, and employee pester-power in medium to large businesses.

The iPhone 3G has faster Wi-Fi connectivity, a better browser, and can be managed via remote network access. Conceivium CEO Jonas Gyllensvaan says the device is "equally secure" as the BlackBerry because of its Cisco IPsec VPN. It also has Microsoft's ActiveSync technology. Gyllensvaan thinks it could be the Trojan horse that leads to enterprise acceptance.

Others are not so sure about the iPhone and point out RIM's dedication to corporate security and the fact that BlackBerry e-mail is 3DES encrypted and compressed, which also makes it far less of a bandwidth hog. In fact, some commentators scoffed at iPhone security, saying it was so loose a teenage hacker could break in easily.

Still, some systems administrators who put down the first iPhone as "executive jewelry" were growing more comfortable with the Apple approach. Now, with a free software development kit (SDK) and rich App Store, the new open Apple was embracing those indie programmers and software vendors it ignored in the iPhone's first release.[11]

When IT managers put the Bold and iPhone head to head, the main strikes against enterprise use of the iPhone are still the following:

11. Eric Lai, "The iPhone 3G could make mobile management legit", Computerworld, July 17, 2008 < * >

1. **Battery Life**. The Bold beats the iPhone hands down. An iPhone can lose its charge by early afternoon; a Bold can get through a full day of similar activity. In a *PC World* lab test, Bold's battery provided seven hours, fifty-six minutes of talk time versus five hours, thirty-eight minutes of talk time for the iPhone 3G. The Bold also is not afflicted by "sudden drain" syndrome. Users can also carry a spare battery and swap it easily. With the iPhone, there is more risk of losing everything if the user cannot reach a charger fast enough.

2. **User Interface**. Using the Bold's contextual menus can be faster than tapping through screens. The iPhone still lacks built-in cut and paste and keyboard shortcuts.

3. **E-mail**. BlackBerry rules mobile e-mail. The iPhone can be slower to load e-mail, and the keyboard can lock-up.

4. **Stability**. The BlackBerry Bold rarely crashes.

5. **Speed**. The BlackBerry Bold is generally faster than the iPhone. The BlackBerry browser will pull the mobile interface by default for many sites, which is swifter.

6. **The Keyboard**. Most business people prefer the physical keyboard to the virtual one.

7. **Voice Activation**. The Bold has voice activated dialing out of the box.

8. **Click versus Swipe**. Clicks can be faster and easier than gestures; for example, with the Bold, clicking to scroll a page or zoom content works better than the two-finger, two-handed equivalent on iPhone. The Bold trackball allows for one-handed use.

9. **Storage**. The Bold lets you swap multiple microSD cards; you can't swap cards into the iPhone, and it has only one internal flash memory.

10. **Video**. The iPhone doesn't record video; the Bold does.

11. **Security**. The iPhone offers limited enterprise-management tools and lacks the security of the Bold's full-device encryption.

⊕   ⊕   ⊕

In Waterloo, RIM engineers had no time to rest on their laurels, as a new set of threats arrived on the horizon, not just from Finland and Silicon Valley, but also from the Far East.

The T-Mobile G1 (originally code-named the HTC Dream) arrived in the market in late spring 2008 as the first smartphone to use Google's Android open source OS. HTC's G1 is a touch-screen "iClone" with a trick up its sleeve—a full QWERTY keyboard that slides out when you want to type and tucks back in when you just want to use the touch screen. The device has HSDPA and Wi-Fi, GPS connectivity with support for Google Maps, a 3.2-megapixel camera, and Bluetooth. It also has access to the Android Market, a developer central such as Apple's iTunes App Store, which ensures there will be no shortage of third-party applications.

T-Mobile's low-cost G1 has been called everything from "a bunch of cheap junk" to "promising but unpolished" to "an unattractive and uninspiring piece of plastic." That's a start: other smartphone makers burdened with Microsoft Mobile licensing fees are lining up to sign on to the Android platform and joining Google's Open Handset Alliance, including Motorola, Sony Ericsson, Vodafone, and chipmaker ARM.

⊕   ⊕   ⊕

RIM's next 2008 offering, the eagerly awaited BlackBerry Storm 9530, code-named "Thunder," was initially rolled out by Verizon in the United States, Telus in Canada, and Vodafone in Europe, which booked more than 100,000 pre-orders before launch. Verizon priced the device at $199.99 (after a $50 mail-in rebate) with a two-year contract and $89.99 for corporate customers. Users could order the Storm backplate in three colors: black, dark blue, and charcoal.

The Storm was RIM's second riposte to the iPhone. While not an outright Apple killer, in many ways the new touch-screen BlackBerry—RIM's first—went beyond Apple's iconic device. It offered many features the iPhone lacked, such as cut and paste, a removable battery and SD card, and turn-by-turn satellite navigation. It also let users run multiple applications at the same time.

Mike Lazaridis called it "the most advanced smartphone ever made. There's no phone that measures up."

First of all, the full-screen Storm came with a huge 360 x 480, 3.6-inch display with fewer colors but 12 percent more pixels than the iPhone. Storm's pixels were denser, making details exceptionally clear and crisp. But the Storm's killer feature was its innovative mechanical Click-Through touch screen. It was the first one with two ways to use your fingers. It smartly married the swiping convenience of a touch screen with the feedback you get from a real keyboard and mouse.

The Storm has regular capacitive touch technology, much like the iPhone and the HTC G1. You scroll around with your finger lightly touching the screen, and it gives you visual feedback with a blue glow. But there's more—nothing happens until you want to confirm a selection or start an action. Then you use a more forceful press on the screen, which results in a "click" and an action. The Haptic Touchscreen technology lets your fingers feel true tactile feedback, so text messaging is like typing on a laptop. The screen is one big physical button that gives you more of a mouselike "3D" experience.

The Storm Web browser has a "cursor mode" that simulates a desktop browsing experience. Your fingertip acts like a mouse, moving the visible pointer across the screen. You can click it when you want action, just like using a mouse. This makes for some clever new features. For example, in your e-mail inbox, you can click to open an e-mail, but if you touch-and-hold, the device will search for all e-mails with the same subject or sender.

Using the Storm in portrait mode, you can tap on a virtual SureType keyboard such as the Pearl's. In wide landscape mode, you get a multi-tap QWERTY keyboard. You type by highlighting the letter on the touch screen and clicking the screen to make it appear in your message or document. You can also use touch-and-hold to pull up accented versions of letters, which is useful for non-English languages. Typing is enhanced by built-in spellchecking and RIM's excellent predictive text entry.

Early reviewers found Web browsing with the Storm better than the Bold, and getting closer to the iPhone's WYSIWYG Safari. They also loved the 3.2-MP video-capable autofocus camera with flash. You can also remove the back cover and insert a new microSD card (up to 16 gigabytes) without having to power down the device.

The Storm is a true world phone, and it packs support for Verizon Wireless's fastest network (EvDO Rev. A), for quad-band GSM/GPRS/EDGE, and for 2100-MHz UMTS/HSPA networks, enabling overseas roaming on any foreign network. The Storm also has a GPS receiver and Bluetooth, but no Wi-Fi.

Overall, while some reviewers had mixed emotions, they found RIM's first foray into the touch-screen universe a promising start, with future iterations no doubt boosting the machine's ease of use and power.

Pre-release reviews of the Storm were generally positive:

Sascha Segan, *PC Magazine*: The Storm is "the BlackBerry that's poised to steal some of the iPhone's thunder in corporate circles."

Bonnie Cha, CNET: Cha found it took time to get used to the Click-Through keyboard but was pleasantly surprised how accurate it was to the touch. She was impressed with the nice design and feature richness, but thought the price would be a big determining factor for sales.

Todd Haselton, *Laptop Magazine*: Haselton called the Storm "drop-dead gorgeous." He liked the turn-by-turn directions that are not found on the iPhone.

Rachel Metz, AP: "I found it much easier to type messages with the Storm's keyboard than with the iPhone's. This could make a big difference to business users who have been lusting after touch-screen smart phones but hesitant to make the switch."

There were, however, a few disappointed thumbs out there on BlackBerry Planet. Some early reviewers of Storm 1.0 griped about OS lag caused by JavaScript, slow list swiping, sudden crashes, awkward number entry, iffy battery life, and some "erroneous touch events."[12] Many of these glitches were caused by an earlier OS on some of the release phones and a somewhat rushed launch before Black Friday. Most were quickly cleared up in later OS releases. But the major gripe was the lack of Wi-Fi, particularly in areas where you couldn't get on Verizon's 3G data network. The Storm providers clearly didn't want buyers to unlock the device, wander out of the data plan, or patch into a Wi-Fi network for free. They were essentially crippling the Storm.

Some critics were hugely grumpy. Danny Dumas at *Wired* liked the Storm's text messaging: "I was able to compose a lengthy detailed SMS without a single typo. That's a feat I have yet to accomplish with the iPhone." But he grumbled that "this isn't the iPhone killer RIM was hoping it would be. OS lag on a piece of

---

12. "Verizon BlackBerry Storm Review," The Boy Genius Report, Nov. 20, 2008 < * >

hardware this gorgeous is unacceptable. Scrolling through menus is jagged, slow and pokey. Accelerometer sometimes takes a good 5 to 10 seconds to orient itself. Lack of Wi-Fi is lame. Verizon's totalitarian control over the Storm's OS is even lamer.

"Would we recommend the Storm? If you're locked into a contract with Verizon, want a touchscreen phone and are willing to put up with an OS that moves like a tranquilized yak, then yes the Storm is for you. Otherwise, your best bet is an iPhone or the very capable BlackBerry Bold. In any case, Apple need not fret; even in the face of a legitimate iPhone killer, they still offer more touchscreen goodness for the money and will undoubtedly, ahem, weather this storm."[13]

Influential blogger Boy Genius Report agreed about the lack of Wi-Fi:

"What about when your carrier is having data outages? No worries, just flip on that Wi-Fi switch, right? Wrong. What about when you travel for business or pleasure and the local coverage in that bad ass remote island location isn't that great. Just flip on Wi-Fi since your hotel (or if you're insane like us, you carry an Airport Express so you can Wi-Fi that shizz) offers Wi-Fi, right? Wrong. What happens when you work in a corporate office that gets horrible reception? Wi-Fi? Nope. What about when you'd like to connect your device to your home network, use VoIP applications, or just get a speedier web experience in general? You're completely out of luck."

Boy Genius was also scathing about the Storm's browser, and made the point that, contrary to rumors, RIM was not using the

---

13. Daniel Dumas, "RIM BlackBerry Strom," *Wired*, Nov. 20, 2008 < * >

open-source WebKit browser, based on Apple's Safari. But the same reviewer raved about the Storm's AV capabilities: "Videos look absolutely stunning on here. Probably one of the best video experiences on a mobile device we've seen."[14]

New York Times tech writer David Pogue, clearly infected with a buggy pre-release OS, was particularly annoyed about RIM's Click-Through touch typing: "How did this thing ever reach the market?" he wailed.

Pogue had loved the Flip and the Bold, but the Storm got him on a very bad day. He called it the BlackBerry Dud. "Was everyone involved just too terrified to pull the emergency brake on this train? Maybe RIM is just overextended. After all, it has just introduced three major new phones—Flip, Bold, Storm—in two months, each with a different software edition. Quality control problems are bound to result; the iPhone 3G went through something similar. Web rumor has it that a bug-fix software update is in the works."[15]

RIM OS patches weren't long in coming, and they restored some luster to the device, but Pogue's article and other negative comments poked some holes in the BlackBerry brand. Reports of a return rate as high as 50 percent also surfaced, which Verizon quickly quashed: "The Storm has the lowest return rate of any of our PDAs and at this point in its life cycle, it has the lowest return rate of any PDA we currently sell."

On RIM's BlackBerry support pages, the forums were ultra active, particularly with questions about the Storm's keyboard, but over all, most reviewers loved the gratifying click they got when "touch" typing and found that the small amount of feedback they

14. "Verizon BlackBerry Storm Review," The Boy Genius Report, Nov. 20, 2008 < * >
15. David Pogue, "No Keyboard? And You Call This a BlackBerry?" New York Times, November 26, 2008 < * >

got boosted their typing efficiency, although one female reviewer found typing on the device "tiring."

Seeking Alpha's Joel West echoed Pogue, calling RIM's Storm "a washout."[16] But OnTheStreet.com's Gary Krakow loved the device, calling it "the best BlackBerry ever,"[17] as did influential blogger Geek.com, who found "a very pleasant browsing experience in both portrait and landscape … For a first generation touch-screen from RIM it's fantastic."[18]

Finally, influential product tester Consumer Reports liked the Storm's "firm, yet responsive, touch screen. With cell-phone touch screens—including the iPhone's—it's too easy to inadvertently launch a program or hit the wrong key on their virtual keyboards. The Storm remedies this with a touch-screen that demands that you press down on it firmly, as you would a real button, before it executes a command. (The screen actually sits on top of a large button that clicks when you depress the screen surface.) While quirky to use at first, we found this unique technology very effective in minimizing time-wasting mistakes. A word of caution: The display won't work with a stylus or long fingernails."[19]

One criticism that stung Mike Lazaridis was the comment that the Storm was a me-too device and a copy of the iPhone.

"I worked on the very first touchscreens," he told one reporter. "Let's go back in time now—Gold Computing, Newton, Envoy, Marco—the very first touchscreens on the Sharp organizers, I had one of those. The very first Palm. I met Jeff Hawkins and (Donna) Dubinsky back when Palm was a block of wood, so I go right back to the beginning. How's that? I've used all the touchscreens, I've

16. Joel West, "RIM's Storm is a Washout" Seeking Alpha, Dec. 5, 2008 < * >
17. Gary Krakow, "BlackBerry Storm: Love at First Touch" TheStreet.com, Nov. 20, 2008 < * >
18. Joel Evans, "Review: Can Verizon's BlackBerry Storm blow over the iPhone?" Geek.com, Nov. 20, 2008 < * >
19. "BlackBerry Storm: First Impressions". ConsumerReports.com, Nov 20, 2008 < * >

known about touchscreens and I've watched NEC and Palm use full touchscreens since the mid-90s.

"This is three years in the making. So I'm sorry but this wasn't a response to another device. Either that or we have a time machine somewhere, or some kind of magic crystal ball or something. This was actually designed three years ago and the actual physical design of this product—I have the original models from 2006."[20]

With its slew of new launches out of the way, RIM now had to contend with the softening of the North American telecom business. It had reliably expanded, sometimes by 10 percent a year, since RIM went into the smartphone business. But it stalled in the summer of 2008, and then tanked that autumn, under the weight of repackaged sub prime U.S. mortgages and elaborate derivatives that left even Warren Buffett baffled.

An alarming drop in consumer spending suddenly changed the whole calculus of the handset industry. While new subscribers still flocked to buy mobile devices, the number of those replacing their devices plunged.

The result? Motorola shares went into the dumpster, plunging 71 percent. Nokia shares fell into a tailspin, dropping 63 percent on the year, and even Research In Motion was off 61 percent. RIM's share price in this period nose-dived from a high of US$147.55 to $40, making it, some said, ripe for a takeover by Microsoft. However, in the same period, Microsoft dropped in value to under $20 a share from more than $35.

Some shell-shocked Wall Street analysts suggested that the most successful phones in the recovery period were going to be

---

20. Natasha Lomas, RIM's Lazaridis on why Qwerty's still working; ZDNet News: May 16, 2008 < * >

smartphones made by RIM and Apple because they had a longer shelf life. Some said RIM, with its one-trick killer app—the ability to deliver instant, secure e-mail anywhere—would keep on ruling the office space and make inroads outside the corporate world. But most agreed that it was shakeout time, and that the industry was going to wind up with fewer competitors a year down the road.

At the Motley Fool website, almost 5,000 members weighed in on RIM's chances of success in the fall of 2008. Most were upbeat in the face of continuing demand. One contributor, DemonDoug, posed the rhetorical question, "What kind of company is most likely to survive a severe downturn, even a depression, and possible US dollar deflation (and therefore beat the S&P 500)?" His answer: "One with no debt, like Research In Motion." But the more bearish and negative members felt that:

1. RIM was falling behind. Some worried about RIM's increased spending for new BlackBerrys and its ability to bring products and applications to market on time. They argued that Apple's iPhone sales in the third quarter of 2008 were 6.9 million compared to 6.1 million BlackBerrys in the same period (although the two companies use different sales tracking, Apple counting sales when they leave their warehouse in Asia). Also, Apple and Google had their application stores up and running in mid-2008, while Research In Motion's own BlackBerry App World didn't open its digital doors until March 2009.

2. The iPhone and smartphones from Nokia and Motorola were causing a drop in prices and creating margin issues. RIM once owned the smartphone market and brought in steady profits. Now it needed to work harder and spend more on marketing to compete on price, features, and fashion.

3. The party's over. Like other huge companies such as Oracle, RIM's best days of growth are behind it, and there are better investment opportunities in smaller companies.
4. New entrants are arriving from Asia Pacific: HTC, Samsung, and LG. The HTC Dream is the first phone that runs Google's "GPhone" Android mobile operating system. It uses T-Mobile's 3G data network on the 1,700 MHz band. Like the BlackBerry, it comes with a tiny "jog ball" trackball device.
5. It would be a mistake to write off competitors such as Microsoft's Windows Mobile and the Symbian operating system of veteran Finnish phone maker Nokia.

At a gloomy RBC Capital Markets conference in November 2008, Jim Balsillie told analysts that "There are more variables, more need to navigate, more need for hands on the wheel and eyes on the road right now. If you don't, you do it at your peril."

Balsillie said RIM was better at what it does now than five years ago and didn't believe that people would give up mobile devices in a tough economy. "I am really quite excited by what we think we can do coming into this season."

UBS analyst Jeffrey Fan felt that RIM would be affected by the slowing market. "Although consumers are unlikely to get rid of cell phones, they may be more cautious about adding incremental monthly data fees, which could slow sales. We expect replacement cycles to continue to lengthen."

Balsillie's take was simple and direct: "The opportunity has expanded, but so has the level of contention."

The lag in getting the Bold to market had hurt RIM's bottom line. Fortunately for Balsillie, in spite of a huge collapse in corporate spending, the trend in purchasing smartphones was staying strong. Companies were realizing that the benefits of the newer, faster, more powerful BlackBerrys far outweighed the price.

Even in the consumer space, *Forbes* magazine reported that cell phone customers were responding to the economic downturn by dining out less frequently (88 percent), holding off on major purchases such as cars, appliances, furniture, and electronics (79 percent), driving less (57percent), and even buying fewer groceries (41 percent). But less than a third (32 percent) were cutting back on their cell phone spending in response to tough times. An Accenture survey found 90 percent of people polled had no intention of dropping their cell phone services.

In spite of the meltdown, 2008 was a good year for RIM. North America was the fastest-growing smartphone market, with a 68 percent increase. RIM with Apple accounted for 70 percent of the total. And sales continued to grow, even with the downturn and lower price points, because of replacement demand for the Bold and stronger than expected sales of the Storm. Indeed, RIM found that at least 75 percent of Storm buyers were new BlackBerry users.

According to a RIM exec, "People who love Storm usually come from the world of cell phones rather than BlackBerry. Where a diehard BlackBerry user detests Storm because of the strange new keyboard experience and latency issues related to touch screen, cell phone users love it because cell phone keyboards are generally slow and hard to use. Storm sales will continue to grow as more cell phone users switch over. Best of all, their costs do not have to increase if they simply opt for cell access and skip data access. Cell phone users are heavy SMS (text) users, so they have no difficulty texting with Storm."

"Through all RIM's stages of growth, our success was a series of very successfully managed evolutions. Everything was an evolution. You just intensely manage what has to be done at that point in time, and that gives you better

facts for the next situation you have to face. Then every
time you face a new circumstance, you have a better set of
facts, and that leads to a more decent probability of suc-
cess. I don't think grandiose, easy plans are the route of
many successful businesses."

—Jim Balsillie

After the Great Meltdown of 2008, Research In Motion still ruled the office as the monarch of mobile e-mail. But RIM's aggressive move into the global consumer space was a different matter, and fraught with danger. For one thing, prices and margins are lower in consumer land. And marketing costs are higher. Since 72 percent of the world's total mobile phone market is prepaid, RIM is having to customize offerings to a whole new set of customers.

Still, in 2009, consumers amount to more than half of new BlackBerry subscriptions. This fact was starting to hit the bottom line; RIM's gross profits were down from 2008, even as sales were higher than expected. Needham & Co. tech analyst Charlie Wolf said he expected low-40s gross profit to be a problem for RIM through 2010.

As prices moved lower, RIM knew it would have to rely increasingly on getting cheaper and better devices to market and giving customers more value by promoting lifestyle applications that run on its planetary platform.

Mike Lazaridis felt RIM was on the right track by aggressively moving into the consumer space because the company was starting with a tried-and-true foundation: the office.

"If you go back in history, just about every major consumer
electronics technology in history started in the enterprise.

So everything from printers, fax machines, telephones, typewriters—you name it, it all started in the enterprise. And then as it became easier to manage, as it came down in price, as it became more ergonomic, what happened was all these businesspeople, who're also consumers—when they saw it available in the store, for a price that they can have it in their home, they start putting fax machines in their home, they start putting PCs in their home, they start putting tape recorders in their home. All of these technologies have their birthplace in business and BlackBerry's following that same path. BlackBerry's really a product that has successfully commercialized the concept of the smartphone for business.[21] "

Jim Balsillie felt that the secret to RIM's success is that the company performed very well in building complete solutions "as we interface everything. We are an interface and we don't compete with the ecosystem. We also have a carrier-channel strategy."[22] In other words, RIM can handle corporate communications from A to Z and can deliver whatever devices its carriers can sell.

Most commentators were optimistic about RIM's chances in a market dominated by Finland's Nokia, which sold 15.3 million smartphones in 2008, giving it a 47.5 percent share, down from 50.8 percent a year earlier. Gartner analyst Roberta Cozza saw RIM as the biggest winner in a slowing smartphone market, roughly doubling its market share from mid 2007 to 17.4 percent.

"RIM continues to execute well at the consumer level, increasing its global market reach," said Cozza. And RIM was finding new

21. Natasha Lomas, "RIM's Lazaridis on why Qwerty's still working". ZDNet News: May 16, 2008 < * >
22. Damian Koh, " The Storm is a Netbook, says RIM's founder". CNET Asia, December 30, 2008 < * >

clients beyond its main business market, especially with its new designs, which were "necessary to keep pace with the competition at the consumer level."

Above all, RIM had to keep pace with Apple and Google in the superphone space. It had to be done to drive the BlackBerry brand forward.

RIM's strategy was low risk in a still burgeoning market. Said Genuity Capital analyst Deepak Chopra, the smartphone market was growing so fast that there was enough room for RIM and Apple to continue to thrive. He said the BlackBerry and iPhone accounted for just 2 percent of the global handset market, leaving ample room for each company to take large hunks of marketshare from Nokia and other rivals.

"We're rocking, we're totally rocking."

—Jim Balsillie

Moving the BlackBerry brand into the consumer space meant targeting early adopters, particularly younger people. Savvy marketers know that adolescence is the time of life when brand loyalties get fixed. But in North America, that's not an easy plan to execute. According to a Piper Jaffray survey of U.S. high school students,[23] Apple owned the lion's share of teen and young adult loyalty.

By 2008, Apple's share of the MP3 music player scene among U.S. high school students had reached a seemingly untouchable 84 percent, up from 80 percent a year earlier. Now that Apple was marketing a handheld that doubled as an iPod, 8 percent of teens with mobiles had already migrated over to the iPhone. A further 22 percent wanted one. And of the students expecting to buy a

---

23. Piper Jaffray 'Taking Stock With Teens' Study Indicates Bottom May Be Nearing for 'Discretionary Recession'. Oct. 9, 2008 < * >

mobile device, 33 percent specified the Apple iPhone. Apple has also moved to sell iPhones in the temple of U.S. consumerdom— Wal-Mart. This made it even tougher for RIM to penetrate the consumer mindspace.

Companies such Nokia and AT&T have built their own music stores to crack the cult of Apple and reach into the teenage market. But RIM wisely avoided this course, releasing the Bold, the Pearl Flip, and Storm with access to Apple's iTunes store so users could easily sync and manage their current music, video, and podcast collections. But RIM is not standing still in music. Led by its rock fan co-CEO Jim Balsillie, RIM is partnering with Slacker, an Internet radio device, and Shazam, a music recognition service, as well as sponsoring the Cannes music conference.

During an interview in the Majestic Hotel in Cannes, Balsillie used his BlackBerry Bold as a remote to control songs on a portable speaker. Singing the lyrics to Soundgarden's 1994 track "Black Hole Sun," he told Bloomberg the music industry is undergoing radical transformation, led by Apple's decision to bring in variable pricing on iTunes and sell songs without copy protection. "This has really gone quite crazy," Balsillie said.[24]

How many of the youth demographic will break free from what cynics call Steve Jobs's "reality distortion field" and migrate over to the new feature-rich BlackBerrys? That is the question, and it may have to do more with carrier loyalty, or slavery, if you prefer.

RIM has to play it very cool to crack this consumer mindspace. The plan is clearly to promote iTunes compatibility, offer a credible touch-screen alternative, rely on parents with office BlackBerrys to spread the gospel, and, finally, promote BlackBerry apps as good or better than those available in the iPhone universe.

---

24. "Blackberry looks beyond lawyers, bankers to add music consumers". Bloomberg News, Jan. 18, 2009 < * >

RIM also has to maintain friendly relations with the world's many telcos, even if they are ferocious competitors with each other and most of them handle Nokia phones.

Inside North America, RIM's carriers are fully engaged in the great superphone war, with Verizon and Bell exclusively pushing RIM's Storm as a counterpoint to AT&T's and Rogers' exclusive iPhone and the BlackBerry Bold. So U.S. customers are now seeing the amazing spectacle of carriers pitting BlackBerry against BlackBerry.

Verizon marketing put its flagship Storm right up against the AT&T Bold, declaring that the Storm had more storage and a better screen than the uncool Bold, which was an old-school device with its trackball and clunky QWERTY keyboard. Plus, who needed the Bold's 3G when Verizon's Storm operated on "the biggest and best network in the USA"? Who, indeed.

Of course, outside Fortress North America, Nokia is an old hand at this game, being all things to all carriers. Nokia is still king of the wireless world, so any movement onto the global stage by RIM means arm wrestling with the monstrous Scandinavian, country by country, channel by channel, in a crazy quilt of complex marketing environments. This is war, or a close substitute, and RIM is making good progress in markets where smartphones are letting people who can't afford computers do real computing. But tackling Nokia is proving to be RIM's toughest marketing job yet.

As Nokia CEO Olli-Pekka Kallasvuo has commented, "If you look at the global mobile devices market, it's very big, it's very versatile. The consumers are many. You need to have 40-plus devices out there at any given point in time. You look at the different consumer segments, the different markets, the different price points and the thinking that we need to tackle every part of the market—as opposed to one or two segments only—has of course led us to high market share. If I look at the competition, they are either smaller or in a niche. Our strategy is to go for all relevant markets. One size will not fit all for mobile communications."[25]

To take on Nokia and build a planetary brand, you have to be flexible, as Apple's Steve Jobs has found out to his cost.

India, with a population of 1.14 billion, is the world's fastest-growing wireless market. Indians buy 8 to 10 million cell phones a month, mostly cheap Nokias on a prepaid basis. But Apple's partners Bharti Airtel and Vodafone Essar sold only 11,000 units of its iPhone 3G in the last half of 2008. According to the Delhi-based newspaper *Mint*, "iPhone's launch in India has been dubbed the biggest failure of a top-notch brand from a well regarded company in recent times."[26]

So what went wrong? Why did the brand with the world's coolest cachet flop so badly?

Price is not the problem, since Nokia, Samsung, and RIM are selling smartphones that cost even more. The problem is marketing. Jobs announced a global price of $199 and couldn't deliver. Cell phone providers in India don't subsidize cell phones with lock-in clauses as they do in North America and Europe. Also, by selling iPhones exclusively at their own outlets, Apple antagonized India's big retail chains.

Nokia is also highly entrenched in India, and its brand is a synonym for "phone," just like Kleenex for tissue in North America. Of course, Apple and to a lesser extent RIM are firmly in Nokia's sights. The Finnish behemoth is plugging the smartphone hole in the market by unleashing its own touch-screen device, the 5800

---

25. Nokia CEO maps out U.S. strategy, by Elise Ackerman. Mercury News interview Oct. 19, 2008 < * >

26. Philip Elmer-DeWitt, iPhone disconnects in India, Fortune, Nov. 13, 2008 < * >

XPress Music, with providers offering 2,000 free hours of music from Nokia's new Comes With Music store.

Business Week's Jack Ewing shrewdly calls the Nokia 5800 the "iPhone triangulator," released "to ensure that Apple remains a niche player in the global handset market." He says, "Nokia will try to smother Apple and other rivals with a range of touch products, aiming to peel away different target groups. And Nokia will launch the products simultaneously around the world, exploiting a distribution system that neither Apple nor any other competitor can match."[27]

⊕　　⊕　　⊕

As the world moves beyond simple cell phones, and the Great Smartphone War spreads across the planet, will a Web giant such as Google or computing behemoths such as Microsoft and Apple end up owning the mobile Web, or will it be nimble competitors from China, Japan, and Korea? Or will it be Nokia? The Finnish giant still sells a phone every eighteen seconds and 40 percent of all cell phones worldwide. It has about 1 billion customers, or one in every six people on the planet. Nokia also builds almost 50 percent of all smartphones, and last year got over 50 percent of its $12 billion in profits from the sector. The company has more than 9,200 applications written for its devices.

Nokia's share of the global smartphone market is getting clipped, and the main gainers are RIM and Apple. But even if Nokia has sputtered, analysts feel they are finding their feet again and starting to compete in the new superphone universe. The Finns intend to be a major player in the mobile web and are investing heavily in music, file sharing, mapping, and advertising, so as to morph themselves into an Internet company.

---

27. Jack Ewing, Nokia's Touch Screen 5800 Nods to iPhone, BusinessWeek, October 2, 2008 < * >

In the spring of 2008, Nokia fired the first salvo against RIM's new offerings, cutting its ties with RIM's BlackBerry brand on its new business handsets, the E71 and E66. These were the first e-series Nokia devices not to house BlackBerry Connect for e-mail, but rather Microsoft Exchange, forcing consumers to make a direct choice between the brands.

As Nokia U.K.'s Simon Ainslie explained it: "RIM are a competitor and have done a reasonable job in a space that is traditionally ours, so it's no great surprise that we see this as an opportunity to give consumers a proper choice on what email solution they want. Our approach is to make email a mass-market proposition for everybody, not just for the corporate boardroom group of individuals where BlackBerry has established itself."[28]

But some analysts felt that Nokia was making a big mistake, since BlackBerry Connect was one of the main selling points for their best-selling devices. For many corporations, BlackBerry Connect is essential, and they will not go any other route for their e-mail services. BlackBerry is the default standard for secure corporate e-mail.

In July 2008, Nokia moved against the RIM OS on another front by spending $410 million to acquire the rest of the Symbian operating system it did not already own. Nokia is making Symbian into an open-source project to "triangulate" Google's Android OS. Symbian sign-ups include AT&T, LG Electronics, Motorola, NTT DoCoMo, Samsung, Sony Ericsson, Texas Instruments, and Vodafone. About 18.5 million Symbian phones shipped during the first quarter of 2008.

Nokia now has its sights firmly on the North American superphone market, currently dominated by RIM, Apple, and Google-based machines. Nokia only occupies a small U.S. niche,

---

28. "Nokia has cut ties with RIM's BlackBerry brand". Mobile Today, July 24, 2008 < * >

primarily because it refused to cave in to the demands of U.S. carriers for control over design and performance. Even though its Nokia N95 has live video and a 5-megapixel phone, it still hasn't locked in consumer eyeballs. But that is changing, as Nokia has decided to mend fences with the U.S. telcos.

For the moment, tech innovation from Research In Motion, Google, and Apple is driving the North American market, but this is having a global effect, as the three supertech companies raise the bar for the whole world.

⊕　　⊕　　⊕

On the one hand, RIM's planetary consumer push will be a great test of Team Lazaridis's ability to deliver desirable devices to market. On the other hand, Team Balsillie is executing in a whole new marketing channel in an effort to bring BlackBerrys to the global masses hooked on Nokia cell phones. They're going to play to their strength—e-mail. Almost 75 percent of the world's population has never used e-mail, even though they might have cell phone access.

Nokia has carefully studied developing use, and in some far-flung places, people use their access to a single village cell phone—usually owned by a storekeeper—to pay bills, transfer money, and keep in touch with family members in the city. A group of farmers can check market data and crop prices to get the best price.

People who can afford to buy a low-cost phone write their cell phone number across the lintel of their front door in place of a street address.

RIM is moving to meet this growing need, and the company's new BlackBerry in a Box and BlackBerry On Demand services, recently rolled out in Indonesia, could be a huge catalyst for growth. With BlackBerry in a Box, people can buy a BlackBerry and one year of the BlackBerry Internet Service (BIS) all in one package at local retail stores. After the first year, they can extend for another year, or get time-based access, or pay by the month, and so on.

With normal prepaid, people purchase devices with no subsidy (at full price). Then they buy prepaid cards to fill up their accounts.

Prepaid is the way to go in markets where people have limited budgets, or can't get postpaid carrier credit. RIM is offering daily or monthly BlackBerry prepaid service. But RIM is also tackling people who do not want to be tied to a long-term contract or even people who don't want to share personal information for security reasons.

Carriers also like prepaid because it removes risk and inventory—instead of buying and stocking hundreds of thousands of devices, carriers can let the retail chains or even small stores market RIM's BlackBerrys directly.

With BlackBerry in a Box, carriers will also experience reduced turnover or churn, which sometimes reaches 70 percent after only a month. An annual fee removes this headache and gives the carriers a direct channel to clients so they can send them subscription deals, money-saving coupons, and other offers to reduce the churn rate.

Another innovation in Indonesia is carrier XL's BlackBerry 1 Data Plan, ideal for price-sensitive users and device sharers. They can buy unlimited daily SMS messaging for 5,000 rupia (about 40 cents U.S.) a day, turning it on and off by simply sending a message "BlackBerry On" or "BlackBerry Off."[29]

BlackBerry On Demand, launched by Indosat Tbk, is available as a seven-day or a thirty-day data plan, with unlimited data

---

29. "XL Launches the BlackBerry 1 Data Plan - a Simple and Cost-effective One-day Usage Plan for BlackBerry Smartphones" RIM News Release, Oct. 31, 2008 < * >

usage for mobile e-mail, attachment viewing, Internet browsing, application downloads, and instant messaging. Indosat customers can activate BlackBerry On Demand via short messaging service (SMS). This prepaid option is available to customers with prepaid and postpaid voice plans.

In the Caribbean, Digicel launched a similar prepaid BlackBerry service. Existing postpaid customers could switch to prepaid service on a weekly or monthly plan. Near the end of the subscription period, customers get a text message reminding them to top up their account for the service to continue. To open up the market beyond business clients, the company highlighted the benefits of a host of services such as web browsing, e-mail, instant messaging, and Facebook.

☠ ☠ ☠

Starting in 2009, RIM went retail in the huge Indian subcontinent, the fastest-growing market on the planet, with a whole new thrust—lower cost BlackBerrys that will work on any network. Originally, Indian BlackBerrys were restricted to telco partners Vodaphone Essar, Bharti Airtel, and Reliance. Now, RIM is starting to crack that segment of the Indian masses who prefer to use unlocked open phones not tied to any carrier. It's a market dominated by Nokia.

To make this leap, RIM chose Redington India, the major player with more than 6,700 IT resellers in more than 450 cities. Redington, which also operates in Singapore, the Middle East, and Africa, already handled popular brands such as Nokia and Samsung.

Redington began expanding RIM's retail footprint in a phased manner, in retail stores and trade outlets in the biggest Indian cities: Mumbai, Delhi and the Capital Region, Hyderabad, Chennai, Bangalore, Kolkata, Pune, and Ahmedabad. RIM is supplying price-wise stripped-down versions of the Pearl, Curve, and Bold smartphones and also launching localized BlackBerry apps in India for areas such as entertainment and sports.

❋   ❋   ❋

"You have to have senior politburo contacts in order to do business in China in the scale that they're looking at."
—*Peter Misek, technology analyst, Canaccord Adams*

The huge Chinese market is entirely a different matter. China is a RIM-marketable country, but the company is in for a wild ride as it tries to tap the world's largest cell phone market.

China didn't even have a wireless network until 1987, and it took ten years for the country to reach its first 10 million cell subscribers. Today, China is the manufacturing center of the world, with U.S.$1.4 trillion in foreign reserves. Among its 1.3 billion people are 640 million cell phone subscribers and more than 300 million Internet users. More than 15 million smartphones are sold in China every year, and the market is exploding.

Imitation is the sincerest form of flattery, and in 2007, China Unicom, a phone company owned by the People's Republic of China, brought out its own low-cost lookalike version of the BlackBerry. The sales copy brazenly boasted that, "The RedBerry name extends the vivid name of BlackBerry that people are already familiar with, and it also combines the new red symbol of China Unicom."

For the moment, RedBerry pushes e-mail like the standard CDMA cell phones China Unicom already supports. It costs a dollar a month plus a few cents per e-mail compared to the $64 per month for unlimited e-mail that BlackBerry users pay in Hong Kong.

RIM wisely declined to take China Unicom to court but instead partnered with China Unicom's competitor, China Mobile, which already markets its own PushMail service. China Mobile has a co-lossal 400 million customers, making it the planet's largest cellco, but most of them rely on low-end handsets. BlackBerry phones have worked with China Mobile since 2006. But people couldn't buy them inside the country, except in Hong Kong.

Now that RIM is inside the Chinese market, they may decide to test the local court system to handle the RedBerry challenge. But for now the company is content to work closely with Alcatel-Lucent, RIM's long-time distributor in Africa, the Middle East, and Southeast Asia, who have been doing business in China for twenty-five years.

The knockoffs keep coming, however. The L900i "Blueberry," a Bold wannabe, is a 2.4-inch quad-band cell phone with RIM-style QWERTY keypad, FM radio, and camera, which you can get for $160 from China Grabber. It even has slots for dual SIM cards.

⊕　　⊕　　⊕

"The big opportunity is in services and applications. We're in the very early stage of this, and a lot of different sectors are just emerging."

—Jim Balsillie

While attacking the macro markets, RIM rolled out its own micro service for the SOHO (small business and home office) market—BlackBerry Unite!

BlackBerry Unite! software is a free download from RIM. It's essentially a stripped-down BlackBerry Enterprise Server (BES) that runs on a Windows PC in your house, and it's carrier independent. You can support up to five BlackBerrys and your family, group and/or home office can collaborate and share content from a central console. Unite! has most of the advantages of its big brother, the full BES, with a setup that gives you and your group mobile access to e-mail, a shared calendar, contacts, pictures, and documents, plus advanced device and security control. Web browsing is available if a BlackBerry is assigned to the Unite! server. However, the PC running Unite! must be running at all times, otherwise the Web browser cannot operate.

While is was not as earth shattering a product as RIM marketing supposed it would be, Unite! is making slow and steady inroads on BlackBerry Planet, and RIM is well positioned to move the software forward, and combine it with other, paid offerings by in house and outside developers. The major push to perform in this arena came from Apple's sudden leap into the smartphone pool and stirrings from Nokia and Google.

In the spring of 2008, news broke that Palo Alto vencap veterans Kleiner Perkins and Apple were starting a $100-million fund for iPhone developers. It also appeared that other major competitors such as Nokia, with its OVI and N-Gage services, were speeding in the same direction. Prodded to act quickly, and better rationalize how it backed outside developers, RIM roused itself and moved briskly to plug that hole in the dike.

The new BlackBerry Partners Fund, based in Toronto, was launched on May 12, 2008, with funding from RIM, RBC, and Thomson Reuters, its mission to spur new mobile apps and services. Funding would be "agnostic" and not restricted to any single mobile platform or any specific industry segment. Platforms would include "mobile commerce (payments, advertising, retailing and banking), vertical and horizontal enterprise applications, location-based and location-aware applications and services (navigation and mapping), communications, social networking, media and entertainment, and lifestyle and personal productivity applications."

Co-managed by JLA Ventures and RBC Venture Partners, and led by John Albright and Kevin Talbot, the fund was looking for companies with:

- potential product and market leadership
- competitive differentiation
- strong management teams
- clear revenue and cost model.

Talbot and Albright were soon knee-deep in thousands of business plans. By the end of October their team had worked through the pile and said they were backing three new ventures to start:

- Israel-based **WorldMate**, whose MobiMate helps travelers by keeping track of delayed flights; raised $8 million in a Series C Preferred Stock financing with BlackBerry Partners Fund, Motorola Ventures, and AMC Communications.
- Austin-based **Digby**, a mobile commerce service provider, which helps retailers set up web stores for cell phone screens; raised $5.5 million Series B Preferred Stock with the BlackBerry Partners Fund and existing shareholders.
- New York City's **buzzd**, which makes a location-sensitive city guide that recommends nearby stores and events; raised $3.2 million in a Series A Preferred Stock financing with BlackBerry Partners Fund, Greycroft Partners, Monitor Ventures, and Qualcomm Ventures.

RIM held its first Silicon Valley developers' conference in October 2008 in Santa Clara, California. The company was expecting 600 attendees and got 900 commercial and corporate developers from twenty-seven countries. At the conference, the BlackBerry Partners

Fund seeded two grand prize winners with $150,000 investments to further develop their applications.

Balsillie is bullish on software development and says RIM is pushing deeper into productivity and cost-saving features for business-to-business, partnering with Oracle, SAP, and others. And he feels that 2009 may also be the year when wireless e-commerce and wireless bill paying finally breaks out. The Bank of America already has 2 million of its 29 million online customers using mobile banking; they released a mobile banking app for the BlackBerry in early 2009. Coming down the pipe is contactless payment, where a consumer pays for merchandise by waving their phone past a reader.

Moving in the same direction as Apple, Google, and Microsoft, RIM also poured the foundations for its BlackBerry App World (BAW) store for mobile apps, add-ons, and games. The store opened in March 2009, featuring free and paid programs and also monthly subscription billing and try-and-buy models.

Developers who want to provide or sell BlackBerry apps must first register in the program and get free access to all the different software development tools. They can then build their application and test it on the simulators for the various devices. They can also request to sign up for RIM's optional partner program in order to get additional support.

Developers then submit their programs for sale in the same way they do at the iPhone App store, but RIM only takes 20 percent of the revenue, versus 30 percent for Apple developers. Carrier partners also have custom kiosks in BlackBerry App World to provide clients with software updates and downloads, but they also can continue to sell from their own sites.

For Jim Balsillie, compelling new mobile applications such as street-level GPS and rich social networking are pulling society in major new directions, and the BlackBerry Partners Fund and BlackBerry App World are ready to help developers move their applications into a booming new marketplace.

The potential for BlackBerry App World is enormous, and it promises to be a valuable profit center on its own, apart from the benefits to the brand. Over at Apple's App Store, the facts speak for themselves: iPhone and iPod Touch users have already downloaded more than 1 billion apps, out of more than 20,000 apps available. Piper Jaffray expects Apple's store to generate more than $1 billion revenue in 2009.

"Once social networking becomes a B2B phenomenon—not unlike IM and texting—I believe every single social networking user will want a data plan."

—Jim Balsillie

The use of Facebook, MySpace, LinkedIn, and other cross-platform social networking programs is booming on the BlackBerry. RIM marketing is also working with carrier and other partners in Taste of BlackBerry demos, to show off other new business- and consumer-oriented applications. These include programs to:

- open your garage door or control your home theater (**Unify4Life** universal remote)
- control your BlackBerry with your voice, using **Vlingo**
- book a hotel room by e-mail and automatically build an itinerary (**WorldMate Live**)
- do a PowerPoint presentation by Bluetooth to a computer display or a projector (**Impatica ShowMate**)
- listen to XM Radio or watch forty live TV channels (**MobiTV**)

- set up channels for whatever interests you with **Viigo**, a lifestyle application that lets you set up your BlackBerry for breaking news, blogs, finance, sports, RSS, and more
- do local search with **Poynt**; find restaurants, local sites of interest and movies, and then buy tickets right from your BlackBerry; won a Best in Show award at BlackBerry Challenge
- remotely unlock your front door with **Schlage LiNK**; a Wi-Fi-enabled locking mechanism; the starter kit costs $299 and comes with a lock, light, and bridge device (which wirelessly connects to your lock to your existing home router).
- view and control live video streams from supported IP cameras and video encoders with **Total Control: BlackBerry Video Camera Edition**.

These shows will continue to be a growing part of BlackBerry evangelism, as the company evolves toward its goal of becoming a lifestyle platform as well as a business device.

RIM is now moving forward with five and perhaps six basic model streams or "evolutions"—the Bold, Storm, Onyx, Curve, Pearl and a possible touch- and slide-screen form factor.

- **The Magnum** (AT&T) aka **The Driftwood** (T-Mobile)—The next evolution of the high-end 3G Bold business communicator line, with QWERTY keys separated by frets combined with a hi-res HVGA touch screen, tri-band UMTS/HSDPA, quad-band GSM/GPRS/EDGE, GPS, WiFi, more RAM. and a 3.2-megapixel autofocus camera.

- **The Storm 2**, with the kinks worked out, will probably sport Wi-Fi and a faster processor. Lazaridis considers it a mini netbook.
- **The Onyx 9600**—A mid-range 3G cross between the Bold and the Curve, with larger separated keys; features a HVGA+ display, 3.2-megapixel camera with autofocus and image stabilization, trackball, 256MB of flash memory, GPS, WiFi, Bluetooth 2.0, 3.5mm headphone jack, microSD slot, quad-band GSM/GPRS/EDGE, and tri-band UMTS/HSDPA.
- **The Gemini** - The low end Curve 8520 will lack 3G, Wi-Fi and touch screen for the best battery life; features an optical trackpad instead of a trackball; with a 512MHz processor, quad-band GSM/GPRS/EDGE, 256MB of flash memory, 128MB of RAM, Bluetooth 2.0, speakerphone, QVGA display, QWERTY keyboard, 2-megapixel camera, microSD slot, dedicated media buttons and a 3.5mm headphone jack.
- The new **Pearl** and **Pearl Flip 3G** have more RAM, better battery life, and faster processors, with new styling and color; targeted to emerging markets, with SureType keyboard, 3.6Mbps HSDPA, tri-band UMTS/ HSDPA, quad-band GSM/GPRS/EDGE, aGPS, Bluetooth 2.0, trackball, a camera, microSD slot, and a 3.5mm headphone jack.
- **The Slider?**—A possible 3G/Wi-Fi touch-screen device with a slide keyboard, for European users, possibly AT&T and Rogers.

Even during the recent downturn, RIM's products were still sought after. And while the Storm received mixed reviews, RIM quickly patched the software glitches, and, says Balsillie, "We can't make it fast enough, and our shipments are off the charts."[30]

---

30. "BlackBerry Maker Sees Competition." Investors.com, Feb. 2009. < * >

Much faster 4G wireless speeds are in the pipe. To give an example, LG Electronics new Long Term Evolution LTE modem chip will support wireless download speeds of 100 megabytes per second and upload speeds of 50 Mbps, which is a major step toward creating a market-ready 4G phone. At those speeds, users will be able to download a 700-megabyte movie file in less than one minute or stream four HD movies at a time without any buffering.

RIM has set up a work team tasked with creating an LTE BlackBerry in order to get a device ready when faster 4G LTE begins to be deployed worldwide. Some networks will be in place in late 2009, devices will be arriving in 2010, and most carriers in the world should be offering LTE by 2011.

According to market research company Strategy Analytics, the global 4G LTE handset market will double from 70 million sales units in 2012 to 150 million sales units by 2013.

3G LTE and WiMax are similar technologies, but it appears LTE will be the standard chosen by 80 percent of the carriers in the world. The competing WiMax standard may be better suited for rural/emerging markets where no GSM infrastructure is in place. It is ideal for countries with large rural populations.

"What other multibillion-dollar seller of high-tech goods can still double both sales and earnings year over year these days?"

—*The Motley Fool*

Competition between RIM and Apple, Nokia, Samsung, HTC, and their carriers is getting hotter by the day. Yet in spite of Apple's entry on the scene, and the explosion of iClones and me-too devices, Research In Motion is stronger than ever, with the following factors in BlackBerry's favor in 2009 and beyond:

- Customers perceive that BlackBerry is *the* business phone; if you don't have a BlackBerry, it isn't a *real* business.
- BlackBerry is a quality name brand that, with the exception of a few stumbles, has been well executed from the days when it was a niche brand.
- RIM has a huge and loyal installed base. The U.S. government is BlackBerry's biggest account, with more than 500,000 users.
- Mobile phones are a 1 billion device per annum market, but older mobile devices are rapidly being replaced by smartphones. In the United States, the traditional cell phone market has declined by 5 percent compounded per annum since 2003, but the smartphone market grew 58 percent.
- Smartphones with Web access currently deliver higher revenue per phone.
- RIM dominated the $12 billion annual U.S. market for smartphones, with a 50 percent share in 2008.
- RIM has doubled its share worldwide, to 14 percent of the market, while still trailing Nokia, which has dropped to 42 percent.
- RIM's base is changing—more than 45 percent of the 25-million-strong subscriber base are now consumers, and 60 percent of new subscribers are consumers.
- RIM is strong in the area of user experience; our personal and business lives have blurred and business versus consumer marketing is no longer enough.
- The new BlackBerry Partners Fund and BlackBerry App World should boost development and create a booming marketplace for apps and solutions.
- RIM is constantly upgrading its product line, with the high-end Bold and the lower end Curves and Pearls getting new

features such as GPS and MP3, as well as regular radio upgrades and battery enhancements.

- RIM is moving into world markets where Nokia rules and offering retail pay-as-you-go options that are more attractive in developing countries.

- Corporate IT managers and CIOs are still loyal to RIM, and several major companies recently decided to pass on the iPhone, which they regard as a consumer or small business device. Many are wary of the iPhone because of perceived security issues and because RIM's enterprise tools make it easier to control corporate devices and write mission specific company software.

- RIM service is faster because e-mail sent through BES or BIS is encrypted and compressed on the BlackBerry before it is sent, allowing more data to be transferred using less bandwidth. Additionally, BES, and BIS in many ways, transcodes e-mail attachments so that they can be sent in much smaller form. Compression is important because network traffic is increasing while bandwidth is finite. One iPhone can use as much bandwidth as twenty BlackBerrys.

- Like Microsoft, RIM has a huge installed base of locked-in proprietary technology: BIS, BES, and NOC.

- Unlike other device manufacturers, RIM provides its own e-mail solutions package. Says Barry Richards, an analyst with Toronto-based Paradigm Capital, RIM's margin on the services business is upwards of 90 percent. "There's a decent net margin on the hardware side, but the service side is enormously profitable." Carriers pay RIM between $7 and $9 per customer every month for BlackBerry service, which gives RIM a steady income stream. Some carriers prefer to take advantage of a model where they remit to

RIM a percentage of sales, even if they do deep discount pricing.

- RIM financials remain stable, largely due to its lock on corporate e-mailing.

Even fans of Apple think it's terrific to have one elite company challenge the other. In the end, consumers all win from the explosion of creativity by the world's two greatest device makers.

5

BlackBerry Jam

"The BlackBerry solves the paradox of modern life. Until you use a BlackBerry, you just don't get it. You are connected for both the crisis and the opportunity. You can respond to your boss, but at the same time you have the freedom to walk to the corner store and get a cup of coffee."

—Mike Lazaridis

So, if smartphones like the BlackBerry are so wonderful, how come there is a growing chorus of complaints from the corporate choir?

Like its namesake fruit, the BlackBerry has a lot of delicious advantages for users. It's a sweet solution to the hunger for connection found in the modern world. Packed with technological antioxidants and flavenoids, it boosts the immune system of the enterprise, enabling workers to perform at their peak. And used in a focused way to do business in groups, it makes an excellent corporate spread.

But BlackBerry consumption has a downside. Some people have problems with dependence. Too much intake can lead to upset employees, who cannot stomach the demands placed on them to be available 24/7. Careless users can easily get entangled in the sharp brambles that surround the BlackBerry environment. You have to exercise extra caution when picking this fruit from a range of other devices on the shelf. And making jam with the BlackBerry can mark the user with stains that are very hard to remove.

✸   ✸   ✸

To be sure, RIM's BlackBerry is a kick-butt tool for productive people, but it is a whole lot more. It has altered our boundaries of work and play and permanently changed the way we behave. It has become an integral part of the modern office and in some cases is the heart of a new mobile office that is more virtual than real: Canadian mining promoter Robert Friedland says his BlackBerry investment has paid for itself many times over—he no longer operates from a fixed office, but keeps ahead of the game from his corporate jet and his BlackBerry, halfway between Toronto and Mongolia.

Productivity counts big when it boosts the bottom line. A 2007 Ipsos Reid survey for RIM claims the BlackBerry gives companies a major and measurable return on investment (ROI). The study looked at BlackBerry deployment across 1,387 IT departments and 1,335 BlackBerry users. It came up with these figures:

- **Personal Productivity**: The typical end user was converting sixty minutes of downtime into productive time per day.
  - This can equate to 250 hours per user per year in recovered downtime.
- **Workflow**: In addition to their own personal productivity, mobile staff use BlackBerry to keep work moving for others while they are out of the office. The average BlackBerry user reports that BlackBerry boosts the efficiency of the

teams that they work with by 38 percent, a marked increase over the 2004 average of 29 percent reported at that time.
  – This can equate to more than US$33,000 per BlackBerry user per year based on international productivity per employee data.
- **Immediacy**: The typical BlackBerry user processes 2,500 time-sensitive e-mails per year while mobile and more than 1,200 phone calls per year.
  – The value of this immediacy is difficult to quantify, but the study estimated the average user saves more than US$5,000 a year, thanks to having immediate access to and acting on BlackBerry-delivered info.

BlackBerry ROI varied by individual. The study calculated a minimum of 238 percent or a payback period of 154 days. This was up from 162 percent in 2004 because of the growing BlackBerry use among operations level staff who likely have more slack time to convert than executives. The higher the percentage of staff with BlackBerry, the more workflow economies.

A separate study also concluded that BlackBerry users tend to put in more hours than your average employee and earn higher salaries.

⊕　　⊕　　⊕

BlackBerrys are no longer executive perks or tech toys. Examples abound on the benefits of BlackBerrys in the modern office, even when that office flies at 30,000 feet. Australian airline QANTAS has 400 cabin staff toting the devices to replace paper-based customer service forms. Answers recorded on the BlackBerry are synchronized with computers after landing, and the data is downloaded. This kind of mobile technology can give rise to ROI periods measured in months.

Still, how do you build a business case for mobile solutions based on ROI modeling alone? You can look at the number of minutes of lost productivity recovered in a day as people use previously "dead" time between meetings or in transit to do useful things on their mobile devices.

But it's not about getting your people to work every minute of the day. How do you put a number value on the visibility, reach, and ease of contact provided by corporate e-mail? And what about the downsides, as ease of use means e-mail boxes grow increasingly clogged?

Mobile use is really about improving visibility and speed. Connected team members can act much more responsively in supporting one another on activities and decisions or when dealing with clients, partners, or subcontractors. It's far easier to do a quick review, confirm a decision, or snag a vital snippet of data.

The real value of mobile e-mail and apps is that they remove artificial delays, slash overhead, optimize resource use, and grease the wheels of trade by better client service and customer response.

⊕　　⊕　　⊕

Some academic and political critics claim that BlackBerry mobile use can have a damaging impact on work-life balance and harm family life. But as Carleton University business professor Linda Duxbury says, "Not all researchers paint a bleak picture with respect to the impact of mobile technology on work-life conflict. In fact, a substantive body of work can be identified which contends that the increased sense of control and flexibility offered by wireless devices helps employees integrate work and family domains."

The essence of smartphone use should be control, she says, and most employees use PDAs such as the BlackBerry to manage the work-life boundary by both integrating and segmenting work and personal life. If you use these devices properly, they can help you maintain flexibility and time at the same time as they give you an edge over your competition.

BlackBerry users are embracing the "anytime, anywhere connectivity that mobile devices enable, valuing the ability to better control the heavy demands of their jobs." The technology makes it easier for users to move between different locations and arrange more flexible working conditions—to "be distant as well as close." Users get more flexibility at business and professional levels as well as in family and personal life because they can multitask work with activities that require basic attention. For example, BlackBerry tech can permit easier "remote mothering," allowing families in the workforce to work "parallel" rather than double shifts to be able to drop or pick up children at school.

Of course, the BlackBerry can enhance corporate loyalty. The device can be an office umbilical cord and almost a membership badge. It can also give people an oasis of privacy in crowded situations and thereby diminishes stress. Look at people getting on an elevator. The second the door closes, everyone reaches for their BlackBerry.

"It always amazes me that security issues are not given an even higher priority."

—Mike Lazaridis

The tragedy of 9/11 first bought the BlackBerry into public consciousness as a device that could work under difficult conditions. But a major selling point for the device today is its NATO-grade security. One of the most security conscious organizations in the world, the U.S. government, is RIM's largest single customer. The FBI gives BlackBerrys to all its agents, although it does not let them use the devices to transmit classified information.

Uncle Sam cannot afford to be complacent: in 2007, U.S. government agencies reported 12,986 cyber security incidents to the Department of Homeland Security—triple the number from just two years earlier.

Apart from a few dedicated and expensive super-spy devices and systems, the BlackBerry is still the best there is, with end-to-end security. Since industrial and international espionage is a fact of life, particularly on the road, wireless warriors are far safer sending e-mails than making voice calls if they are discussing policy, sales numbers, patents, pricing, or a current mergers-and-acquisition bidding strategy.

BlackBerrys with sensitive data can also go missing. Proofpoint research found that 27 percent of U.S. companies investigated a data breach due to loss or theft of a mobile device. But RIM has bolted in a number of security features that minimize the danger of data loss.

So how does BlackBerry security work?

First, it's the NOC and BES systems. Before an e-mail arrives at your BlackBerry and passes through your corporate BlackBerry Enterprise Server or your provider's servers, it is compressed and then encrypted before it is sent. If you are using RIM's BlackBerry desktop redirector then it's compressed and encrypted before it leaves your local mail server. It's never de-encrypted mid-stream. If an e-mail is received on your BlackBerry, then the device handles de-encryption and decompression. All messages you compose on your BlackBerry are compressed and encrypted before leaving the device, and BES de-encrypts and decompresses them before they are passed through to the mail server for delivery to the addressee. BES also detects a growing range of events within your mailbox, like new messages arriving, deleting of messages and messages sent from your local desktop. These events are mirrored on the BlackBerry device to help the user keep track of the state of messages within their own mailbox.

Second, every time you send an e-mail out from your BlackBerry, it is compressed using standard AES-128 or Triple DES (AES-256 or elliptic-curve cryptography) that effectively encodes the message so that it can't be cracked by anyone else. A Canadian company called Certicom, recently acquired by RIM, provides the algorithms and encryption systems used in the BlackBerry service. They are deemed by the U.S. National Security Agency (NSA) as the best available for top-secret protection, and the NSA has licensed twenty-six of Certicom's elliptic curve cryptography (ECC) patents. The Fraunhofer Institute for Secure Information technology in Germany also gave a thumbs-up to the BlackBerry's use of cryptographic algorithms and life-cycle management of shared secrets or keys and passwords.

Third, inside an office or site, companies can add security features by using BlackBerry Smart Card Readers, which give users controlled access to BlackBerrys via Bluetooth and advanced AES-256 encryption.

Fourth, with the BlackBerry Enterprise Server, companies can enable remote kill of lost or stolen devices, since each BlackBerry device is assigned a unique eight-digit number called a personal identification number (PIN) that can be managed by the BES. Companies using the BES can also customize BlackBerry use to meet their internal security needs; for example, by disabling cameras or controlling access.

Finally, most users enable password protection on their devices. Once the device is locked, no one can get in without the correct password. By default, a BlackBerry allows ten password attempts before the device is wiped. Toward the final attempts, warning prompts are shown, and the user has to enter "blackberry" to proceed. The tenth password you enter is shown in extra clear text to make sure you have the highest chance of getting it right.

⊕　　⊕　　⊕

RIM's fussiness over security still satisfies all but the worst corporate paranoiacs, but this stance has sometimes tested the patience of national security services.

In June 2007, the French Secrétariat Général de la Défense Nationale (SGND) banned BlackBerry use by anyone in the president's or prime minister's offices on the basis of "a very real risk of interception" by third parties. The SGND argued that phone calls and e-mails routed through BlackBerry servers in the Canada and United Kingdom were too easy to intercept.

"It's not a problem if you're writing to your mother-in-law," said Deputy Pierre Lasbordes. But if a minister going to a G8 meeting "sends information to his colleagues and it goes via Canada and the United States ... that's it. Game over."

A confidential study carried out in 2005 by French functionary Alain Juillet, had concluded that the BlackBerry posed "a data security problem." Juillet said that "U.S. bankers would prove their bona fides in meetings by first placing their BlackBerry on the table and removing the batteries." In a fiercely competitive, global economy, governments and corporations covet information about what their rivals might be up to: "This is economic war."

French oil company Total had also banned the BlackBerry for "security reasons." "There are plenty of other perfectly good PDAs," the company said.[1]

RIM officials were quick to dismiss French fears, stressing that e-mails sent through its NOCs were more thoroughly encrypted than banking transactions over the Internet. But this did not satisfy the

---

1. Mark Solomons, "BlackBerry Ban for French Cabinet," *Financial Times*, June 19, 2007 < * >

French, who may have only themselves to blame. Says Cambridge University computer security expert Ross Anderson, the French originally opposed strong cryptographic algorithms on GSM cell phones, making them vulnerable to eavesdropping. "The delicious irony in this is that the A5 algorithms used to encrypt GSM traffic came from France and are now fairly easy to break. It was the French authorities who pressed harder than anyone for the strength of generally available cryptography to be limited during the 1990s."

Says Anderson, if the Echelon signals intelligence operation of the United States, United Kingdom, Australia, Canada, and New Zealand, which listens in on global wireless traffic, wants to hear what French ministers are saying on their BlackBerry, their electronics can break GSM keys "in under a minute."

Research In Motion is ahead of the game. According to RIM security chief Scott Totzke, BlackBerry e-mail is far harder to crack since it uses AES256, a stronger cryptographic algorithm than the A5 used for GSM voice calls.

The French ban may not work anyway. Paris newspaper *Le Monde* soon reported that French managers and heads of companies "cannot live without this jewel of technology." The paper quoted an unnamed member of the French cabinet: "They've tried to suggest to us something to replace the BlackBerry, but it doesn't work, and certain people are still using their BlackBerrys in secret."[2]

In India, for more than a year before the horrific Mumbai attacks, India's security services had also been lobbying against Research In Motion's mobile device. But unlike the French, they were claiming

---

2. Jacques Follorou, "La complainte du Blackberry dans les ministères," *Le Monde*, June 20, 2007 < * >

that criminals, militants, and terrorists could use BlackBerrys to send encrypted messages that passed through RIM NOCs, messages that the agencies could neither intercept, trace, nor decode. They suggested that RIM should be required to install servers in India proper to allow the security services to monitor and intercept traffic or else the devices should be outlawed.

RIM refused, and stuck to its guns, pointing out that they had designed the BlackBerry service to exclude any third party, including RIM themselves, from reading the encrypted transmissions. In June 2008, after meeting with RIM executives, the Indian Ministry of Telecommunications concluded that BlackBerry devices did not pose a security threat and that, therefore, it would not be closing down BlackBerry's service in the subcontinent.

The Mumbai attacks highlighted another growing problem for RIM, when several news reports used the term "BlackBerry-toting terrorists"—not good optics for a firm that prides itself on secure service to corporations.

However, the BlackBerry is being used effectively by soldiers fighting the war against terror in Iraq or Afghanistan. In the field, they can communicate silently and securely as they deploy across open ground or block to block in villages against enemy positions.

The fact remains that BlackBerrys have become just one part of the terrorist arsenal along with off-the-shelf satellite phones, GPS, VoIP, Google Earth, and other tools used in the Mumbai attacks. But this is already yesterday's terrorism. Future commercial tech will let terrorists use remote-control attack devices programmed via GPS and flown or driven into buildings.

RIM has certainly tightened up plant and manufacturing security. Wireless Internet tools have all security services concerned about the insertion of malicious code into electronic devices while they are being made. U.S. experts have already unearthed counterfeit hardware with backdoors that could be used to spy, detonate, or do other damage. Sites such as power plants or chemical factories now have to contend with potential infected firmware or software used in wired and wireless Internet devices.

⊕　　⊕　　⊕

Because BlackBerrys are so secure, and users feel so confident about communicating with the devices, they can often be careless about using all its features to secure personal or office data and passwords. So, modern secret agents clearly see BlackBerrys as targets for espionage stings.

In January 2008, a senior advisor to British Prime Minister Gordon Brown had his BlackBerry stolen by Chinese intelligence while on a trip to Shanghai. Apparently, the Downing Street aide fell victim to the world's oldest intelligence ploy, the "honeytrap." He was lured to the hotel disco by a glamorous secret agent and returned to his room with the woman. He sheepishly reported the loss of his BlackBerry to the Prime Minister's Special Branch protection team the next morning and was informally reprimanded.

The *Sunday Times* warned "that even if the aide's device did not contain anything top secret, it might enable a hostile intelligence service to hack into the Downing Street server, potentially gaining access to No 10's email traffic and text messages."

Even lost BlackBerrys pose an intelligence risk. White House Deputy Chief of Staff Karl Rove lost his device more than once. But stolen ones are also becoming common. In 2008, a Mexican press aide was caught taking BlackBerry devices belonging to White House staffers at New Orleans meetings between U.S. President George W. Bush and his Canadian and Mexican counterparts.

One of the main dangers here is that agents can temporarily steal the devices and install virtually undetectable software that can turn a BlackBerry into a mobile surveillance system. Originally designed to trap cheating spouses, the software lets a spy hear everything that the phone's mike can pick up, get copies of every e-mail sent and received, and preview data on the device—a single BlackBerry can store the equivalent of about 28,000 printed pages.

Phil Zimmermann is a fellow at the Stanford Law School's Center for Internet and Society, who created Pretty Good Privacy (PGP), the public-key encryption and authentication system, in 1991. He says that today's smartphones are programmable and are "increasingly vulnerable to attacks by injecting hostile software onto the device." If that code can gain control of your device, it can record your conversations and transmit them somewhere else. "You're being ratted out by the device in your pocket."

The stolen BlackBerrys in New Orleans were returned to their owners, presumably after the U.S. Secret Service gave them a full, bare-metal wipe.

Other risks come from selling used BlackBerrys that have not been properly erased. One company in Washington who bought a batch of used smartphones off eBay found that they contained data about corporate mergers and acquisitions, earnings announcements, product announcements, and even extramarital affairs, information that bad guys could use to exploit a company, the market, or an individual.

BES operators can easily deal with this kind of risk on the BlackBerry platform—they can erase all of the information on a BlackBerry remotely and then overwrite the data so that it is not recoverable.

Mobile police and cops on the beat are finding that BlackBerrys help them do their jobs better, and even save lives. Many victims of accidents and natural disasters who use the device are able to e-mail the police for help because data sent to and from BlackBerrys relies on servers and satellite networks different from the networks cell phones use.

Quick access to vital information can also mean the difference between life and death. The Seattle Police BlackBerry Program, which began in 2004, lets bike officers, who don't have access to an in-car computer, tap directly into the National Crime Information Center (NCIC), Washington Crime Information Center (WACIC), and Department of Corrections (DOC) databases, allowing officers to pull up records within five to ten seconds. Before this, officers had to radio in to the dispatcher in the 911 center and wait up to five to ten minutes for a response depending on how busy the dispatcher was. The BlackBerrys allow the officers and detectives to be much more proactive, while also cutting down requests to the 911 center by hundreds of hours. Since the program began, police in the field have run more than 35,000 queries.

In Britain, Tony McNulty, minister for policing, says the country is investing £50 million to deliver 10,000 mobile data devices to forces. "It is just one element of a range of improvements that we are delivering to cut unnecessary bureaucracy, exploit new technologies and enable police officers to spend more time on front line policing."

The East Midlands police forces have just invested £8.3 million from the fund in 4,000 BlackBerrys and vehicle-mounted computers. One suspect caught in Nottingham surrendered immediately when the officer called dispatch and got them to send a picture that matched his description.

In 2009, the officers on the beat were given direct access to driving license records. Richard Hitch, project manager for mobile systems, says, "Before, officers were radioing in name checks and getting the control room to run police national computer checks. Now those with BlackBerrys can do that themselves."

Nottingham desk sergeants are using the devices to issue missing persons alerts. They can also decide, based on GPS and images
from the field, whether a site needs evacuation or roadblocks.[3]

The Thames Valley Police are also supplying BlackBerrys to police officers and community support officers (PCSOs). The devices
will combine their phones, e-mail, and calendar and give officers
access to Britain's police national computer (PNC) system.

⊕   ⊕   ⊕

*"The indicator of a good speaker is how many BlackBerrys
are out. When you see half-a-dozen BlackBerrys come out,
it's time to end the meeting."*
— *Kim Nelson, CIO, U.S. Environmental
Protection Agency*

Many managers adopting BlackBerrys find unexpected benefits in
the day-to-day use of the device:

- When an employee leaves the office for vacation or
  business travel, there is no longer much need to designate a
  colleague to take over. The BlackBerry reduces the need for
  extensive backup.
- BlackBerry users make better use of their time away from the
  office, and they get a heads-up on what's happening so they're
  not hit by a tidal wave of information when they return.
- Employees can respond to e-mails anywhere in the world
  while on the go; they can also update their schedules using
  the calendar function, eliminating the need to call back and
  forth to a secretary.

---

3. Guy Woodford, "BlackBerry Cops Taking the Fight to Notts Criminals," This is Nottingham,
   Dec. 27, 2008 < * >

- BlackBerry e-mailing and messaging are perfect for quiet and secure interpersonal communications when you don't want to use your phone in a public place.
- Managers can approve travel vouchers and purchases directly on their BlackBerrys.
- Laptops can sometimes be left at home for business trips.
- Replacing printed materials with wireless Internet and e-mail can save offices thousands of dollars a year in paper and recycling costs.

BlackBerrys also have another, less publicized function: they provide a way to pass the time, even during dull meetings or endless presentations.

⊕   ⊕   ⊕

BlackBerrys have become not just time savers but life enhancers as well. Now, it's been shown that older users of BlackBerrys and other smartphones can save brain cells as well. A UCLA study, published in *The American Journal of Geriatric Psychiatry*, suggests that searching the Web helps stimulate and improve brain function.

In its 2008 study of twenty-four healthy people between the ages of fifty-five and seventy-six, UCLA's Memory and Aging Research Center found all participants showed the same brain activity when asked to read a book, but the group who were Web-savvy also registered activity in areas of the brain that control decision-making and complex reasoning. "Our most striking finding was that Internet searching appears to engage a greater extent of neural circuitry that is not activated during reading— but only in those with prior Internet experience," said principal investigator Dr. Gary Small. "The study results are encouraging that emerging computerized technologies may have physiological effects and potential benefits for middle-aged and older adults."[4]

More and more people realize the benefits of quick and convenient Web access and what are called Work Extending Technologies (WETs). In a 2004 survey, Ian Towers and Linda Duxbury found that 95 percent of office workers they interviewed said they would keep their WETs, 50 percent would upgrade, and 33 percent wanted to get a BlackBerry.

Using BlackBerrys can stimulate our minds and help us solve problems, but there is a growing body of people who argue that the use of e-mail, Web search, blogging, twittering, social networking, and so on can actually do the opposite.

Some psychologists say that office e-mail is driving us to distraction. In his *Atlantic* magazine article, "Is Google Making Us Stupid?" Nicholas Carr suggests that we are drowning in data and distracted by an ocean of facts. With powerful Google search at our fingertips, the Web is doing our thinking for us and flattening our intelligence.

So what are the downsides of BlackBerry use, and can we learn to cope with the mobile power it provides us?

"Well, it is addictive and on Wall Street they call it CrackBerry for exactly that reason. Once you try it you can't live without it, so they say."
                                        —Geoff Colvin, RIM CFO, 2000

---

4. Gary Small, *iBrain: Surviving the Technological Alteration of the Modern Mind* (New York: HarperCollins, 2008).

The ubiquity of the BlackBerry in the business world and the compulsive use of its quick e-mail service has earned it the nickname CrackBerry. The term may have been coined by Dr. Paul Levy, president of Boston Medical Center. He confesses to being "a recovering BlackBerry addict" himself.[5]

Ten years after the birth of the device, CIO.com asked David Placek, originator of the BlackBerry name, to comment on the *CrackBerry* word and whether he saw that one coming. Placek said, "No, we didn't. In a way, it's just a measure of the popularity and the addiction of the machine. We've talked with RIM about that. I think it's just a harmless thing, and I'd take this just as a compliment. If it was a losing product, it wouldn't have a nickname like that."[6]

"There is a difference between addiction and attachment."
—*Robin Bienfait, RIM CIO*

For some people, BlackBerry dependence can develop into a problem, and not one to take lightly, particularly if your career revolves around being connected all the time. ABC News Washington reporter Rick Klein didn't know how badly he was wired until a BlackBerry blackout at 3:30 p.m. on February 11, 2008, which was caused by a glitch during a RIM software upgrade. Klein was riding home from work on the Metrorail when the outage hit. It was to last more than three hours, but for Klein the half-hour he was on the train without e-mail was torture. It was the day before the Potomac primary, and he had been dealing with hundreds of e-mails all day for his blog, The Note.

5. Columbus Business First (Jan. 4, 2008)
6. Thomas Walgom, Meet Tech's Product Name Guru, The Industry Standard < * >

Klein said, "It was like being underwater without an oxygen tank. It felt like every minute was an hour." Klein finally made it to his home PC, but the damage was done, and he had missed a story contact. "It couldn't have come at a worse time for me, but I think it was just an occasional problem. I'm too wedded to the technology at this point to change."[7]

So how did we arrive at this state of affairs, where a networking platform designed to help people be more productive can turn into something akin to drug addiction?

Engineers such as Mike Lazaridis are by their nature optimistic and forward-looking about technology. Most believe you can solve problems and generate progress over time if you pose the right questions and use the right tools. And engineers love to make tools that free people from wasting time on mundane tasks—the BlackBerry is a perfect example of such a tool. But other scientists see the rise of technology as an affront against nature and the natural ways of doing things.

This is an old, old fear. Socrates believed that writing would interfere with our ability to think. Critics of the printing press bemoaned the fact that thousands of scribes were put out of work. Forty years ago, Hewlett Packard's new HP-35 scientific calculator was banned from classrooms when professors feared that engineers would use the handheld as a crutch and lose the skills to do penciled calculations or use a slide rule.

Today the BlackBerry and other mobile devices are generating the same fears. Many people worry that the BlackBerry—the iconic symbol of our always-on society—is to blame for many modern ills.

So what is the truth? Does BlackBerry use lead to social problems? Is RIM responsible for unleashing a new plague on the

---

7. Cecilia Kang, BlackBerry Blackout Strands Users, Washington Post, February 12, 2008

world? Or are we blaming the BlackBerry for digital addiction the same way we blame murder on guns and knives.

⊕ ⊕ ⊕

It's increasingly clear that BlackBerrys can be dangerous in the wrong hands.

RIM's instant real-time communication ecosystem makes people who have power or crave power dangerous to others. Even ordinary managers can get intoxicated with devices that give them more power, and they can lose perspective on that power. Instead of letting their employees make decisions on their own, they micromanage them and expect immediate responses. They wait anxiously to respond 24/7 to even the most trivial of requests.

And while RIM propaganda trumpets the finding that BlackBerry use can turn an hour of "downtime" into working time each day, other research on workplace interruption suggests that being wired is making us less effective, not more. One study, based on observing workers at two U.S. high-tech firms, found that people interrupted in the middle of a task took an average of twenty-five minutes to return to it—if, indeed, they returned to it at all.

In certain work-life situations (for example, in an office with a "toxic boss" who demands 24/7 availability), the benefits of BlackBerry e-mailing are seriously overweighed by the downsides. Some consultants are warning corporations to gird themselves for potentially costly lawsuits from employees claiming they are addicted to CrackBerrys.

Yes, all is not rosy in office land. As Carleton University business professor Linda Duxbury and her team found, for many people, mobile technologies are causing severe stresses and strains. Here are a few salient comments from the almost 30,000 people she and her colleagues interviewed:

- "Corporate objectives and expectations continue to increase faster than the resources allocated to support the expected growth. The result is that you must work longer hours to do the same job as the year before."
- "We have fewer people to do the same jobs, but jobs have also changed due to technology. We are constantly revving the engine and if not enough oil gets on the pistons, the engine blows up."
- "E-mail is widely used as the primary method of communication with employees at all levels; however, there is a universal expectation that everyone reads, clears and responds to all e-mails on a daily basis, actually a constant basis. This is unrealistic. Memos sent in late afternoon are expected to be read by morning for discussion. This is unreasonable."
- "Technology has had a major impact on workload. It is not unusual to receive 40 to 50 e-mails per day, most of which require either a response or some actions."
- "Everyone needs to understand that communications need to be managed, time must be allowed to read, understand and be able to respond. We waste time on computers and software due to an inability to plan and to set priorities."
- "The amount of work, regardless of organization, has increased dramatically in the last decade, mainly due to the increased use of technology. With today's technology, we can have someone in our office, an incoming phone call, voice mails and e-mails—all of which we are supposed to respond to at once. Technology has added the expectation of immediate response—and solutions—to the workplace."

- "Job sharing, compressed work weeks, and working at home just don't appear to be options in our area, although they could be with today's technology."*

⊕　　⊕　　⊕

"In our increasingly wired world, most of us live in a state of shattered concentration, so distracted that we don't even notice how much we don't understand."

—*Tina Brown*

Office workers were formerly deluged with paper. Now the deluge is a rain of data, from bosses, clients, co workers, and family.

The BlackBerry was designed as a tool to help people make more productive use of digital data, but critics say it can become a crutch that causes distraction and destroys productivity. It can save us time, but it can also cause us to waste time. This is because the BlackBerry is now far more than an e-mailer. It is now a Web browser, music and video player, and a game machine in your pocket. So instead of using a BlackBerry to break our e-mail logjam, we play BrickBreaker to escape it.

So how can we better manage the deluge and the damage? Experts say the best modern organizations have leaders who set clear objectives and expectations. They give employees the space and the resources to get the job done. But in offices where BlackBerry addiction happens or is tolerated, frustration grows between managers and employees. Many people get distracted with too much trivial to and fro. They feel compelled to check new messages the instant they arrive and to answer immediately or they will let down the team or lose their chance at promotion. They exist in a state of hazy semi-focus, and don't have time to think or to be productive.

---

* Voices of Canadians; Duxbury et al

Says software executive Linda Stone, being connected electronically "makes us feel alive and important." But the mantra of "connect, connect, connect has brought us to a place where we feel overwhelmed, overstimulated, and unfulfilled."

In the years to come, before the workplace learns how to cope, this double-edged device mania may cut deeper. As we pack more and more lifestyle applications on our smartphones, the proportion of time-wasters to time-savers will grow. So the great time-saving devices promoted by RIM, Nokia, Apple, and Google risk becoming time-sucking machines from hell.

⊕　　⊕　　⊕

"As our attentional skills are squandered, we are plunging into a culture of mistrust, skimming and a dehumanising merger between man and machine."
—*Maggie Jackson, Distracted: The Erosion of Attention and the Coming Dark Age*

BlackBerry Planet has its own growing slate of physical and mental ailments caused by improper or inappropriate use of the device.

BlackBerrys and other messaging devices are being blamed for minor bodily maladies such as Tech Neck and BlackBerry Thumb. But the real dangers come from BlackBerry Distraction, the state of being enthralled by your e-mail and messaging, a state that can lead to mental breakdown and even loss of life.

This is the age of distraction. One study says the average American knowledge worker is interrupted 2.1 hours every day. Others estimate this lost concentration is costing the U.S. economy almost $600 billion a year in lost work time. But all these interruptions have an even darker side.

The greatest physical risks of BlackBerry Distraction relate to multitasking and multitexting. Multitexting means being able to send text messages and do other things at the same time. Like walking around or driving a car. In mid-2008, the American College of Emergency Physicians issued a warning to multitexters that they were endangering their own lives and those around them.

Most injuries involve scrapes, cuts, and sprains, suffered when text-walkers collide with walls, hot dog vendors, lampposts, or innocent civilians or trip over sidewalk cracks or curbs. It's hilarious in some ways, and we all laugh at the pompous person tripping on a banana peel. It's classic Keystone Kops comedy. But bones can be broken, and real human suffering can ensue. It happened to Senator Barack Obama's advisor Valerie Jarrett, who fell off a Chicago curb while happily thumbing away on her BlackBerry. "I didn't see the sidewalk," she wailed, "and I twisted my ankle."

Jarrett was one of the lucky texters. Emergency room doctors are reporting a growing number of pedestrians struck and killed in the line of duty, crossing the street while replying to an urgent message from home base or the office. Cyclists, in-line skaters, and motorists are also not immune from this growing danger, not confined to the BlackBerry but common to all texting devices. But as usual, the jackal pack that is the lifestyle press blames the BlackBerry for the crime.

Many concerned citizens are stepping up to the plate and rescuing those poor wandering souls consumed by irrational texting. Ben Martin, executive assistant to Canadian Member of Parliament Pat Davidson, tells of walking to work one beautiful day:

"All around me were other people hustling and bustling to get to work, morning lattes in hand. One particular gentleman, I noticed, was precariously balancing not only his morning coffee, but a briefcase and a BlackBerry to boot!"

"Despite his obvious struggle with the load he was carrying, nonetheless he fearlessly checked his inbox while walking through the sea of people toward a busy intersection."

"To my fright, he was about to walk right across the intersection, despite the red light, as he was fixated on his CrackBerry fix .... Only when he was two feet from the curb did I notice the bus oncoming."

"I desperately lunged at the man, grabbing him from behind on both shoulders and pulling him away from the fatal step he was about to take in to the street."

"His only response other than a frantic thank you for saving him?"

"'Geez, these damn CrackBerrys, eh?'"

"'Yes, sir. Those damn CrackBerrys ...'"

＊ ＊ ＊

Many digital zombies engage in dangerous behaviors while driving. This problem is spreading around the planet, and media in England, Australia, New Zealand, Malaysia, and Switzerland are reporting a rash of deaths from text-distracted drivers hitting cyclists or pedestrians.

One driver in San Jose, California, saw one driving through heavy traffic with his BlackBerry attached to his ear with a large rubber band. Another in Mumbai, India, filmed a motorcyclist happily texting away on his way to work, leaning back in his seat and driving with no hands.

Says Dr. Patrick Walsh, an emergency physician in Bakersfield, California, "We think we're multi-tasking, but we're not. You're focusing on one task for a split second, then focusing on another one, and with something moving at 40 mph like a car, it just takes a couple of seconds to be hit."[8]

Talking on your phone or looking at your GPS is bad enough. But texting while driving? You're dicing with death, and threatening the lives of your fellow creatures, and it's time you unplugged yourself.

David Meyer, professor of psychology at the University of Michigan, is a specialist in attention disorders and knows all about the dangers of distraction. In 1995, his son was killed by a distracted driver who ran a red light.

Meyer says how we focus on one thing rather than another is how we survive and define ourselves. The opposite of attention—distraction—he sees as an unnatural condition. He argues that chronic, long-term distraction is as bad for the health as smoking.

Multitasking is seen as some kind of office ideal, but multitaskers are fooling themselves, says Meyer. There is no way a human can effectively write an e-mail and speak on the phone at the same time—the language channel in the brain just can't cope. By rapidly switching attention over time, a person's work output deteriorates.

Meyer says talking on a mobile phone while driving—even legally with a hands-free kit—is the same. As you listen to language on the phone, you lose the ability to read the language of road signs. And if your caller describes something visual, it gets worse, because as you picture what your caller says, your visual channel gets clogged and you start losing your sense of the road ahead.

"For tasks that are at all complicated, no matter how good you have become at multitasking, you're still going to suffer hits against

---

8. Lindsey Tanner , "Emergency-room doctors: Don't text and walk, skate or cook", Associated Press, July 31, 2008

your performance. You will be worse compared to if you were actually concentrating from start to finish on the task," Meyer says.

Multitasking causes a kind of brownout in the brain, he says. All the lights go dim because there isn't enough power to go around, and the brain starts shutting down neural connections to other information. He gives an example of a teenager named Alex doing his homework who is interrupted by a text message. As Alex replies, his brain starts losing the connections it was using for his French history report. The pathway to Napoleon fades quickly, and Alex will have to repeat much of the thought process that created it in the first place when he goes back to his homework and tries to take up where he left off.[9]

With manic multitasking and work interruptions, some ordinary BlackBerry users are now experiencing chronic distraction and the same kinds of symptoms as burnt-out air traffic controllers. Chronic distraction kills you more slowly, says Meyer. People in chronically distracted jobs might get stress-related diseases, even irreversible brain damage.[10]

People known as PDDs (Personal Digital Dopes) are a subset of hard-core BlackBerry users. These individuals are regarded as ill mannered by most of the rest of the planet. You probably know PDDs who check their BlackBerry under the table when you are sitting beside them at dinner. They are clearly signaling they'd like to be somewhere else, like back at the office. But, maybe, life is their office.

Strange to say, most PDDs don't think they are being rude; it's just that they are super-busy. They justify their behavior by

---

9. Jon Hamilton, "Multitasking Teens May Be Muddling Their Brains", NPR, Oct.9, 2008
10. Brian Appleyard, "Stoooopid .... why the Google generation isn't as smart as it thinks," Times Online July 20, 2008

telling people that they would *never* answer a cell phone in public because it interferes with other people. Now *that* would be rude.

For this subset of mobile maniacs, rudeness is irrelevant. They are perfectly capable of multitasking, and working on their e-mail while they are talking to you. Why get upset? they think. It just gets in the way of work.

These people much prefer the company of other PDDs, because if everybody is rude, then nobody is rude. They're not offended if somebody breaks off to check and even answer a message. Life with BlackBerry goes on, and if you don't get it, that's your problem.

People thumb-dancing with their BlackBerrys during business meetings is the worst faux pas.

"It's extraordinarily rude," says Debbie Fiorito, president of Houston-based 20K Group, a communications strategy and consulting firm. "The worst offenders are investment bankers and hedge fund managers—the deal makers. They can't put it down." She says this kind of behavior "sends the message that my business is so much more important than what I'm hearing in this meeting."

Strange to say, these people don't think they're being rude at all. "They think they can multitask and listen and text at same time. But it's not true," she said.

Fiorito coaches her clients to lay out the rules in advance and say something like: "I realize you may have to go out and take a call, but I'd appreciate it if you wouldn't use your BlackBerry or text while I'm speaking."[11]

BlackBerry use can also enable boorish behaviour, and people who generally behave badly and bully others are much worse when toting their BlackBerrys. For example, the British yacht broker in Portsmouth who kicked and punched a builder who threw

---

11. Richard Roth, "BlackBerry users want payment for overtime use." CNN 6/20/2008

his BlackBerry into a pint of beer. Or actress Reese Witherspoon, who allegedly attacked her assistant with a bejeweled BlackBerry.

Supermarket tabloid writers love to fabricate serial sagas about rash behavior by angry celebrities. Over the past year, the tabs featured several reports about BlackBerry enabled divorces. One story had Britney Spears checking her spouse's BlackBerry, finding amorous e-mails, and then filing for divorce. Another had Tori Spelling using her BlackBerry to serve notice to her spouse that she was filing divorce papers.

Of all the pathetic behavior associated with BlackBerry use, surely texting in church is the worst example, and a major highway to hell. The media deems such behavior noteworthy, especially on slow news days. For example, a recent AOL Survey found that 15 percent of people interviewed had used their handhelds in church (up from 12 percent last year). On June 11, 2004, Vice President Dick Cheney's daughter Liz was spotted messaging on her BlackBerry during Ronald Reagan's funeral at the National Cathedral. In Canada, one woman was even caught tapping on a BlackBerry during her daughter's wedding.

According to AOL, the other top times for texting are:

- on a date: 25 percent
- during happy hour: 34 percent
- in a business meeting: 38 percent
- in a bar or club: 39 percent
- while driving: 50 percent (up from 37 percent last year)

and the favorite location of all,

- in the bathroom: 59 percent (up from 53 percent last year).

By the way, here's how to save your BlackBerry if you drop it in the toilet.

- Open it and remove the battery and memory card and SIM card if possible.
- Wrap your BlackBerry in a dry washcloth and aluminum foil.
- Bake it in the oven for several hours at the lowest setting. Apparently the foil and washcloth insulate it, and the cloth sucks in the moisture.
- Put back the battery and cards and see if it works.

If it goes crazy and starts dialing random phonebook entries or emergency services, you're out of luck. Get a new one.

The BlackBerry is a perfect enabling device for the narcissist, who simply knows that he or she is the most important person living in that time in that place on this planet. All external living things and objects, except other BlackBerry narcissists who keep their distance, are simply annoyances.

You'll find these people on the road, usually in an SUV, endangering everybody else around them. However, the most evil of this tribe, with a special place reserved in hell, are the ones who light up in movie houses or theaters.

What's the fuss? Well, try sitting behind one of these little Gollums when you're trying to enjoy the show. You hear a gentle *clickety-click* as their thumbs fly over the keys and an annoyingly dull glow lights up your peripheral vision. But the worst is the flash that comes when they have successfully sent or received a precious e-mail or "LOL" message.

Concertgoers are warned to turn off their cell phones during performances. Why is this edict not being extended to FZX$&KQG texters?

Many of us are concerned with the lack of civility we see all around. In some toxic offices, politeness is a sign of weakness. Civility is redundant. The squeaky wheel gets the grease and the promotion. Everybody checks their BlackBerry at any time, so what's the big deal?

Out on the street, you'll find more incivility. Digital zombies abound, taking up space as they talk or text in doorways or stairs, on sidewalks, or on the walking side of the escalator. Nothing can budge them as they teletransport into home base, completely oblivious to others.

Theories abound about technology and the decline of modern manners. Some say it's because we live in a more self-centered world, and BlackBerrys are part of the problem. Others say it's because we are now surrounded by new generations who were raised to believe in their own self-esteem. Parents protected their little ones from feelings of guilt and shame and loss. They end up as narcissists, who see the needs of others as only a distant concern.

🌐 🌐 🌐

There is something pathetic and yet so modern in people taking their BlackBerry on vacation and then being sucked into viewing the screen while the ocean's waves are beautifully slapping on the shore. This kind of behavior can grow until the user loses all perspective and the BlackBerry ultimately becomes an object of worship, indeed a magically charged talisman. How else are we to explain these comments on the CrackBerry.com weblog:

- "This is my BlackBerry. There are many like it but this one is mine. My BlackBerry is my best friend. It is my life. I must master it as I must master my life. Without me,

my BlackBerry is useless. Without my BlackBerry I am
useless."—alan8385
- "My BlackBerry is a lifeline to love, work, knowledge, friendship and experience. Who wouldn't be
addicted?"—anonymous

Have these people no life, that they can invest their devices
with near-magical powers? Magical thinking related to objects is
nothing new, but this kind of device worship is a frightening form
of mental disability.

⊕　　⊕　　⊕

More and more wired-up workers are fed up with always-on culture,
and want to stop the insanity. So, it's no wonder that a backlash
against smartphones such as the BlackBerry has been growing
in offices around the planet. Many employees are exhausted by
BlackBerry-enabled multitasking. Workers can't escape or unwind.
They feel there is an unwritten team rule that they must always be
available. Others are afflicted by the demands of toxic bosses, or
harassed by co-workers who copy them constantly with the most
mundane e-mails.

"Some people they feel like they're missing out on something.
I think for others there really is a genuine fear that they'll appear
not to be a team player," life coach Valorie Burton said.*

Some workers are fighting back, and there is a growing field
of litigation on requiring employees to use their BlackBerrys outside of work hours without pay. In 2008, writers and producers
at ABC News negotiated a settlement for after-work BlackBerry
usage.

------
* Valorie Burton Interview, CNN 6/21/2008

But most of the backlash against BlackBerrys is, in fact, coming from the home front, as BlackBerry dependence and addiction are starting to take a large toll on family life and relationships.

⊕　　⊕　　⊕

"Technology does things for us, but also to us, to our ways of perceiving the world, to our relationships and sense of ourselves."

—Sherry Turkel

Technology is changing how we relate and the ways we behave, and it's doing so faster than many thought possible. According to a recent America Online poll, 41 percent of adults check their e-mail first thing in the morning, even before they brush their teeth. A recent Pew Internet Project poll says that families are now using cell phones, wireless messaging, and Internet access to create a "new connectedness."

Technology is now a central feature of the day-to-day lives of busy families. They are less likely to share meals together but compensate by staying connected and sharing Web experiences. Sure, tech can blur traditional lines between "work" and "home" and make it harder to put aside time for hobbies or relaxing. But most people say technology actually makes family life closer than when they were growing up. For one thing, they spend less time watching TV.[12]

Another Pew poll says that most people who own BlackBerrys never really stop working. Seventy-one percent of people who own BlackBerrys say the device has increased their flexibility. Regarding use outside the office and at home or on vacation:

- 70 percent of smartphone owners check work-related e-mails on the weekend.

---

12. Pew Internet and American Life Project

- 40 percent do so often.
- 55 percent check work-related email on vacation.
- 25 percent do it often.
- 70 percent check work-related email when they're taking a sick day and most regularly check in before going into the office and again when they get home at night.
- 43 percent check work-related email when they're shopping or commuting.
- 48 percent say they are required to read and respond to e-mail when they are away from work.

The problem with BlackBerrys in the family lies with stress related to maintaining a work-life division: almost half the people interviewed by Pew said smartphone technology had made their lives more stressful.

          ⊕   ⊕   ⊕

"There are a lot of brownie points you have to make up every time there's a phone call at home from each other. You get this look when they hand you the phone and say, It's Jim. We developed BlackBerry just to deal with that situation—so we could keep talking without our wives giving us a hard time."

—Mike Lazaridis

Mike Lazaridis fully admits that his invention can upset family relations or cause marital tensions if people get too attached to their BlackBerry or don't act in respectful ways to spouses and children. But originally things were different, and the telephone was the culprit. In a November 2007 TV interview, he recalled:

In those early days we both had young children and we'd go home but the workday wouldn't end. We'd be on the phone to each other constantly and there were times when our wives would say, "Why do you even come home? Stay at work, keep talking, and come home when you're done." It even got to the point where I bought secure phones for Jim and I. We were starting to use cordless phones so we could spend more time with the kids and play with the kids and not be tethered back with a wire, but of course those phones weren't very secure. So we bought secure cordless phones.

Meanwhile, said Lazaridis, new technologies such as push e-mail and instant messaging were coming on the scene. It struck him and Jim Balsillie that these innovations were going to finally free them from being on the phone all night when they should be playing with their kids. They started taking the prototypes home and found they could type messages back and forth without annoying their families with phone calls.

"When you're doing that, you're realizing, 'Gosh, as the world becomes more competitive and people become more ambitious and they spend more and more time working to stay on top of their game and be more successful, wouldn't it be nice if they could stay on top of that data and not go to work the next day to a mountain of e-mail and still be able to go home and move around and go to kids' baseball games and spend time with them in a non-obtrusive way?' That was something we had glimmers of. I don't think we had anywhere near the idea that it would become as big of a hit as it is today and what it's turning into."[*]

Admittedly, if families hate you being on the phone all the time, and if separating home and work life is not always possible, then using a BlackBerry can help keep your work contacts

* CBC Interview Peter Nowak, CBC News, November 21, 2007

relatively covert. But today's BlackBerrys also have phones. Today Mike Lazaridis sees the irony in having a work tool that originally promoted domestic bliss now contributing to family disharmony in its own way. He admits to taking a holiday "occasionally" but says there are fewer and fewer places to go that don't have BlackBerry coverage. "It's good for me," he smiles. "My wife doesn't like it."*

When told about a birthing mother who complained in *The Wall Street Journal* that her husband was tapping on his BlackBerry while she was pushing their child into the world, Lazaridis concedes, "There is a time and a place," yet he ignores his "only while sleeping."[13]

Today, work and family are not "separate spheres" but are interdependent domains or roles with "permeable" boundaries. The BlackBerry has played a major role in changing the rules.

Research on electronic workplace interruptions suggests that connectedness is making us less effective at work. Apparently, the syndrome is following office workers home:

U.S. psychiatrist Edward Hallowell sees the problem as the "attention deficit trait" and feels it affects home life. "A patient asked me whether I thought it was abnormal that her husband brings the BlackBerry to bed and lays it next to them while they make love," he told *Time* magazine.

In the worst cases, intimacy becomes a chore. Now if you're a busy professional neglecting your personal life, and you can't tear yourself away from your beloved e-mail to share time with your spouse, you can now send flowers by BlackBerry using

---

* Interview with Josephine Moulds, Daily Telegraph, 2007/10/23
13. Erin Anderssen, Mike Lazaridis, 2002; Globe and Mail Nov. 18, 2008

1-800-Flowers.com. As CEO Jim McCann says, his company's target audience are "affluent, thoughtful people who have a need to express themselves."

On the other hand, when you are away on a business trip, the BlackBerry lets you keep in touch with home base. A survey of 6,500 professionals done for Sheraton Hotels says 85 percent of business travelers say they sneak a quick peek at their smartphones if they wake in the middle of the night, and 80 percent check their e-mail before morning coffee. Sheraton also found that 81 percent say they're working harder now than five years ago, and many are enjoying it.

Unfortunately, 35 percent of those surveyed said if forced to choose, they'd stick with their PDA over their spouse. A horrifying 62 percent said they love their little high-tech companions. Ah, the romance.

⊕　　⊕　　⊕

Teen mobile Internet use is rising, and with it Internet addiction. In South Korea, the most wired nation on the planet, there are "PC bang" Internet cafés on nearly every street corner. Parents who want to rescue their Web-addled kids can send them to the Jump Up Internet Rescue School, which uses obstacle courses, calisthenics, group therapy, and even pottery and drumming workshops to cure teens used to spending seventeen hours a day playing online games.

Texting is also a big problem with the young and connected because it makes already distracted teens more so.

Young people going into the workforce have to be taught the do's and don't's of texting at work because most companies have no tolerance for poor texting etiquette.

Randall Morton, president of the civic speaker organization Progressive Forum, tells a story about having a nice conversation with his son in the car when suddenly his son got a text message and started texting back. All of a sudden it was a one-sided conversation because the kid was lost in his electronic message. Then one day Morton's son was at a dance, and his girl got buzzed and started to text a friend right in the middle of the dance floor. He told his father he couldn't believe it. "See, that's how I felt," he replied to his son.

⊕　⊕　⊕

New technology has radically changed the world of work over the past fifteen years, and none more than the BlackBerry.

Some WET experts feel that managers are giving BlackBerrys to employees without thinking about the effects of always-on mobile in the workplace. BlackBerrys are far more intrusive than cell phones because it is more socially acceptable to send e-mail messages during meetings or after work than to call someone.

It's also clear that peer pressure and expectations from above often make it difficult for employees to set limits about work intruding into personal life. At home, some husbands and wives complain that when their spouses have their BlackBerrys with them, there is always an obsessive edge, and it often feels like somebody else is in the room. In many cases, relaxation and time spent with children suffer when BlackBerrys come home.

The boundary between work and life divides two different domains of activity: the workplace and the home. But BlackBerry use is now helping to blur the typical differences between work and non-work spaces by boosting the number of micro-transitions between work and non-work domains. The boundary between work and life becomes more porous, and transiting between work and family gets a lot easier.

BlackBerry use can also erode time by letting companies dictate a 24/7 expectation, with "electronic leashes" on employees.

While a BlackBerry can let an employee respond almost instantly to a request, it can also require the user to disengage from whatever else they are currently doing. This causes real problems in people who get easily distracted, or who can't manage the work/life boundary by turning off their device or not answering business calls or e-mails.

Linda Duxbury of Carleton University and Chris Higgins of the University of Western Ontario are publishing new evidence from a massive study on how people are using BlackBerrys and other PDAs and the impact of smartphones on workload. The team interviewed more than 100,000 WET-using Canadians and their families from 2006 to 2008.

Originally, Duxbury, Higgins, and colleagues set out to answer the following questions:

- How much use do knowledge workers (i.e., managers, professionals, technical workers) make of the following types of technology: cell phones, laptops, home computers (with and without access to e-mail), BlackBerrys, and PDAs?
- How do employees use these different types of technology?
- What are the perceived advantages and disadvantages (for the employer, the employee, the family) of using WET?
- How can employees and employers manage the use of WET so as to enhance the usefulness/reduce the challenges associated with the use of these technologies?

In 2007, the team started focusing on the BlackBerry almost exclusively and zeroed in on the following work/life boundary issues:

- Why and how do employees use mobile technologies including BlackBerry devices?

- What advantages and disadvantages do mobile technology/BlackBerry users perceive that the use of such technology offers them in their personal and professional lives?
- What impact does the adoption of mobile technology / BlackBerry devices have on:
  * The demands employees face at work and at home?
  * Perceived control of the work-life interface?
  * Work-life balance and employee well-being
- What impact does the use of mobile technology have on the work-life boundary?

After digesting the data from this very large and long-term longitudinal survey, the Duxbury-Higgins team came up with the following findings:

- 25 percent used their BlackBerry devices to schedule appointments and meetings
- 23.3 percent sent short e-mails to colleagues or clients
- 23.3 percent read/checked their e-mail
- 23.3 percent made contact with their customers
- 19 percent checked for and answered urgent questions
- 19 percent kept on top of e-mails, and
- 13.3 percent sent reports or presentations.

Half the respondents said they used their BlackBerry when traveling on business, just under 50 percent used their BlackBerry to work at home (telework and supplemental work at home), and 25 percent said that they used their device "everywhere." Also,

- 37 percent checked their BlackBerry occasionally.
- 37 percent checked their BlackBerry frequently.

- 26 percent said they checked their BlackBerry only when they were traveling/away from the office, but then used the device constantly.
- 10 percent said they checked their BlackBerry constantly (more than twenty times per day).

Respondents said they handled an average of 24.7 BlackBerry messages per day.

BlackBerry benefits are clearly skewed toward work. While having a BlackBerry can ease the workload, it benefits the family only occasionally, such as during a crisis or while traveling.

While almost all new users interviewed felt their use of the BlackBerry had stabilized in the past few months, their spouses had a different impression. Most felt their partner's BlackBerry use was continuing to rise. One in three said that their partner was making frequent use of the technology when they were together outside of office hours. And most wanted them to stop using their BlackBerry at home.

The bulk of new BlackBerry users had good intentions, expecting to use their device only during work hours or when traveling. But seven months after getting their BlackBerry they were using it to extend their workday and work from home. Many spouses weren't at all pleased, and 55 percent said their partner was making "inappropriate" use of their BlackBerry several times a day, using it constantly to check their e-mails at home or in a social or family setting.

Some spouses also complained that the BlackBerry made it harder for their partner to get away from work. Their partner had more work-related calls and e-mails when home. Almost

50 percent of spouses interviewed felt that the BlackBerry "tempted" their partner to work more. They found it harder for the family to compete for the partner's attention, and they noted that their own stress levels had increased after their partner got a BlackBerry.

And finally, "respondents reported a significant drop in the amount of time per week they spent in childcare activities and the amount of time that they had to reflect."

Of the spouses in the sample,

- 56 percent felt that the only appropriate use of the BlackBerry was during business hours or when traveling for work—that the device should remain turned off when the individual was at home.
- 22 percent felt it was okay if their partner used it once a night to check e-mails (i.e., disciplined use) and one individual felt that it was appropriate to use the technology to reply to urgent queries only.
- 55 percent said it was not appropriate for their partner to constantly check e-mails when at home.
- 44 percent said it was not okay to use their BlackBerry in a social or family setting.
- 11 percent did not like any BlackBerry use at home.
- 55 percent felt that their partner made inappropriate use of their BlackBerry several times a day.
- 22 percent said that their spouse never made inappropriate use of the technology.

In spite of their feelings, 44 percent of the spouses were pragmatic about the value of the device and said they would like their partner to keep using their BlackBerry because of its work benefits.

But the rest said that "from the perspective of the family and a balance between work and life, they would prefer that their partner abandon its use."

Near the end of the survey period, the Duxbury-Higgins team asked the spouses one final question: "What one change would you like your partner to make with respect to their use of the BlackBerry, and why this change?"

- 33 percent would ask their partner to refrain from checking e-mails when at home.
- 33 percent would ask their partner to turn off the e-mail notification feature when at home.
- 22 percent would ask their partner to leave the device at work.
- 22 percent would ask their partner for a moratorium on use until after the children went to bed ("do not be on it right away when you walk in the door").

Why the change?

- 44 percent noted that that their partner did not contribute to the family when he/she was on the BlackBerry.
- 33 percent said too many e-mails were very distracting to family life.
- 22 percent would like their partner to give priority to the family when at home.

Half the sample spouses felt they were not successful in their efforts to control their partner's use of BlackBerrys, and 81 percent of those spouses thought their problem was due to the fact that there were no longer any boundaries between work and non-work time. But they recognized that families had to bite the bullet—career advancement and stability depended on longer working hours and 24/7 availability.

🌐   🌐   🌐

Faced with such evidence of family distress, what can business managers do to help workers cope with the CrackBerry Dilemma?

Duxbury and Higgins conclude that BlackBerrys are great at work but not so great at home. Rather than making work easier, these devices increase pressure and expectations. Because people are assumed to be available at all times, they can't balance their work and their lives. People in this state have lower levels of job satisfaction. They are less committed to their organizations and less loyal. They report higher job stress and they're more likely to be absent from work as well as take a higher number of days off. This is a lose-lose situation. Absenteeism costs North American companies about $50 billion a year in direct costs.

Duxbury and Higgins say the key driver that lets employees lead balanced lives is flexibility in terms of when and where they work. "How easy is it to vary when you come in or leave? Can you interrupt your workday and come back? If the situation warrants it, could you work at home for a day? That makes a phenomenal difference. But the biggest predictor of how much flexibility somebody has is the person they actually work for. If you work for a supportive manager who demonstrates respect, who communicates with you, who gives you positive feedback, who focuses on what you do not where you do it, then you're going to have a lot more balance."

The Duxbury-Higgins team concludes that employers must set some rules and regulations about when and how new technologies should be used.

To help employees cope with mobile technology, they suggest putting the following standards in place:

- The corporate culture has to be supportive, with good managers rewarded for behavior that's not normally seen as businesslike. Really good people managers need to be supported, since they often put their own mental health or career in jeopardy taking time to help others.
- The whole value chain has to be present—with open communication, good programs, and support, with investment in training and development, so managers learn to give employees more flexibility around when and where work is done. With more flexibility and control, employees are in better physical and mental health and have more loyalty toward their organization.
- Executives have to get personally involved and informed about bringing in work and family supports for sound business reasons.
- Managers should use outcome measures to create a balanced scorecard for measuring employee well being. A major criteria for upward mobility should be how well you manage people, not just how well you do the technical piece of your job.
- Executives should understand that a "show me the data" attitude in terms of work-life balance can negatively affect the bottom line. Companies with short-term focus don't see the negative results of not treating people well because the negative effects on the bottom line aren't immediate.

Rules and standards will help families already afflicted with BlackBerry obsession, but demographics are finally forcing a change in attitude by employers. At a time when North America is facing a skilled labor shortage, with millions of baby boomers retiring, we're only going to have enough workers to replace half the baby boomers who are leaving the workforce. We're moving into a seller's market, and employers will have to see that it's not good enough to talk about best employment practises, you actually have to walk the walk.*

⊕   ⊕   ⊕

BlackBerry ills can be managed, and should be managed, especially by companies and institutions. Corporate leaders are derelict in their duty if they do not educate their employees with techniques to manage their new power to communicate.

It's also becoming apparent that how you use your BlackBerry tells a lot about how you manage, and your level of confidence, coolness, and command. At a meeting, if you turn off the device, or place it at the table, and avoid the temptation to look at it, you are demonstrating leadership and good manners. Conversely, if you surreptitiously check your BlackBerry during a meeting, you are showing that you are afflicted with a twitchy insecurity.

Ringing cell phones have long been forbidden at business meetings, and so it should be with BlackBerrys. Maybe the best option is to have a ten-minute BlackBerry breaks every hour so people can check in and sync with their server. Or if that doesn't work, ban the little beepers from the room.

Experts have warned that if you have too much dependence on your BlackBerry, you are at risk of developing a real addiction. People who reach for their BlackBerry first thing in the morning before doing anything else aren't much different from people who light up a cigarette upon rising.

---

* Data primarily from Linda Duxbury, Christopher Higgins, Rob Smart, Maggie Stevenson, Ian Towers. The "Myth of Separate Worlds": An exploration of how Mobile Technology has redefined Work-Life Balance

If you experience these warning signs, there are simple steps you should take:

1. You find your efficiency is slipping. You let e-mail, phone calls, voicemails, RSS feeds, tweets, or whatever constantly interrupt your workday.
   - Dr. Edward Hallowell, author of *CrazyBusy: Overbooked, Overstretched, and About to Snap!*, says multitasking can cause the brain to overheat, like a car engine. Your brain needs periods of rest, so take time off to get away from technomania and the data deluge.
2. You find e-mail is stressing you out and affecting your health and sleep patterns.
   - Reading e-mail can be stimulating, but it can also make you tense. Don't read it before bedtime. Dr. Mark Rosekind, former head of the Fatigue Countermeasures Program at NASA Ames Research Center, says that if your brain is revved up you won't get a good night's rest.
3. You feel office technology is putting your life out of balance. Your work is causing you to neglect your life.
4. Turn off the device outside the office if you are losing contact with important people and areas in your life.

"I like the concept of mobile e-mail and carefully make sure I don't have it myself. Thinking time is precious and I find it much harder to think deep thoughts when connected in to the company communication network."
—Ed Moore, OpenWeb product manager, OpenWave Europe

Some lucky people can operate perfectly well without push e-mail. Others can easily deal with data deluge by simply turning off their BlackBerry when they leave the office and turning it back on when they arrive at work in the morning.

But others have to be wired all of the time. It's just part of their job. Tech support people, account managers, consultants, and freelancers all need e-mail to solve client problems or get alerted to new opportunities. Sales people know that one single message can mean the difference between a deal won instead of lost.

Your ability to respond to an emergency, or grab new business, can pay for an entire mobile e-mail infrastructure. Improving your office efficiency with e-mail—approving a travel request or pricing quote, or ordering new chairs for the office—can save hours of time for you and your colleagues.

Unfortunately, making e-mail mobile also makes mobile all those thieves of time, people who plague you with constant commentary and stuff your inbox with copies of copies, the latest gossip, links to cute cat videos, viral jokes making the rounds of cyberspace, all "Sent from my BlackBerry Device."

U.S. Postal Service CTO Robert Otto agrees that BlackBerrys can take a toll on spouses and children. "I've had managers' wives come up to me and say they hate me," he says. "They say their husbands pay more attention to their BlackBerrys than to them at dinner." Otto advises his managers to make a personal choice: "If you don't want to use it after 5:30 p.m., turn it off."

Michael Miller, a cognitive psychologist by training and a CTO at the National Defense University, agrees. "People have to develop the discipline to turn them off," he says. Miller personally sets his BlackBerry to automatically shut off at 10 p.m. and on weekends. "People feel pretty comfortable not answering the phone," he says.

"You need to control the technology rather than having the technology control you."[14]

One commentator in *The Wall Street Journal* professed he was baffled by the whole problem: "Why is it that that we want to blame the device for ruining our time off. The last time I checked a BlackBerry didn't include an electro-shock feature if you let an e-mail sit for a few hours. I've had a BlackBerry or other smart phone for the last five years and yes it was disruptive until I decided to manage it instead of vice versa. To blame the technology is wrong-headed. If there is a problem, it is unrealistic expectations in our work environments and an unwillingness to take risks by exerting control to have a more balanced life."[15]

Some understanding bosses urge their maxed-out employees to get away from it all by going out of cell phone reach. Take a cruise, visit another country, or go hiking in the mountains, away from those pesky radio waves. But don't forget to leave an out-of-office memo saying "no access to e-mail."

If you're an e-mail stress victim, you can reward yourself with luxurious alternatives to restore your inner calm. You can enter a Digital Detox program, now available at Fairmont hotels such as the Banff Springs and Château Lake Louise. At the front desk, you agree to hand over your BlackBerry or other PDA and opt to get massages, not messages.

This kind of pampering can be pricey. The Hyatt Regency Scottsdale Resort and Spa in Arizona offers a special half-hour BlackBerry Balm Hand Massage for $80.

In Chicago, the Sheraton Hotel offered for a time a popular free option, the BlackBerry Check-In Program. Vacationing or business travelers could hand over their PDAs or BlackBerrys so they

---

14. Alina Tugend, Blackberry Jam; Government Executive November 1, 2004
15. Ben Worthen, "BlackBerrys Ruin Vacations, Sick Days." Wall Street Journal, Sept. 26, 2008

could better focus on their business meeting or families instead of their e-mails. The program was so successful, after one year, hotel general manager Rick Ueno, a recovering CrackBerry addict, announced another special March initiative: The BlackBerry Detox Challenge. Addicts had to agree to go into "detox" by locking away their PDA or BlackBerry, and if they could stay "clean" for forty-eight hours, they would win a complimentary three-night return stay and dinner for two at the hotel's Shula Steak House.

The programs ran their course and are no longer offered, but manager Rick Ueno was pleased with the results. CIO.com's Al Sacco talked to Ueno about why he started them up. Two years earlier, he realized his own BlackBerry use was getting out of control. "If you really get addicted the way I was, it's a problem," he says. "I would wake up in the middle of the night to get a drink of water and have to check my messages. I'd check the BlackBerry at traffic lights and everywhere else."

Ueno went cold turkey. He says he found it really hard at first, but soon saw he could be more productive if he put time aside to read e-mail on his laptop. This gave him more face time with customers instead of being tethered to a handheld. "The BlackBerry was stressing me out. I'm a hell of a lot more creative now," he said. "I felt like that's all I used to do, e-mail all day, as opposed to working on customer connections. I feel a lot better without it."[16]

Many tech-obsessed professionals have fingers and thumbs that can feel painfully cramped from trying to type on small keys. The condition can become permanent, and it's called BlackBerry Thumb.

BlackBerry Thumb used to be worse when BlackBerrys had thumb wheels, and the trackball, introduced with the Pearl, eased

---

16. Sharon Begley, "Will the BlackBerry Sink the Presidency?," *Newsweek*, Feb. 16, 2009

some suffering. But road warriors who thumb exhaustive reports to home base are just asking for trouble.

BlackBerry Thumb is a serious repetitive-stress injury (RSI) that can require long-term therapy or even surgery to relieve. People in their fifties and sixties used to be victims of RSI. Now New York orthopedic surgeon Thomas Scilaris says he is getting cases in people in their thirties and even twenties.

Tech Neck is another BlackBerry-related syndrome, caused by holding yourself too long in the hunched-over BlackBerry Prayer Position.

Help is at hand. The Dorit Baxter Spa on West 57th Street in New York offers Tech Neck and Tech Hand treatments. You can get a weekly half-hour treatment for $59 per half-hour, which combines hot compress and acupressure to relieve the inflammation and "pins and needles."

There's a good reason God rested on the seventh day, and most major religions have imitated his almighty wisdom. You can too, by going to church, or joining a religion that engages you to shut down your work flow and spend a day a week in contemplation, or simply meditating or doing yoga.

Professor David Levy teaches in the Information School at the University of Washington in Seattle. He is also a practicing Orthodox Jew. "The Web is a fantastic tool," he says, and he would never consider giving it up, but "the contemplative dimension of my life is very important to me." Every Friday at sundown he disconnects for the Sabbath, until Saturday night.[17]

We can't turn back technology, but we have to learn to cope with the wired world if we are to take advantage of its benefits. One way is by practicing good mobile manners.

---

17. Al Sacco, "BlackBerry Addiction and You: The Detox Challenge," CIO Feb. 22, 2008

Judith Martin, better known by her pen name Miss Manners, has been writing an advice column since 1978, and she has seen it all. Martin says the old rules are best, and we should apply them to the modern world of instant connection.

In a recent CBC interview, Valerie Pringle asked Martin, "Tell me the rules about electronic toys." Martin replied:

The rules were in place long before these things were invented. You know, can you sit there and have a cell phone conversation in the middle of a concert? Well, no! You're not supposed to be making noise. Right? That's an old rule. Whether you make it with a trumpet or you make it with a cell phone, it's still wrong. I don't like the people who say, "Well, cell phones are terrible. They're rude." We all have them. They're very useful. It's how you use them.
What people don't understand is that they do not abolish all the rules. They do not exist in an etiquette-free zone. And that the more technological tools you have available, the richer life is, and you should use them each for their own purpose. And not, "Okay, now I'm gonna text message or e-mail my ... condolence letter to you." Ah! People do that. No. That's the wrong use of it.[18]

More and more of us are concerned with smartphone etiquette. Most of us know it's rude to talk loudly on our cell phone and bother bystanders with long-winded conversations about our babysitter or stock option plan. And we do know that text messaging is more discreet and less ill mannered. But when is it okay to check our BlackBerry in public? Certain standards seem to be emerging:

---

18. Valerie Pringle, "Rude: Where are our Manners?, CBC, Dec. 27, 2008

- In a meeting: A recent survey said 31 percent of senior executives think it's not acceptable.
- In the car: Only when you pull over to the side. Increasingly, this isn't a question of etiquette; it may be a question of breaking a local law, the same as for mobile phones.
- At dinner: Generally thought to be offensive behavior. You must have a very good reason for checking your e-mail, and excuse yourself from the table before doing so.
- In the bathroom: BlackBerry use is more acceptable than cell phone use. Enough said.
- In the bedroom: This is risky behavior, but if you both text each other in bed, it might enhance your relationship. Apparently there are emerging technologies that enable the use of love toys with smartphones. Enough said.

Coping with smartphone use can be hard when most of us are amazed at the power that the BlackBerry and its cousins can give us. But cope we must, because we are facing even more profound technological shocks that will change our planet utterly and forever.

What we are presently seeing with the BlackBerry, the iPhone, and other emerging superphones is a major revolution in human history linked to the future of the mobile Web.

In the following chapter, we'll look at where these devices are headed, as they evolve from smartphones to superphones to a new machine I call the TeleBrain—the brain in your pocket.

6

The Rise of the TeleBrain

"Applications and devices taking advantage of wireless networks will revolutionize the way people interact. These connected data devices will become the closest thing we have to mental telepathy on a world scale."

—Mike Lazaridis

Superphone technology is exploding fast, and these devices are going to morph in the next few decades into a new mobile platform I call the TeleBrain—the brain in your pocket. The TeleBrain, possibly powered by quantum computing, will let you manage your life and interact with the planet in what we can only describe as techno-telepathy.

"The medium is the message."

—Marshall McLuhan

Media and culture critic Marshall McLuhan predicted the advent and the effects of the TeleBrain, although he did his best work forty years ago and died of a brain tumor in 1980 just as the world of the PC was emerging. But he would be fascinated by the effects of mobile computing and how this new medium is reshaping humanity.

As a student at the University of Toronto, I often sat in on English Lit seminars given by McLuhan. He was a man charged with a brain that gave off sparks.

McLuhan had a wicked sense of humor and believed in Henri Bergson's dictum that true comedy happens when we see "the mechanical encrusted on the living." One of his first books, *The Mechanical Bride*, was a masterful skewering of the advertising business.

I found McLuhan a great antidote to professors who droned on and on in packed and stuffy lecture halls. You never knew what would come out of his mouth, but we waited for his light to shine, and when it did, it was always original and sometimes quite profound. I remember once, speaking of British tactile poet Gerard Manley Hopkins, McLuhan said Hopkins was "Braille for the poetically blind."

I know McLuhan would have loved the BlackBerry Bold and the Apple iPhone because they were new and more powerful extensions of the human senses, including the hand—in the same way Harry Potter's wand is an extension of his hand. The human hand can do magical things, with the right technology. But smartphones are also starting to extend the human nervous system as well.

In his masterwork, *Understanding Media*, McLuhan anticipated the TeleBrain when he called humans "an organism that now wears its brain outside its skull and its nerves outside its hide." We employ older technologies to merely extend our hands and feet and teeth and skin, but with electric media we extend our whole brain and nervous system. He said that even cities, which are extensions of our bodies, will be translated into information systems.

McLuhan concluded that Man must serve his electric technology with the same servo-mechanistic fidelity with which he served his coracle, his canoe, his typography, and all other extensions of his physical organs. But there is this difference that previous technologies were partial and fragmentary, and the electric is total and inclusive.

McLuhan was always highly amused at the passing parade of humanity and how we were dealing so obtusely with the electronic technology that was changing us so utterly and completely. He portrayed us thinking we were outside, looking down at our reflection on the surface of the water, instead of grasping that we were immersed in a new electronic ocean: "As long as we adopt the Narcissus attitude of regarding the extensions of our own bodies as really out there and really independent of us," he warned, "we will meet all technological challenges with the same sort of banana-skin pirouette and collapse."

"With the advent of humankind, Life had a means of solving many problems much faster than natural selection."
—Vernor Vinge

Culturally, and in many ways beside, electronic technologies are becoming part of our being and what it means to be human. And they are rapidly making us into interconnected citizens of McLuhan's global village.

A recent AT&T survey found that the most popular phrase among text-messaging adults ages eighteen to fifty-five, on the same romantic wavelength, is "thinking of you." Yes, indeed. But are lovers like us really reading each other's thoughts, talking to each other without speaking, and in a way messaging/massaging each other's brains? Or are we just operating in what Carl Jung called a state of "synchronicity?"

So far, science has failed to show that our brains are capable of true telepathy, where identical thoughts occur at the same time in different places. If they do, it's just coincidence. And yet we yearn for it, fantasize about it, and feel it somehow must exist. So where biology is lacking, we are turning to new tools, to force evolution upon ourselves faster than biology can do it. We're creating artificial or techno-telepathy and in doing so, unifying the human race.

The BlackBerry and other smartphones, plugged into the planetary platform of the Internet, are starting to project a new world where we humans will be always thinking, connecting, or contributing in real time to our various tribes and families, and through cloud computing, to a World Wide Whatever.

With this movement, we are leapfrogging mere technology to embrace a whole new world. It's a world based on a fantasy, but one that may have a basis in biological fact.

Telepathy—it means, literally, "distance feeling"—seems to exist in nature. Watch a flock of birds bunch and swoop to evade a hawk. Or marvel how a school of fish escapes from a seal by suddenly turning with a single unified flash of scales. What you think you are seeing is electric telepathy in nature.

Many humans feel that telepathy, ESP, and the paranormal must exist and often fantasize about it as it should exist. It's certainly a staple of literature and video. Mandrake the Magician used telepathic powers to solve crimes. The Jedi in *Star Wars* were a telepathic race, and *Star Trek*'s Deanna Troi's Betazoid empathy is telepathically endowed. Various TV shows, books, magazines, and websites promote the fantasy. But alas, biological human telepathy does not yet meet the test of scientific proof, based on empirical observation. It's wishful thinking, based on the human need to connect.

A 2005 Gallup poll found that 41 percent of Americans believe in ESP, down from an astounding 50 percent in the 1990s. So why does almost half the population believe in this pseudo-science? Perhaps because there are many human phenomena that we often confuse with telepathy.

People with keen senses and instincts, which can be learned skills, often prosper. A good fortune teller or magician can elicit a lot of information by closely observing another person and asking leading questions, not by mind reading. Or they can simply trick us into believing.

Romantic love can sometimes seem telepathic. A courting couple can be so totally in tune with each other that we can describe them as being "on the same wavelength." People at an Obama rally or World Cup match seem in the grip of a common emotion. Frantic traders in a commodity pit waving hand signals and color cards seem to move as a wave when suddenly the price of wheat moves north or south. And we humans never learn to distrust instinct, even though it often leads us astray. Every generation experiences its own stock market or property bubble, as young investors exhibit herd behavior, stampede in one direction, then all go over the cliff together.

What we are seeing here is a kind of electric empathy in human nature, but related to senses that already exist—touch, taste, sight, smell, and hearing—which can cause a kind of herd or group instinctual reaction.

We humans are also inherently suggestible creatures, which means we can be induced, hypnotized, or even brainwashed to act in close concert, even to the point of committing suicide for our religious faith.

We also have a strange ability to feel what is not there. For example, BlackBerry users who set their phones to vibrate on receipt of a call are developing a phantom relationship with the device. They sense vibrations even when there is no call coming through.

Watch a modern office communicate and you see a kind of electric empathy in action, but this time it is accomplished with speedy electronic devices, such as BlackBerrys and other mobile computers. It still looks a lot like telepathy—people collaborating and sharing their thoughts and feelings—only it's artificial.

The computer and the Internet also contribute to group social action and rapid communications and movement, almost as if we had restored the old jungle telegraph used by our ancestors. A rumor about mad cow disease goes viral over the Internet and in short order rioting breaks out in Korea to prevent U.S. food imports. Web organized flash mobs gather around the world to do silent disco demos or world wide pillow fights.

My point being, we have invented these artificial communications devices to fill a need and extend part of ourselves that in some cases exists in a fantasy, that we can share thoughts magically. But who knows. We have nervous systems based on electrical impulses between neurons. Maybe we will discover that there is a deeper quantum level of communications between and among human beings, an electromagnetic ocean that is beyond the rational and the sensual. In the meantime, we will be relying more and more on machine telepathy where real telepathy fails, and this will change our civilization utterly.

It's time to study where we are going with this coming technological medium and listen to what it is telling us.

If you have a BlackBerry, iPhone, or Google Android in your pocket, you already have a primitive TeleBrain companion.

Let's see how it works. First, it needs a name. I'm calling mine Deanna, after the doe-eyed Betazoid empath and ship's counselor in *Star Trek, The Next Generation*. You can call yours Spock, or perhaps Scotty, after the irascible Scottish engineer in the original *Star Trek*.

Beam me up, Scotty.

So, we're in San Francisco walking around. It's lunchtime. You ask Deanna, via the radio in your sunglasses, "Deanna, know any good restaurants around here? Mexican. Authentic. 4.5 stars."

"Sure," she says. "La Taqueria. $8.95 for the burrito special. Voted Best Burrito in San Francisco. Vibe: boisterous. Cash only."

"Okay."

"Want to see the menu? Say menu. Want to hear a review? Say review."

"No, reserve for three at twelve-thirty."

"They don't take reservations."

"How do I get there?"

"It's twenty blocks west and south on Mission. Want a projection? Bus or BART?"

"Projection. BART."

"Here's the street. Get off at 24th and walk south half a block on the west side."

This is a simple TeleBrain activity and is available right now to varying degrees, including a street view in Google maps, from a voice-activated device with a browser. To come up with La Taqueria, Deanna simply went into speech recognition mode, accessed the database in the cloud and then passed over to local resources. She then found out where you were and then looked at the location database and the businesses database and then gave you all your local Mexican 4.5 star restaurants by name.

Here's another example, with more subtle recommendations based on the weather and other less obvious options.

After lunch, we want to go to Sausalito to visit Lexicon Naming, the company that came up with the BlackBerry name.

"Deanna, what's the best way to get to Lexicon Naming in Sausalito?"

"It's a nice, sunny afternoon. I recommend the Sausalito Ferry from Pier 43, Fisherman's Wharf. In Sausalito, turn right and walk up Bridgeway Boulevard past Dunphy Park and turn right on Liberty Ship Way. It's number thirty. I see no fog in the forecast. Want to ride there and take the ferry back?"

"Sure."

"Okay, I recommend Blazing Saddles, Bike the Bridge, or Bike and Roll. Twenty-five dollars a day, but I can get you a $5 discount. Helmets and bike locks are included. They have outlets by the ferry. Reviews say be careful your bike is properly tuned before you start off. Watch for scams. Don't pay anything extra on return. Want a map of the route? Want to ride on to Tiburon?"

And so on. All this Deanna activity is a programmed use of databases that already exist, as well as technologies such as Bluetooth and GPS. If you want to dig deeper, you can access an increasing number of reviews, geo-tagged images and videos, and so on.

So if this is what we can do now with a smartphone, what's coming in the future with the mobile TeleBrain?

First, let's look at evolving and converging technologies.

"Neither the naked hand nor the understanding left to itself can effect much. It is by instruments and helps that the work is done, which are as much wanted for the understanding as for the hand."

—Francis Bacon

We already have all the ingredients in place for digital telepathy. And we already use primitive TeleBrains. Increasingly sophisticated ones will arrive in the next twenty years through a number of engineering advances:

1. **Storage**. TeleBrains with multi-terabyte memory will soon surpass the storage capacity of your own brain. Science still does not know exactly how the human brain stores and represents information, and what are the storage limits, but Yoshihiro Shiroishi of Japanese computer maker Hitachi estimates our brains store around 10 terabytes of information. He says that by 2010, two Hitachi 3.5-inch, 5-terabyte hard drives will provide the same storage capacity. Next-generation 2-terabyte SDXC (eXtended Capacity) memory cards will be available before then. A terabyte is 1,000 gigabytes; it's been estimated that the Library of Congress holds 175 terabytes of text.

2. **Processors**. We're seeing the dawn of ultra-fast, dedicated processors, superior to the human brain in certain specialties. However, biological computing currently has silicon-based computing beat by a country kilometer. The processing capacity of a typical desktop computer is 25 billion instructions per second; your brain can do 100 trillion instructions per second, or 100 teraflops. In June 2008, IBM's Roadrunner supercomputer was the first to break what has been called "the petaflop barrier" of 1,000 teraflops.

3. **Radios on a Chip**. One billion Wi-Fi chipsets are being built every year. Professor Jan Rabaey of UC Berkeley says chipmakers will soon pack hundreds of dedicated radios on a single chip, and each person will link to thousands of these miniscule radios. Radio devices, he says, will become

"cognitive." They will automatically find the most uncluttered spectrum and use the best protocols available. Radios will also become more collaborative, joining a mesh network to collectively transmit large amounts of data faster and more efficiently. These radios will connect you directly with other people and other TeleBrains on more sophisticated networks and frequencies.

4. **Spectrum**. The amount of data you can get through a radio spectrum channel is rapidly increasing, and radios are on a similar trajectory as computers. Wireless broadband connectivity and the open Internet will wire your TeleBrain to the planet.

5. **Speed**. Cheap Millimeter-wave Technology (MWT) will soon deliver data short distances over the air at more than 20 gigabits per second, close to the speed you get over fiber optic connections. MWT operates at radio frequencies of between 60 and 100 GHz, on an uncrowded part of the radio spectrum used for radio astronomy and high-res radar. A system on a chip (SOC) with transmission speeds 100 times faster than Wi-Fi and 350 times faster than 3.5G cell phones has been created by Professor Jri Lee of National Taiwan University. It will cost about $1 to produce.

6. **Video**. High-definition (HD) onboard cameras and projectors will let us stream what we see anywhere live or to a storage medium in the cloud. Texas Instruments' soon-to-be released OMAP 4 family of low-power dual-core mobile chips will allow 1,080 pixel video playback, ten times the Web surfing speed, a 20-megapixel camera, and 130 hours of audio playback.

7. **Implants**. In some cases, people will prefer TeleBrain implants with brain-machine interfaces. We are already using rudimentary versions of this technology to help people with

nerve damage to do tasks using microprocessors. Adding advanced Wi-Fi and Bluetooth will eliminate intrusive wiring and enable something akin to tele-twittering.

8. **Personal Medicine**. Your TeleBrain will contain all your personal medical information and genomic maps and will be able to monitor your health and suggest preventive supplements and activities to improve your odds of survival. Medical devices such as Dr. "Bones" McCoy's portable scanner from *Star Trek* will be able to scan your TeleBrain and use the information to reveal internal problems, and in some cases cure them.

9. **Custom TeleBrains**. We are now starting to customize, personalize, program, tailor, and train our TeleBrains through free and cheap programs we can download. We are using them to extend our own brains, senses, and connections to our world. When needed, we will also link with custom-programmed TeleBrains, for, example, to operate our smart cars and smart houses. Our personal information in the cloud will be permissions based, using social networking and a form of what Tim O'Reilly calls "personal CRM"— customer relationship management.

10. **Whole Brain Emulation**. In future, your TeleBrain will be able to hold a software model of your brain that is so faithful to the original that, when run on appropriate hardware, it will behave much like your original one.

11. **TeleBrain Power**. Wireless power management is a big problem, and things may get worse before they get better. RIM has pioneered many power-saving technologies, but we need superbatteries or power cells that can hold a charge longer so they can power hot processors and super-high-speed data transfers. Every increase in CPU power or data transfer speed equals a further drop in battery life between

charges. The good news is, wireless charging is already here, with adapters that use magnetic induction to trickle electricity to your device. Future advances in electrical generation and storage will let your blood glucose or heart activity recharge your TeleBrain.

12. **Googlepedia**. You can already use Google Mobile App to speak your queries to the Googlepedia without pushing any buttons and do local searches without specifying your location.* Future TeleBrain tools will perform a lot of simple tasks the Internet is already doing, only better, faster, and with an ethos tailored to your needs. For example, it will:

- answer questions and suggest alternatives
- look for and contact new friends, or even a life partner
- do real-time speech interpretation, letting you talk effortlessly in other languages
- find the best interest rates and get you money or credit
- make you happy with its own artificial sunlight
- let the dog out and get a meal ready for you at home
- recharge the electric car; ask it to get some milk and eggs
- train you in microsurgery, with programmed AV learning, real-distance internship, and hands-on operation simulation
- vote and pay microtaxes, and handle your relations with governments
- check for potential danger on the road, rate your chances of being seriously injured, and take appropriate action.

13. **Net Culture**. Your TeleBrain use will help net culture continue to expand, creating dynamic commercial, educational, and social resources; what you put on the Web will only be limited by your imagination and local bylaws. Vast search

---

* See Google Mobile Apps in Action on the Web Support Site

databases created by peer production such as yours will be held in the cloud and managed by database search engines such as Google Mobile App.

14. **Life Recording**: Canadian filmmaker Rob Spence is having a video camera implanted in place of an artificial eye. For people who want a less intense experience, mobile 12-megapixel camera phones with HD video recording (720 pixels at 60 frames per second) will soon become commonplace. Your TeleBrain screen can always be on, with touchable multiscreens, and options such as 3D. Cameras will be able to record the entire timeline of your life. Your TeleBrain will also build a record of every call, meeting, email and activity of your lifetime, letting you access any data you ever come in contact with.

"My life is my message."

—Mahatma Gandhi

Essentially, the TeleBrain will be a personal, programmable life-support system you can tailor to your needs. RIM calls its version The Lifestyle Platform, but it will turn out to be far, far more.

With the arrival of the BlackBerry Bold, the Apple iPhone, and other advanced superphones, we are seeing a clear morphing of the personal digital assistant (PDA) into the mobile personal computer (MPC)—the precursor to the TeleBrain. And with the growth of the mobile Web, power and business are shifting away from the PC to the network. Research In Motion is playing a leading role in this shift.

Computing pioneer Alan Turing once famously predicted that "software can always be substituted for hardware." And as RIM's mechanical devices start to reach plateaus of speed and power, software is indeed coming to the rescue. With the current explosion of free and cheap programs on mobile app stores, we can more precisely customize our devices. Our smartphones are becoming superphones—individualized, indispensable, interactive companions.

The rise of the World Wide Computer is also seeing the demise of the traditional mobile phones and PDAs, in the same way that color TV sets drove out black and white in the 1960s, or FM radios drove out AM in the 1970s. The cell phone business is shrinking by about half a percent a year, while the smartphone market is growing by more than 50 percent a year.

RIM's Jim Balsillie also notes a shift from business-only or consumer-only devices to all-in-one superphones for both the consumer and business markets. He's seeing "a large proportion of B2B users who also use B2C apps. They like games, social networking, personal navigation, e-commerce, multimedia, and music. Every B2B person is also a B2C if their policies let them load up. People think of this as a lifestyle terminal."[1]

"If you look back through history, every industrial revolution has come from a breakthrough in theoretical physics."
                                        —*Mike Lazaridis*

A crucial stage in the evolution of the Lifestyle Platform into the TeleBrain may come with the advent of quantum computing. This technology will enable incredibly high-speed, low-power computing that will usher in a new age for humanity and perhaps take us to the stars. Mike Lazaridis has his eye firmly on giving this technology a shove.

---

1. Damian Koh, "The Storm Is a Netbook, Says RIM's Founder," CNN Asia, Dec 30, 2008

As Mike Lazaridis strides across the RIM campus in Waterloo, his wavy mane of white hair makes him instantly recognizable to the passersby. This is his town, and all the buildings around the square are RIM territory, bought up when the company he founded to make glorified pagers ended up creating the essential mobile device for global business.

He has a BlackBerry Bold cupped in his palm. He ignores the little green flash and the insistent buzzing the machine makes as another one of his 200-odd e-mails a day slides into its assigned slot on his docket.

He is going to the Black Hole Bistro to talk to Stephen Hawking about the universe.

The famed Cambridge University mathematician, author of the bestseller *A Brief History of Time*, is the first distinguished research chair at the Perimeter Institute for Theoretical Physics, the quantum theory and cosmology institute founded by Mike Lazaridis in 1999.

On accepting the position, Hawking said, "The institute's twin focus, on quantum theory and gravity, is very close to my heart and central to explaining the origin of the universe."

"I grew up on Star Trek. I believe in the final frontier."
—*Barack Obama*

A child's imagination can be as limitless as the universe. In some children, it can actually lead to the stars. In the case of three boys who grew up together in Windsor, Ontario, their dreams and imagination are today helping the world move in important new directions.

Mike Lazaridis and Doug Fregin are spearheading BlackBerry development at RIM, and Ken Wood is deputy director of the

Chapter Six

Microsoft Research laboratory in Cambridge, England, doing R&D on the "SenseCam" and human/machine interaction.

The wireless handheld communicators, scanner, and tricorders, cloaking devices, laser surgery, and programmable computers that the boys adored on Gene Rodenberry's *Star Trek* are all coming true, and even the force fields that Mike and Ken failed to create, using wires, switches, and chemicals, are now being explored and exploited through the near-magic of quantum physics.

Mike Lazaridis carried his dreams to college, and as an undergraduate engineering student, he was inspired further by a physics teacher, who told his students, "During the day, I'm going to teach you the curriculum, but I'm going to hold a night course once a week, and I'll talk about the latest developments."[2]

So, this Dead Poets Society of physics students—a kind of Dead Physicists Society—met and were blown away by the latest developments in string theory and other delights of quantum physics, discoveries such as those of French physicist Alain Aspect, who was working with crystal prisms to generate what he called entangled photons.

In the early 1980s, Aspect and his partners performed the crucial "Bell test experiments" that showed that when twin photons were separated, a change in the polarity of one photon influenced the polarity of its twin. This so-called "ghostly action at a distance" was strong evidence that a quantum event at one location can affect an event at another location without any obvious means of communication between the two locations.* The pure science behind this phenomenon should eventually have practical use in the fields

---

2. David Fielding, "Leaps of Faith," *Globe and Mail*, April 25, 2008 < * >
* Since 1997, Aspect and colleagues have been studying Bose-Einstein condensates of ultra-cold atomic gases, as well as atom lasers, especially with a view to using them in atomic interferometers that may lead to accurate measurements of gravitation and to test general relativity.

of secure data transmission (quantum cryptography) and quantum computing in future BlackBerry devices.

Mike Lazaridis and friends have given the study of the field a tremendous boost with the creation of the Perimeter Institute for Theoretical Physics.

⊕ ⊕ ⊕

"Certainly it is agreeable to reason, that there are at least some light effluxions from spirit, when men are in presence one with another, as well as from body to body."
— *Francis Bacon*

In 1999, Mike Lazaridis pulled together a non-profit independent think-tank called the Perimeter Institute for Theoretical Physics, gave it C$20 million in seed money, and launched it a year later, on October 23, 2000. The institute (known to most as "the PI"), started operations a year later in an old tavern, formerly the Waterloo post office, where a core group of nine world-class physicists started pursuing research in quantum gravity, string theory, quantum information theory, and foundations of quantum mechanics.

Lazaridis endowed the PI with an additional C$80 million, with Jim Balsillie and Doug Fregin chipping in another $20 million. With this backing, the PI was able to attract $43 million more from the Canada Foundation for Innovation, the Ontario Innovation Trust, the Ontario Research and Development Challenge Fund, the Government of Canada and the Government of Ontario. The Prime Minister of Canada, Jean Chrétien, turned the sod for the permanent building.

The PI was also linked to the Institute for Quantum Computing at the University of Waterloo, so faculty can be cross-appointed to teach undergraduates.

In 2003, the PI moved into its elegant new quarters, a complex that looks more like an upscale resort than a think-tank, with courtyards, working fireplaces, foosball tables, a grand piano, and a reflecting pool, where brainiacs can ponder how to unify relativity and quantum mechanics, what Lazaridis calls "the holy grail of physics." Most rooms have wall-to-wall blackboards with dusty floors, where physicists meet to chat and chalk up their formulae. The main dining area has no long refectory tables, the theory being shorter tables encourage particle physicists to eat at the same table as astrophysicists and mathematicians.

The goal of Perimeter is to create an atmosphere where physicists and other leading theoreticians can brainstorm to their hearts' content, free of academic distractions. Some of the planet's best hang out at Perimeter, including information theorist Raymond Laflamme, originally from Los Alamos National Lab, together with several dozen five-year appointees and post-doctoral students. Laflamme is known as the person who changed Stephen Hawking's mind about the direction of time in a contracting universe.

Another PI appointee, John Moffat, is a self-taught physicist. In 1953, he was a starving artist in Copenhagen when he wrote Albert Einstein a letter questioning the assumptions of his unified field theory. Einstein wrote back, a friendly letter, and he and Moffatt remained lifelong correspondents.

Perhaps the most radical of the PI theorists, Lee Smolin, puts forward the suggestion that we may live in a "fecund universe," where every black hole leads to another universe.

Lazaridis wanted the PI to have a practical orientation from the start, exploring and developing technology that could change the world. "What we have and enjoy today is a result of physics discoveries," he says. "Maxwell's equations are an example of physics discoveries that have been commercialized. Marconi invented wireless transmissions from Maxwell's discoveries."

Laflamme agrees. "Think about the Industrial Revolution," he says. "Suddenly, people see steam and they are able to harness it, control it, and make machines. Locomotives changed the landscape of cities and, at the same time, the fabric of society itself . . . when we think of quantum computing, that's the vision we have."

Developing practical ways to compute by the use of quantum interactions is a major thrust at Perimeter. Another focus is refining the "loop quantum" theory of gravity, where space-time is a foamy network of intersecting loops (spin networks).

This particular project is not a politically correct one and has raised the radar of some conventional "superstring" quantum theorists, perhaps envious of the PI's funding. They believe that the fundamental particles in the universe are actually multidimensional strings vibrating at different frequencies. For some superstringers, the PI's loop quantum approach is clearly contrarian, even heretical, and some have insinuated that the PI is a rich man's toy. In 2001, Harvard physicist Lubos Motl stepped over the line and publicly insulted Lazaridis, posting on a newsgroup that it was "a well known fact that the billionaire's opinion of what theoretical physics means is naive."

Back on BlackBerry Planet, the billionaire shrugged off the trash talk, joking that the physicists merely humor him and are kind enough to tolerate his presence. But Laflamme recognizes that Lazaridis is an intensely practical man seriously in awe of what they are doing at Perimeter. "Mike Lazaridis's curiosity is beyond bounds. He wants to know the little details of how things work and the big pictures of where things are going. And he wants to connect the dots in between."

"The idea of entanglement grabbed me in my second year of university because it was so nonsensical. You couldn't

believe what the mathematics was telling you because it made no sense physically."

—Mike Lazaridis

Scientists around the world, including those at the Perimeter Institute, are starting to figure out how to teleport—move atoms from one place to another using quantum mechanics.

We use a fake form of teleportation today—when we phone, fax, or send an e-mail. All of these messaging technologies involve making a copy of the original object, sending it to a new location, and then reading it out on the other side.

Quantum teleportation is a bit like *Star Trek*'s transporter technology, but instead of beaming trillions of atoms down to the planet in a couple of shimmering seconds, physicists are finding they can nudge a few atoms at a time from one place to another instantly. Copenhagen scientists using a new method, called a Bose-Einstein condensate, can cause about 5,000 particles to disappear from one place and appear thirty centimeters away. At the Perimeter Institute in Waterloo, Laflamme has been able to manipulate a grand total of seven quantum bits ("qubits") to run a calculation.

On the surface, this seems to be the same as scanning a message into pixels, faxing it, and recreating it at the other end, except the scientists are adding in "entangled quantum states" to send the real thing, not a copy.

It works something like this: when two atoms or two laser beams are inextricably dependent on each other, i.e., "entangled," it is possible to make a link between two ends of a line. In the case of two "entangled" particles, if one is rotating in one direction, the other one will always be rotating in the opposite direction and vice versa. When you measure one particle, it instantaneously influences its entangled partner. When you act to change the state of one, then the other reacts and makes the same change.

What excites Mike Lazaridis in all this basic research is the promise that quantum techno-magic will some day make it possible to transmit and process data at near light speeds—quantum computing. Unlike electronic bits, quantum bits don't have to be recorded as either a one or a zero—they can be both at the same time. A quantum computer with only 40 or 50 qubits may some day perform the same tasks as today's supercomputers.

"Moore's law will run out between 2010 and 2020," he says. "After that, we approach circuitry that's just one atom in size. If we can't get past classical computing methods and learn to use quantum interactions to convey information, we'll bounce off the wall, and things will start getting bigger. That will slow technological development.

"Fundamental research is hit or miss. You have no idea what could happen or when. The only guarantee is that if you invest in it and prioritize resources well enough, eventually it will change everything."[3]

It's not a stretch to think that one day, while tinkering with some qubits, one of the PI's junior physicists will have a small but significant eureka moment and come up with a quantum application that Team Lazaridis can build into a next generation of BlackBerrys.

Then we'll see some big, big changes.

---

3. *Infoworld*, February 27, 2002; Duff McDonald, "The BlackBerry Brain Trust," *Wired*, January 2005 < * >

Afterword: RIM on the Plateau?

"In answer to the question of why it happened, I offer the modest proposal that our Universe is simply one of those things which happen from time to time."
— Edward P. Tryon

Mike Lazaridis is proud of the legacy he and his team have built with the BlackBerry, but he admits he couldn't stop "tinkering with the BlackBerry" if he tried.

Just before the birth of his second child, he took some time off to help his wife Ophelia. But his brain didn't turn off, and to keep it running hot, he worked out a series of algorithms to determine the best way to place the components for his home entertainment system. He confesses that he only "stopped tinkering with it" when he had what some of his acquaintances have described as the best home theatre in the world, with a ten-foot HD screen. He loves to watch films—Monty Python movies are a favorite. But he is also a voracious reader, and reads Dr. Seuss to his kids before bed.

Lazaridis is giving it his best shot, to keep BlackBerry's momentum going, but he is keenly aware of the danger of missed opportunities. He keeps on his desk a wooden model of the Avro Arrow, an advanced Canadian jet interceptor cancelled in the early 1960s. Many of the Avro engineers left Canada for Houston and Cape Kennedy, where they quickly found work meeting John F. Kennedy's goal of putting a man on the Moon.

He and Jim Balsillie are also keenly aware of "the Kleenex Dilemma." This happens when a market leader slides into being just a generic product, when patents and pioneers get exhausted by battles in the marketplace, and more nimble and lower cost competitors nip at your heels and steal your lunch.

RIM is starting to look ordinary in the eyes of some analysts. Perhaps the entry of the Apple iPhone and the lukewarm reception of the Storm have marked the plateau or highwater mark of Research In Motion. Perhaps RIM will be increasingly cornered by cheaper Asian imports and smothered by Nokia's worldwide range.

In a frank MD&A (Management Discussion and Analysis) paper, team Balisillie shows it is fully aware of the risks RIM faces moving forward, including:

- RIM's ability to successfully obtain patent or other proprietary or statutory protection for its technologies and products;
- RIM's ability to obtain rights to use software or components supplied by third parties;
- RIM's ability to enhance current products and develop new products;
- RIM's ability to establish new, and to build on existing, relationships with its network carrier partners and distributors;
- RIM's dependence on its carrier partners to grow its BlackBerry subscriber account base;

- RIM's dependence on a limited number of significant customers;
- the efficient and uninterrupted operation of RIM's network operations center and the networks of its carrier partners;
- the occurrence or perception of a breach of RIM's security measures, or an inappropriate disclosure of confidential or personal information;
- RIM's ability to manage production facilities and its reliance on third-party manufacturers for certain products;
- RIM's reliance on its suppliers for functional components and the risk that suppliers will not be able to supply components on a timely basis or in sufficient quantities;
- the continued quality and reliability of RIM's products and services;
- risks associated with RIM's expanding foreign operations;
- restrictions on import and use of RIM's products in certain countries due to encryption of the products and services;
- and so on[*]

With over 10,000 employees around the world, and the inevitable corporate empire building and infighting, perhaps RIM now risks becoming what Mike Lazaridis saw CDC becoming when he worked for them as a young co-op student—a work environment where marketing trumps engineering. Like other big operations—Microsoft for example—RIM risks drowning in bureaucracy, becoming a company that doesn't really matter any more.

Will RIM do what many a company does when faced by a cooling market or hostile competition, do a sharp inward turn and

---

[*] Research In Motion Limited management's discussion and analysis of financial condition and results of operations continued FOR THE THREE MONTHS AND FISCAL YEAR ENDED MARCH 1, 2008 Special Note Regarding Forward-Looking Statements; RIM Annual Report, 2008.

retreat into a PR shell, doling out self-congratulation to the one person listening, itself? Will it believe its own spin?

Sure, there are enough addicted office workers and enough major offices happily plugged into the secure BlackBerry contact solution to ensure a long run still. But that advantage won't last forever, as other, cheaper solutions will emerge and network security gets commoditized.

At the very least, RIM can beaver on, making well-engineered smartphones that telecom providers and their customers continue to appreciate. Perhaps it will even engineer some quantum communicator in a future time. At worst, RIM will go into a shell, with most outward contact dictated by feeding the needs of financial analysts, by the need to put out media firestorms (such as the Storm's truly terrible reviews) and shore up the share price. Marketing and trade shows will become more lame, tightly scripted, well-rehearsed performances for the converted.

At best, RIM will start to innovate in new directions and exhibit some of the scrappiness it showed during the NTP patent case. Fans of Apple's rival iPhone are turning up the heat on RIM, and RIM has to meet the challenge. In a scathing *Infoworld* article called Deathmatch: BlackBerry versus iPhone, reporter Galen Gruman calls the BlackBerry browser "a Pinto in an era of Priuses," "the Lotus Notes of mobile" and "yesterday's mobile messenger, way past its prime and heading toward retirement. The iPhone is light-years ahead of the BlackBerry on almost every count. RIM should be ashamed."*

Right now, Jim Balsillie doesn't buy that scenario at all:

"We work with 400 carriers in 150 countries, we have 125,000 corporations on BlackBerry service and 1,000

---

* Galen Gruman, Deathmatch: BlackBerry versus iPhone, Infoworld, May 26, 2009. Gruman does not address the speed, bandwidth savings and longer battery life that come from RIM's approach to browsing. < * >

application partners. And, of course, we have this very high-performance, up-tempo team. In many respects, we feel like Venice in the 1300s—all travelers somehow crossed through Venice, and they all cross through BlackBerry, they intersect, they interface with us. To be relevant to everything that's going on in technology and telecom is an enormous privilege. Everything we work with is intellectually stimulating, creatively interesting, personally fascinating. People think of the growth and the money. But it really is the excitement of the environment."***

The situation at RIM may not be as bad as that painted by Dan Lyons of *Newsweek*, who quipped about Apple, "Imagine what it might be like if the Church of Scientology went into the consumer electronics business, and you'd have a pretty good picture of how Apple operates."

Companies rise and companies fall. The sleepy old RIM culture of summer employee picnics and company ball games and hanging around with Mike and Herb and Doug and Gary has gone forever, after a spectacular 25-year run. And a new and tougher corporate predator has muscled out the older, gentler RIM guard, as it arms itself to fight giant Nokia on the global battleground.

For Mike Lazaridis, other concerns are now clouding his focus, issues such as family security, and other perils of being a modern billionaire. A bodyguard shadows his moves, and scans his surroundings. One RIM watcher reveals that he's built a large secure fortress outside Waterloo, apparently with canine security. Quite

---

** *Globe and Mail*, Jim Balsillie Interview, Nov. 26, 2008. < * >

a change from the good old days, when he could hang around with employees, or stroll over to the Perimeter Institute for an afternoon chat with his quantum buddies. But to the north, outside the light polluted town of Waterloo, the night sky is blacker and the stars are clearer, and he can gaze upward, dream the dream of his boyhood hero, the Captain of the Enterprise, and murmur "Engage."

Index

Index

Index

Index

Index

Index